Museum of Fine Arts Boston: 1870 to 2020
An Oral History

Charles Giuliano

Berkshire Fine Arts, LLC
North Adams, Massachusetts

berkshirefinearts.com

Copyright © 2021 by Charles Giuliano
Published by Berkshire Fine Arts, LLC
Book Design by Studio Two, Amanda Hill
All images, except when indicated, by Charles Giuliano, copyright 2021.
All rights reserved. No part of this book may be reproduced or transmitted in any form or by any means, electronic or mechanical, including photocopying, recording, or by any information storage and retrieval system without the written permission of the author. For information or permissions contact Berkshire Fine Arts at 243 Union Street, Unit 208, North Adams, Mass. 01247.
ISBN-13: 978-0-9961715-7-1
Library of Congress Control Number: 2021916454

This book is dedicated to my wife, Astrid Hiemer,
and sister, Pippy Giuliano. Their inspiration
and support has been indispensible.

Also by Charles Giuliano

Counterculture in Boston: 1968–1980s

Topsy Turvy

Gloucester Poems: Nugents of Rockport

Ultra Cosmic Gonzology

Total Gonzo Poems

Shards of a Life

Love Made Visible: Scenes from a Mostly Happy Marriage, by Jean Gibran (Introduction)

100 Boston Painters, by Chawky Frenn (Essay)

Selected Exhibition Catalogues

Pioneers from Provincetown: The Roots of Figurative Expressionism, by Adam Zucker (Essay: "Sun Gallery and a Return to the Figure in the 1950s")

Lester Johnson: In Memoriam (Essay)

Randall Deihl: An American Realist (Essay)

James Aponovich Recent Paintings (Essay)

Harriet Casdin Silver: The Art of Holography (Essay)

Lester Johnson (Essay)

Contents

Preface vii

Acknowledgements xi

Matthew Teitelbaum Guides the Museum Through Crisis and Change 1

MFA 100 15

The Rathbone Years 35

Centennial Introspection 49

The Brief and Turbulent Tenure of Merrill Rueppel 59

The Museum as a Business 71

Board President George Seybolt Wanted to Manage the MFA Like a Business 85

Jan Fontein, from Asiatic Curator to Museum Director 95

Former MIT President Howard Johnson Chaired the MFA Board 125

Board Member Lewis Cabot Was Also a Private Art Consultant 135

Kenworth Moffett was Founding Curator of the Department of Contemporary Art 147

Barry Gaither, Curator of Afro-American Art 159

Ted Stebbins Chaired American and European Painting and Contemporary Departments ... 177

Contemporary Curator Amy Lighthill's Brave New Works 203

Director Alan Shestack Succumbed to Downturn 217

Peter Lacovara of the Egyptian Department 243

Malcolm Rogers, Expansion and Controversy 253

Malcolm's Union-Busting Blues 275

Matthew Teitelbaum, from the ICA to MFA 283

Preface

In 2020 the Museum of Fine Arts observed its 150th anniversary. Though Boston has been the subject of numerous scholarly books, remarkably, this publication is only the second attempt to write a history of the museum. It takes up where the commissioned *Museum of Fine Arts Boston: A Centennial History* by Walter Muir Whitehill, board member and director of the Boston Athenaeum, left off in 1970. His history was an invaluable resource, as was Hina Hirayama's 2013 book *With Eclat: The Boston Atheneaum and the Origin of the Museum of Fine Arts Boston*.

This volume includes a summary of the first hundred years, as well as a discussion of issues and controversies regarding remarkable acquisitions that occurred before nations passed laws regarding the export of art and artifacts. From the 1960s on, the book comprises an oral history drawn from interviews with directors, curators, and administrators, as well as observers and critics of the museum.

Both the Museum of Fine Arts and New York's Metropolitan Museum of Art were founded in 1870. They are often compared as the nation's foremost encyclopedic museums. They both explored unique opportunities, particularly in the early decades. Through 1900, they competed for masterpieces on a level playing field. That changed when the MFA raised money to move from Copley Square to a larger structure on Huntington Avenue, which it occupied beginning in 1909. In stages, it took until the 1920s to complete the initial design of Guy Lowell.

The scale and depth of the Met is vast, but for Classical, Ancient Egyptian (Old Kingdom and Nubian), Asiatic, and American Art (from Colonial through 1900), the MFA is second to none. The collection comprises some 500,000 objects, including great depth in European art and 19th century French Impressionism. Where the MFA falls short, compared to other encyclopedic American museums, is in 20th century art. Exceptions include superb collections of prints, drawings, and photography.

This book is a culmination of a lifelong relationship with the MFA. That started in 1949 when I was nine years old. My uncle, Dr. William Giuliano, a professor of romance languages at Queens College, took my sister Josephine and me to the museum. My most vivid memory of that experience is of the mummies, Japanese swords, and samurai armor.

During high school, I was within walking distance of the museum from Boston Latin School. Accordingly, I was a frequent visitor. My parents were members and I used their invitations to elegant openings during the era of Perry T. Rathbone.

In the fall of 1963, having graduated from Brandeis University, I went to work for the museum. I walked into Rathbone's office to ask for a job. His secretary informed me that guards and maintenance apply in the basement. I told her that I was interested in a curatorial position. She replied "It just isn't done that way."

That may be, but I worked in the basement storage area of the Egyptian department for two and a half years. I worked for Dr. William Stevenson Smith. After a period of basic cleaning and organization, I was trained by William Young in the restoration of Old Kingdom stone vessels. Given permission to open crates, I set up tables and sorted through a jumble of shards. That resulted in some 60 completed objects.

My first task was to sweep eight barrels of dirt, for nobody had entered the basement for decades. When I interviewed Dr. Peter Lacovara in 2020, he told me that he later followed me to the basement. It was fun to share memories of the "basement tapes." He told me that my restoration of the shallow Ka Ba, trompe l'oeil plate was "famous" in the field. I restored rare objects related to the Dynasty Three pharaoh, circa 2670 B.C. Lacovara was also familiar with a stunning, large Coptic painted vessel that I restored.

During lunch breaks I explored the galleries. In particular, I liked to ask the guard to unlock the dimly lit, atmospheric Asiatic temple room. It astonished me one time when a family of tourists came in and commenced chanting and praying. What for me were works of art, to them were sacred objects. On other occasions I sat in the Catalonian Chapel. Over time, I explored the museum's many treasures and secrets. This book reveals some of them.

After living in Manhattan's bohemian Lower East Side from 1966 to 1968, I returned to Boston as a writer and editor of *Avatar*. That launched a career in arts journalism. It entailed positions with *Boston After Dark/Phoenix*, the *Boston Herald Traveler*, the *Patriot Ledger*, *Boston Ledger*, Boston correspondent to *Art News*, columnist and frequent guest editor for *Art New England*, and other publications. Starting with the end of the Rathbone years, I interviewed every MFA director from then to now.

In 1976, I wrote a cover story for the *Boston Phoenix*, "Knocking the Stuffiness Out of a Brahmin Stronghold: The Renaissance at the Museum of Fine Arts."

The pullout quote for the article was "The MFA has an image and we did not talk with as many as we would have wished. The image is that of a rich, austere, acquisitive, dignified and not particularly welcoming institution deeply representative of the Boston establishment culturally, financially and socially." It was taken from the museum's 1970 ad hoc report.

For that assignment I had the full cooperation of the museum through Clementine Brown, the director of publicity and marketing. I had complete access to the director, Dr. Jan Fontein, board president Howard Johnson, administrators, curators, educators, and patrons.

I stuffed those interviews and others into file cabinets. Now, however, warts and all, this book is a remarkable tale told in the participants' own words. Considering current initiatives to deconstruct that legacy, the frankness and arrogance of some of their statements are astonishing.

The intent of this book is to interest the general reader, while for art historians and scholars, there is unique original source material. During an interview with Dr. Jan Fontein, for example, I asked about the museum's justification for owning several of Japan's greatest national treasures. Considering that he was one the foremost Asiatic scholars of his generation, Fontein's frank and detailed discussion is insightful.

Given the many difficult circumstances of the pandemic, the museum has been cooperative. In January 2021, Matthew Teitelbaum gave me twice the allotted time for an interview. I had also interviewed him in 2019 and when he was ending his tenure as a curator of the Institute of Contemporary Art in 1993.

Those one-on-one encounters comprise this oral history. The book conveys the history of a great institution in the words of its directors, curators, administrators, trustees, sources, and critics. This is their story as much as it is mine and the museum's.

Acknowledgements

While it has taken a lifetime to create this oral history, intensively over the past couple of years, I am grateful to the many who have supported this project. There, every step of the way, has been my wife, Astrid Hiemer, a former administrative officer of the Center for Advanced Visual Studies at MIT. She has provided many insights and edits.

Another unending source of material and aesthetic support has been my sister Mary Louise "Pippy" Giuliano. For many years we shared immersion in the Boston arts world.

This is now the seventh book created with the superb skills of meticulous editor, Leanne Jewett and creative designer, Amanda Hill.

There were long and insightful discussions of her father with Belinda Rathbone. Her book, *The Boston Raphael: A Mysterious Painting, an Embattled Museum in an Era of Change & a Daughter's Search for the Truth*, was an invaluable resource. The family paid to transcribe the extensive interview of Perry T. Rathbone with the *Archives of American Art*. The material about such a colorful and vital museum director deserves to be published in its entirety. I knew Perry well and enjoyed talking about him and the controversies of his legacy. He was one of the last of the old-school museum directors.

On the scholarly end, there was valuable discussion and advice from my former Boston University professors, Carl Chiarenza, Patricia Hills, and Peggy Smith. As some chapters were posted at *Berkshire Fine Arts* there was lively feedback from avant-garde gallerist Mario Diacono and former ICA director Sydney Rockefeller. Michael Conforti, former director of the Clark Art Institute, intriguingly discussed former Board President John Coolidge, trustee Whitehill, and curator Hanns Swarzenski. Collector and patron Ed Shein shared knowledge of Bloom and the Boston Expressionists. Jean Gibran, widow of the sculptor Kahlil Gibran, shared research on Bloom, Karl Zerbe, and Boston's renowned African American artist, Alan Rohan Crite. Documentary filmmaker David Sutherland provided access to his subject, Jack Levine, and discussed Bloom in depth.

While I was an intern for the Egyptian Department, Jim Jacobs was a volunteer for the adjacent Classical Department. Today he is a private art dealer. We have shared memories of our formative years. My consigliore, Robert Henriquez, and arts entrepreneur Steve Nelson were valued first responders.

For the MFA, Karen Frascona helped by answering questions and fact checking. Jennifer Riley facilitated use of nine vintage images for the book. Maria Daniels also provided images from the archive of the Boston Athenaeum. The Dallas Museum of Art provided images for former director Merrill Rueppel.

Of course, I am indebted to all those I interviewed and wrote about over the years, including the MFA directors Perry T. Rathbone, Cornelius Vermeule, Merrill Rueppel, Jan Fontein, Alan Shestack, Malcolm Rogers, and Matthew Teitelbaum. I knew them well, some more so than others. It was always exhilarating to go one-on-one with such remarkable individuals.

Matthew Teitelbaum Guides the Museum Through Crisis and Change

The Museum of Fine Arts, founded in 1870, turned 150 in 2020, but there was little time or mood for celebration. The Covid-19 pandemic devastated the nation, including cultural institutions.

Then generations of elitism and racism caught up with the museum.

I have known Matthew Teitelbaum since he was a curator at the Institute of Contemporary Art, which he left in 1993. He subsequently rose to the position of director of Canada's Art Gallery of Ontario (AGO). In 2015 he joined the MFA as director. In 2019 I interviewed him and, by Zoom, in 2021. Much had changed in the intervening time.

On May 20, 2019, Marvelyne Lamy, a middle school teacher at the Helen V. Davis Leadership Academy, wrote on Facebook recounting her students' experiences during a visit to the MFA. She related that students endured racist jokes and sexualized comments from adult patrons.

Lamy wrote that she and several other teachers brought a group of 26 non-white students to the museum. "At the very beginning of the tour, one of the staff gave an overview on what to expect and told the kids 'no food, no drink, and no watermelon.' "

The incident was widely reported in the media.

A release from the museum states, "After a thorough and integrated process, the MFA has achieved a forward-looking and productive memorandum of understanding (MOU) with Attorney General Maura Healey that builds on our ongoing work to foster greater diversity and inclusion at the Museum. 'There's nothing more important to us than making sure everyone feels welcome at the MFA,' said Matthew Teitelbaum, Ann and Graham Gund Director. 'Working with Attorney General Healey and the Davis Leadership Academy, we have the opportunity to create a new model of inclusion and diversity to serve Boston and we hope to set an example for others to follow. We look forward to our partnership and embracing this important work. It will build upon the foundation established by our strategic plan over the past three years. We have learned a great deal during the past year and through this process, and while we have more to learn and more work to do, together we will succeed. Whether you walk through the doors of the Museum every day, every week, once a year, or just once, everyone is welcome at the MFA.'

"The Museum will make a number of investments and commitments, including a $500,000 fund devoted to diversity and inclusion initiatives."

The museum announced, "Toward that goal Rosa Rodriguez-Williams was appointed as the MFA's first-ever Senior Director of Belonging and Inclusion. The newly established position will play a critical role in delivering on the MFA's promise to be a Museum for all of Boston. In her role, Rodriguez-Williams will empower others within the MFA to prioritize inclusion as a key practice in their own work, creating an internal culture that places a priority on visitor experience.

" 'Rosa's deep experience and passion for equity and inclusion will be invaluable as we continue our important work in ensuring a true sense of belonging at the MFA,' said Matthew Teitelbaum, Ann and Graham Gund Director. 'She will be integral in reimagining how we welcome and engage historically underrepresented audiences, truly reflecting the communities we serve. This is one of the most important issues for museums in the 21st century, and I look forward to working alongside her to achieve our goal of becoming open and accessible.'"

On 12 January 2021, I spoke by Zoom with Teitelbaum about challenges the museum faced during its chaotic anniversary. I asked how the museum is coping with the ongoing pandemic, as well as how he is addressing diversity and filling gaps in the modern and contemporary collections.

During a 2019 visit to the Art Gallery of Ontario, as well as other Canadian museums, my wife, Astrid, and I noted the degree to which First Nation artists were prominently integrated into galleries displaying permanent collections. Fresh from that experience, I discussed his role in that process. Those insights are included in the final chapter of this book. In that effort, he takes great pride in what was accomplished.

With his focus on modern and contemporary art it was anticipated that Teitelbaum would upgrade the MFA in modern and contemporary art. As director, however, he has broader responsibilities.

Navigating through a year of challenges, he conveyed the reassuring sense of being in control of the museum.

We started by crunching the numbers, and I asked about the endowment. "That fluctuates day to day," he said. "I can check if you need to know. We can put you in touch with our CFO if you need exact figures on debt that Rogers passed on."

Museum spokesperson Karen Frascona responded, "When Malcolm Rogers arrived in 1994, the budget was about $77 million; it rose to $101 million. The number of visitors was 864,179 in 1994, and 1,227,163 in 2015. The endowment grew from $180.6 million to $623.7 million. The 2021 value of the endowment is $608 million. The museum's debt, however, grew from $35 million; to $189 million at its peak, through construction and the 2007 acquisition of the adjacent, former Forsyth Institute. The American Wing cost $345 million; the Rogers campaign was $504 million and included endowment. He left a debt of $140 million, which in 2021 is $105 million."

She later emailed further clarification, "It is important to keep in mind the following when writing about endowment:

- Endowments are not cash reserves, which is a common misunderstanding.
- The $608 million is the total amount held in endowment, not the annual budget for the institution (or a general savings account). Endowment means that the principle is invested and we can only spend a percentage of the income generated at a spend rate set by the Museum's Board of Trustees (currently 5.1 percent).
- The MFA's endowment is made up of literally hundreds of restricted funds that can only be spent according to the donor's intent. For example, the income from an endowed fund to support a particular curatorial position cannot be spent to pay for building maintenance.
- Endowment funds for art acquisitions are part of the Museum's

total endowment and just another type of restricted fund. If there is approximately $18 million in endowed funds for acquisitions, that means we have 5.1% annually in spendable income (about $900,000) that can be used to buy art each year. And that income is allocated between many separate restricted funds with donor specifications for their use (i.e. American paintings, Japanese prints, etc....).

- Each separate restricted fund has its own purpose defined by the documented donor's intent."

Regarding the endowment, which has declined, Teitelbaum said, "We haven't made that much progress but have reduced debt." He described the debt left by Rogers as "significant" particularly when faced with $14 million in debt during the 2020 year of pandemic. The debt for 2021 is projected to be even greater at $21 million.

The Rogers' mantra of "One Museum" conflated independent departments into rebranded conglomerates like Art of the Americas, Art of the Ancient World, Art of Africa and Oceania. Renowned curators were fired and others resigned. The restructuring disrupted the independence of departments, which traditionally functioned as fiefdoms.

I asked Teitelbaum to define his mandate for the museum.

He declined to comment on the administration of his predecessor, but was clear in articulating his vision for the museum. "From the moment I arrived here I wanted a museum for all of Boston. Regarding my relationship to curators, we talk a lot and reach across departments. That makes our relationships richer and deeper from within and we also reach outside the museum to diverse communities, including artists. My two imperatives are to work more together and across departments as well as with outside communities. We want to open up and work with others. When you work with shared narratives to show and interpret work, that results in interesting ideas."

One of which is the notion of modernism. He deconstructed the concept that modernism originated in Europe and spread from there. He is developing a team to explore how this was a global movement. The challenge is to find space and programming to present this as well as funding support. This will also be applied to collections. Through the lens of contemporary art and theory, for example, how do we look at and activate our relationship to classical art?

When renovated classic galleries are reopened, six sculptures by Cy Twombly

(1928–2011), on extended loan from the Twombly Foundation, will be displayed. The juxtaposition will convey to visitors concepts of how artists draw from and are inspired by the past. It demonstrates how classicism in embedded in abstract art. On the occasion of the 150th anniversary *Il Parnassus*, 1964, by Twombly is a promised gift by Ann and Graham Gund.

The museum is moving forward with new galleries for Dutch Art and The Ancient World. The Museum has unveiled a new gallery of Old Kingdom Egyptian art with an adjoining gallery of portraits drawn from all periods. Teitlebaum said that they have been working with Harvard, Emerson, communities and artists to explore: "How to bring ancient works alive in a contemporary setting with ideas about democracy and leadership."

I asked how the museum had coped with a time of crisis.

"This has been a time of health crisis, crisis of recognition, questions of financial engagement, and institutional authority," he said. "For me it has been deeply personal, as well as deeply institutional. We have had a staff deeply concerned about their positions. With the financial crisis, we have been deeply challenged and it is here to stay for a long time. There have been existential questions."

Cultural institutions have struggled to survive. The best-endowed museums can tighten belts. The performing arts, music, theatre, and dance, function on the edge and depend on ticket sales and subscription series. Their crisis is more critical.

The loss for the MFA in 2020 has been reported at $14 million. "We ended the year with a balanced budget," Teitelbaum reported. "It is projected that the 2021 loss will be about $15 million. (Frascona suggested $21 million.) We have managed through cost containment, fundraising, drawing on cash reserves, layoffs, and early retirement. We have tried to handle severance packages in a very thoughtful manner. The staff has been reduced by 18 to 20%."

Regarding the visit of the Davis Leadership Academy, he stated, "First we tried to determine just what happened and what precisely was said. We have been following the agreement with the Attorney General on our hiring practices. We are adhering to sensitivity training, which actually had started prior to the incident. It entailed a challenge for the visitors and their sense of identity. This involves all institutions. (He stated with intensity) I do not believe for *one minute* that what occurred at the MFA is unique. It concerns all institutions. Through our actions, perhaps we can be a leader."

On the occasion of its centennial in 1970, the museum's board formed an ad hoc committee which examined the museum and made key recommendations. They reached out to leaders in the community, including Elma Lewis (1921–2004) the founder of The National Center for Afro American Artists and The Elma Lewis School of Fine Arts in Roxbury. She raised issues of diversity.

An agreement emerged from these discussions for the MFA to support the National Center, which was initially a part of her school. Arson, in 1985, destroyed the school, but not the museum. It occupied a former mansion on Elm Hill Avenue. The MFA paid the salary of its director, Barry Gaither, and his assistant, the artist Harriet Kennedy. Gaither, now retired, curated several major exhibitions for the MFA.

Initially, the MFA followed the diversity recommendations of the ad hoc report, including the appointment of an African American board member. In 1976, Board President, Howard Johnson, formerly president of MIT, appointed Phyllis A. Wallace (1921–1993) an economist and activist. She was on the faculty of MIT's Sloan School of Management.

From then until now, there were many missed opportunities to address issues of diversity. Social justice, in fits and starts, has simmered on the museum's back burner. I asked Teitelbaum if the museum continues to have a relationship with Gaither and the National Center? In recent years the National Center has fallen off the radar screen.

He responded that the commitment continues, "Gaither has now retired but acts as a consultant to the museum. Our discussions have been very thoughtful with them. They have to decide what they want to do in the future."

To which I replied that since the 1970s, the MFA's support was "the tip of the iceberg" and could have been more substantive. There have been many opportunities to avoid conflicts of social justice that have pervaded society, including arts and culture, particularly in the past few years.

He agreed, "Yes, responses have been inconsistent across the country. Today, we are not the same museum that we were when I came here in 2015."

While there has been focus on the community of color, the museum has a legacy of elitism and anti-Semitism. In addition to African Americans and Hispanics, the museum has not been welcoming to Boston's Irish American, Italian American, Asian, and other ethnic communities. During the court-ordered desegregation of Boston Public Schools (1974–1988) the city was revealed to be deeply racist.

The museum embraced Boston artists until the leading artists emerged as the Jewish Boston Expressionists during and after the 1930s.

I stated, "The Museum honored Maxim Karolik (1893–1963, a Russian Jewish immigrant and with his wife Martha Codman Karolik, 1858–1948, a great collector). He was named a Great Benefactor but was never appointed a trustee. That didn't happen until Sidney Rabb (who died at 84 in 1985) in the 1960s. You are the second director of Jewish heritage. The first was Alan Shestack (1987–1993). What is your position on the museum's legacy?"

He responded, "I don't have a developed thought on that. Concerning the current crisis, diversity is a good thing. Invitations to many groups have not been made."

Regarding Judaica, Frascona stated, "The MFA acquired the Charles and Lynn Schusterman Collection of 119 decorative and ritual Jewish art objects. Many of these objects are on view throughout the MFA's galleries, demonstrating the dynamism and importance of Judaica through time and cultures. Simona Di Nepi joined the MFA as its first-ever dedicated curator of Judaica in 2017, an endowed curatorial position funded by Charles and Lynn Schusterman. The MFA has continued to collect Judaica in recent years, including purchasing two pairs of Torah finials in 2019 as well as a Torah shield, wine cup, and finials in 2020.

"Exhibitions featuring work by Jewish artists include *Memory Unearthed: The Lodz Ghetto Photographs of Henryk Ross* in 2016. Erica Hirschler curated *Hyman Bloom: Matters of Life and Death* in 2019. Since 2013, the MFA has partnered with local Jewish cultural organizations such as the Jewish Arts Collaborative and Combined Jewish Philanthropies to host an annual Hanukkah Community Celebration welcoming visitors into the Museum for free to learn about its vast collection of Judaica—this year's Hanukkah Community Celebration was hosted virtually."

I asked how many trustees the museum has and its diversity? "Some 37 or 38 voting members," he said. "I can get you those numbers. The board is getting more diverse points of view and overall is getting better."

(Fact checking revealed that as of September 2020, 23 percent of voting Trustees and 32 percent of voting Advisors identify as people of color. Edward E. Greene was elected as the Museum's first-ever African American President of the

Board of Trustees, also in September 2020.)

Museum directors bring their curatorial vision to the position. Dr. Jan Fontein (1927–2017), for example, focused on renovation on Asiatic galleries. Sources have revealed that he diverted funds designated for other departments toward that end. I asked Teitelbaum for his priorities.

He responded about a range of projects and renovations. "Our new, expanded center for conservation has no rival in North America," he said. "New Dutch, Greek, Byzantine, and Ancient World galleries are a high priority by the end of 2021. We are creating a diverse *Table of Voices*. That includes seats for artists who are being developed to become trustees. Contemporary art will be on display across the institution. There are robust conversations with collectors. There will be more sculptures sited in areas surrounding the museum. We are creating spaces for the voices of artists to be heard. We will have Cy Twombly's in Greek and Roman galleries. They will be on loan from the foundation."

From its founding in 1870, the MFA was committed to Boston's artists. That started with the establishment of the Museum School. Instruction was initiated in the galleries. Eventually, with the move to the Fenway, there was a separate building to house the school. The program employed and trained artists whose work was displayed at the museum. That went on robustly until the 1930s. That's when the German Jewish artist Karl Zerbe represented a class shift for the school's faculty. The MFA lost interest in showing and collecting Boston artists because of this ethnic shift. There was significant progress, in 2019, with the special exhibition curated by Erica Hirschler, *Hyman Bloom: Matters of Life and Death*.

By email Hirschler conveyed updated programming addressing diversity for the museum. "Diversity has been an integral aspect of the Museum's collecting strategy for quite some time. In advance of the opening of the Art of the Americas Wing in 2010, the MFA made significant acquisitions—through both gift and purchase—of works by (African American artists) Henry Ossawa Tanner, Loïs Mailou Jones, Norman Lewis, John Wilson, Allan Rohan Crite, and Wilfredo Lam.

"Our curators continue to seek out and acquire works by Black artists—significant additions to the collection since the John Axelrod (acquisition of 67 works) include a 2012 gift of paintings and works on paper by Eldzier Cortor from the artist's family, *Lancaster, New Hampshire* (1862) by Robert S. Duncanson in 2015, *The Annunciation and the Adoration of the Wise Men* (1957) by Clementine Hunter in 2018 and *Elizabeth (Mrs. Andrew) Aitkin and her Daughter Eliza* (about

1805) by Joshua Johnson in 2019.

"The Art of the Americas department continues to make acquisitions that represent geographic diversity, with purchases of works by Mexican artists (Frida Kahlo, Miguel Cabrera, José de Alcíbar, Ignacio de Castro, and David Alfaro Siqueiros), South American artists (from the 18th century and up) and a number of Native American objects in a variety of media. Gender diversity and LGBTQIA+ representation have also been top of mind, with acquisitions of works by women artists (as evidenced by the current exhibition *Women Take the Floor*) and queer and trans artists including Paul Cadmus, Arroh-ah-och, and Charles Winslow Hall.

"In recent years, the MFA has also added to its holdings of American Jewish artists. In 2006, the Museum received two monumental works—a sculpture and a painting—by David Aronson, and the momentum has picked up again recently, following the success of the Hyman Bloom exhibition. The Museum acquired two works by Bernard Chaet in 2016, two paintings by Bloom in 2018, two more Aronsons, and a Karl Zerbe in 2020. Several other acquisitions of works by Bloom, Aronson, Samuel Bak, and Harold Tovish are currently in progress."

Later Hirschler added additional details, "...We have Jack Levine's work in the collection, of course, and another very fine one has been made a promised gift. The painting you may recall is *Street Scene No. 1*, which has been in the collection since 1946 and is a favorite of mine. There are three other oils, including a late political one, *Vermeer Goes to Washington*, and a number of works on paper—alas, not all of these have images on the website.

"While I understand very well indeed that there has been concern in the past about the museum and anti-Semitism, I can assure you that it plays no part in our collecting strategy, and we are working actively to diversify our holdings in every way. The establishment of the Judaica collection and Simona's curatorship has helped enormously to build trust in the museum's intentions in that regard, as I hope the recent Bloom show did as well. When I visit collectors, that's one of my main goals—to reassure owners that despite what they may have felt or heard about the museum in the past, the MFA is indeed an appropriate home and a caring steward for these works, and that we are looking ahead, not back, with an eye toward inclusion and renewed narratives about American art. And yes, we keep an eye out for potential purchases as well, although our funds are limited (we tried for a Bloom at auction a few years back, for example, but were outbid)."

If the museum honored Bloom with a special exhibition, it owes equal recognition to Allan Rohan Crite, (1910–2007). A graduate of the Museum School, he is regarded as the dean of his generation of African American artists. I asked Teitelbaum about his commitment to telling the story of Boston's artists.

He affirmed his interest, "The Museum School was important in the 1870s, 1880s, 1890s, and beyond. More than training artists, it created a broader interest in the arts. It helped to grow visitors to the museum. Other than the Art Institute of Chicago, it has become increasingly difficult for museums to maintain art schools, as it is for us. As the result of the Bloom exhibition, we are in process of increasing acquisitions of his work. There is a larger observation in the collection of Bloom, Crite, print-making, and photography. We must be committed to Boston artists and we are purchasing works by Boston artists."

In 2011 the museum acquired 67 works by African American artists from the Boston attorney John Axelrod. The sale at between five and ten million dollars was reported as below market rate. Overall, the collector has donated some 700 works to the museum.

Asked about the Axelrod acquisition Teitelbaum said, "It's on us to maintain a commitment to black voices. It's on us to continue."

Given limited resources, it is a mandate for curators to advocate for space and funding of their departments. Responding to pressure from a potential donor of Greek heritage, Rogers reassigned the prime Ancient Egyptian gallery to Classical art. It was formerly located on the axis from the museum's rotunda. The collection, regarded as the finest Old Kingdom collection other than Cairo's, is now less imposing, facing the atrium of the American Wing.

"You will be surprised by the new galleries," he said. "Particularly, the installation of the collection of Nubian art. (It is regarded as the world's finest). It's a matter of geography and finding space for it. To install the collection means removing and relocating works. It is also a matter of funding. It's something that I regard as important to do."

During the 21-year tenure of Malcolm Rogers there was a great range of programming with an emphasis on populism. Exceptions were exhibitions and acquisitions of works by Ellsworth Kelly, David Hockney, and Dale Chihuly. There wasn't a strong sense of closing the gap on modern and contemporary art.

In that field, the appointment of Teitelbaum raised the bar of expectations. That paradigm shift is a work in progress. To date we have seen *Writing the Future: Basquiat and the Hip-Hop Generation*, which was disrupted by pandemic closings.

At the AGO he initiated the first major Basquiat exhibition in Canada. Other noteworthy MFA projects have been: *Women Take the Floor; Black Histories: Black Futures; Community Art Initiatives; Exchange Codes; Personal Space: Self Portraits on Paper, Elsa Dorfman: Me and My Camera;* and *The Banner Project: Robert Pruitt.*

The program hit a speed bump, however, with *Philip Guston Now* a project in partnership with National Gallery of Art (Washington, D. C.), Tate Modern (London), and the Museum of Fine Arts, (Houston). Having worked on the project for four years there was a collective decision among the museum directors to postpone the traveling exhibition.

In the 1960s, reacting to the Vietnam War, Guston (1913–1980) abandoned abstract expressionism and adapted a cartoonish style that initiated the movement of neo expressionism. From an early age in LA he was aware of the Ku Klux Klan's persecution of Jews. In 1923, perhaps caused by that American pogrom, his Ukrainian-born father (Goldstein) hung himself in the family shed. Philip discovered the body.

The planned exhibition entails 24 images that evoke the Klan and two more where the imagery is less obvious. In total, there would be a selection of roughly 125 paintings and 70 drawings.

When Guston made a shift from abstraction to figurative expressionism he was shunned by the art world and vilified by conservative critics. Boston proved to be a port in the storm. From 1973 to 1978 he taught a monthly graduate seminar at the Boston University School of Fine Arts. His presence recharged the tradition of Boston Expressionism, which had continued at the Museum School. David Aronson, the director of the BU studio program, was a second-generation Boston Expressionist.

In gratitude, Guston offered the MFA its choice of work in the studio. It was perceived as an insult when MFA curator Kenworth Moffett asked the artist for one of his older, abstract works.

There were all the right reasons for a major Guston show in Boston. I was among critics who protested the decision to cancel or postpone it.

Teitelbaum commented that he read what I wrote and was not surprised by pervasive criticism. What happened next says a lot about his moral fiber, leadership, and commitment to problem solving. The museums had to reconsider contextualizing the Klan paintings and develop educational programming around them.

The museums hoped to avoid the protest that was unleashed during the 2017 Whitney Biennial, when it displayed a painting *Open Casket* by Dana Shutz that depicted the brutally mutilated corpse of Emmett Till. The 14-year-old who was lynched in Mississippi in 1955.

"It's not acceptable for a white person to transmute Black suffering into profit and fun," said artist Hannah Black. There were demonstrations including protestors blocking view of the painting.

The challenge was to convey the intent and social justice commentary of Guston's powerful and disturbing Klan images. It raises deep issues of the rights of Caucasians to depict and interpret black history and culture. What are the boundaries of that discussion?

In an MFA release Teitelbaum stated in part, "In considering the presentation of *Philip Guston Now*—both before and after the decision to postpone—I have engaged with artists, academics, community leaders, colleagues at other institutions, and a wide range of staff and stakeholders within our MFA community. I listened to those who live in the art world and who have a profound interest in Guston's life and work, sought the views of those proximate to the world of art, but are not directly part of it, and solicited feedback from others who are deeply committed to a broader definition of the cultural and social missions of museums. I continue to learn from all of them."

The exhibition was initially planned to be launched at the National Gallery. The MFA was to be the last venue. Teitelbaum retained that slot, and the exhibition will now start at the MFA on May 1, 2022 and run through September 11, 2022. As reconfigured and programmed, the Guston exhibition will represent a great teaching moment for the museum and its audience. It is emblematic of a museum embracing change and moving forward.

Frascona sent additional diversity-based updates:

In summer 2020, the MFA announced a new initiative to acquire works by 24 contemporary artists based in Boston and throughout the U.S. and Puerto Rico. An upcoming exhibition titled *New Light: Encounters and Connections* will include many of these newly acquired works placed in conversation with historical objects in the MFA's collection, which will illuminate and trace the timeless threads and themes that artists capture in their practice.

In the MFA's Art of the America's Wing, curators are reinterpreting key works in the galleries and interrogating the definition of "American" through a new installation at the entrance of the wing.

The MFA announced the creation of a dedicated curator of Islamic art in winter 2020 through a grant from Lilly Endowment Inc. The new curator will oversee the MFA's collection of arts from Islamic cultures and the MFA's dedicated Arts of Islamic Cultures gallery, which was recently redesigned in summer 2019.

In winter 2018, collector Wan-go H.C. Weng donated a landmark gift of 183 Chinese paintings, works of calligraphy, ink rubbings, and textiles spanning five imperial dynasties. This gift elevates the MFA's Chinese paintings collection into one of the foremost outside of China. Many of these works are on view in *Weng Family Collection of Chinese Painting: Family and Friends*, part of a series of three exhibitions celebrating the major acquisition.

The MFA launched its *Table of Voices* program in 2018, a new program that embeds community perspectives into the exhibition planning process. During exhibition planning, the MFA invites a group of local individuals with a wide range of expertise and backgrounds, including musicians, artists, educators, academics, financiers, social workers, and creative professionals, to help guide the interpretation of exhibition objects and in some cases write labels that appear in the galleries. *Table of Voices* has been utilized in major exhibitions such as *Gender Bending Fashion, Ancient Nubia Now* and *Writing the Future: Basquiat and the Hip-Hop Generation*.

American Art Curator Erica H. Hirshler. Giuliano photo.

Matthew Teitelbaum in his office. Giuliano photo.

Interviewing Matthew. Astrid Hiemer photo.

MFA 100

In the aftermath of the Civil War (1861–1865) the city of Boston was prosperous and progressive. Inspired by London's South Kensington Museum, founded in 1852 and later renamed the Victoria and Albert Museum, Boston's Museum of Fine Arts (MFA) was founded in 1870.

The Structures

Initially, the MFA occupied floors of the Boston Athenaeum on Beacon Hill, which had been founded in 1807. From 1827 the Athenaeum featured an art gallery and program of exhibitions. In 1847, after several moves, it constructed the building designed by Howard Clark Cabot that it still occupies.

Works from the Athenaeum were loaned to the MFA. That generosity took an odd turn with Athenaeum's decision to sell its pair of George and Martha Washington portraits by Gilbert Stuart. They had been displayed at the MFA for a hundred years, but in 1979 were sold to The National Portrait Gallery for $5 million. An agreement was reached for the pair to be shown in Boston for one out of every five years.

By 1876 the MFA moved to its own building in Copley Square. The ornate structure was designed by John Hubbard Sturgis and Charles Brigham in the Venetian Gothic manner with brick and ceramic exterior panels. Like London's

South Kensington Museum, it displayed plaster casts of classical and renaissance sculptures. It allowed visitors to experience facsimiles of masterpieces at a time when travel was less accessible.

By 1907 the MFA outgrew its home in Copley Square. Through serendipity it came to acquire great works and ran out of space to display them. After some debate the plaster casts went into storage or were scrapped.

The Copley Square plot, which had been gifted by the city of Boston, was sold with the proceeds helping to purchase land on Huntington Avenue in the Fenway. Construction of a design by Guy Lowell would continue in stages into the 1920s. The section comprising the granite, Neoclassical façade and rotunda was started in 1907 and occupied in 1909.

The Lowell plan created confusion. The ground floor was intended for offices and study collection galleries. From the Huntington Avenue entrance, visitors were intended to ascend the grand staircase to galleries on the second level, the impact of which was augmented with murals above the rotunda by John Singer Sargent. From the grand staircase one could proceed left into galleries of the Asiatic collection or right into the Ancient Egyptian and Classical galleries. Straight ahead, one passed though the Tapestries galleries and, after 1915, into the Evans Wing of European paintings.

Visitors, however, were diverted to the ground level cloakrooms and wandered beyond them into a warren of galleries with little thematic continuity. When Merrill Rueppel was director 1973–1975 there was a committee that suggested moving the staircase. He went along with the plan, which was turned down by the board and became one of the issues cited in his removal.

When I.M. Pei's West Wing was completed in 1981, the main entrance was redirected from the Huntington and Fenway entrances. It was Pei's plan that created two loops leading visitors coherently through the museum from the parking lot on the side of the museum.

There was further tinkering with traffic flow during the construction of the American Wing by Lord Norman Foster during the administration of Malcolm Rogers in the 1990s.

After the Great Chicago Fire of 1871, the era of Chicago's revolutionary tall office buildings, or skyscrapers, was largely financed by Boston's banks. In 1872, there was a similar fire in Boston that destroyed wooden structures in the downtown vicinity of Washington Street. It was reconstructed as a mercantile area with large department stores.

While Bostonians financed Chicago skyscrapers, they shunned skyscrapers for their own city. A single exception was the addition to the Custom House near Quincy Market. Constructed 1837–47, it was designed by Ammi Burnham Young in the Greek Revival style. The tower designed by Peabody and Stearns was added 1913–15. It is now a Marriott property.

The MFA and Boston's Visionary Plan

The original location of the MFA was part of a visionary plan to expand and reinvent the city. Starting in 1859, there was the project to fill the Mill Pond and create the area now known as the Back Bay. There was a grand design modeled on Baron Georges-Eugène Haussmann's renovation of Paris from 1853 to 1870.

Commonwealth Avenue emulated Avenue des Champs-Élysées. The Back Bay was laid out as a grid with alphabetical cross streets: Arlington, Berkley, Clarendon, Dartmouth, Exeter, Fairfield, Gloucester, and Hereford. Crossing Massachusetts Avenue, the landfill ended with Bay State Road, which is now part of the Boston University Campus.

There were corner lots for great mansions and row houses in between. Those closest to Boston Common were most elegant. The later ones, approaching Commonwealth Avenue, were developed by speculators.

The architectural accomplishment of this development was the subject of Bainbridge Bunting's 1967 book *Houses of Boston's Back Bay: An Architectural History, 1840–1917* (Harvard University Press, 494 pages, illustrated).

That it resulted in one of the most beautiful and livable cities in America, was the theme of the 1969 Museum of Fine Arts' exhibition *Back Bay Boston: The City as a Work of Art*. The 149-page catalogue included essays by Walter Mumford and MFA trustee Walter Muir Whitehill.

In a 1986 exhibition, curated by Trevor J. Fairbrother, the MFA celebrated the aesthetics of that period with *The Bostonians: Painters of an Elegant Age, 1870-1930*. Boston artists created in the genteel manner of American impressionism and some taught at the School of the Museum of Fine Arts.

Notably, the MFA lost interest in collecting and exhibiting Boston artists after 1930. During the depression years there was a change at the Museum School when Karl Zerbe, a German born expressionist, became its head. He was one of three leaders of The Boston Expressionists, along with other Jewish artists Hyman

Bloom and Jack Levine. The MFA shunned these artists until quite recently. Expressionist figuration, however, became a signifier for art created in Boston and remains so even to this day. In 2019 the museum exhibited *Hyman Bloom: Matters of Life and Death* curated by Erica Hirshler.

"Bloom's work has been neglected for much too long," Hirshler stated. "As we reassess the histories we tell about 20th-century American art, we need to include those bold figures who, like Bloom, remained committed to the figure and who sought to explore the complex nature of human existence, in which beauty and horror are often inextricably linked."

The concept of the residential Back Bay was that merchants and bankers would live in their mansions or "French Flats" and walk to work. They could take a carriage to the thriving financial district and waterfront. Boston was still a viable port and Quincy Market functioned as such. For many residents homes in the Back Bay were occupied in season. During the summer months families resided in mansions on the North Shore, Pride's Crossing, Cape Cod, Newport, or Northeast Harbor, Maine.

The needs of these wealthy families would be met by visiting Copley Square and Newbury Street. They worshiped at H.H. Richardson's Romanesque Trinity Church (1872–1877) or Charles Amos Cummings and Willard T. Sears Old South Church, completed in 1873, in the Gothic Revival style. There were other churches within walking distance.

Their literary interests were met by The Boston Public Library, designed in the Neoclassical style by Charles Follen McKim which opened in 1895. It emulated French Beaux Arts design.

On the corner of Copley Square and Huntington Avenue, in 1887, S.S. Pierce opened an eclectic Romanesque building designed by S. Edwin Tobey. Groceries purchased there were delivered to the ground floor kitchens of the Back Bay by public alleys. The landmark was later razed and the location is now occupied by a Westin Hotel. Prior to development, in the 1960s, that stretch of Huntington Avenue was home to jazz clubs like Storyville, The Stables, and Mahogany Hall.

There were other shops and cultural institutions along Newbury Street, including The Copley Society and Guild of Boston Artists. Men were properly attired at Brooks Brothers while silver and jewelry were sold by Shreve, Crump & Low.

Massachusetts Institute of Technology was founded in 1861. Its Rogers

Building, later razed when the campus moved to Cambridge in 1916, was nearly identical to its neighbor, The Museum of Natural History, which opened in 1863. I recall visiting as a child and marveling at the skeleton of a dinosaur hanging from the ceiling. In 1951, the museum relocated as the Boston Museum of Science. The landmark building, between Boylston and Newbury Streets, became home to Bonwit Teller and then Louis Boston.

Around the corner from Copley Square on Huntington Avenue, William Gibbon Preston designed the sprawling Mechanics Hall as well as the MIT Rogers Building. Growing up in Boston I attended the annual Flower Show and Autorama as well as the traveling rodeo and circus.

Cultural development continued along Huntington Avenue and into the Fenway. The MFA relocated within walking distance of the Isabella Stewart Gardner Museum, which was built according to her notions working with Willard Sears from 1896 to 1903.

The Boston Symphony Orchestra (BSO) was founded in 1881. It moved to a building designed by McKim, Mead, and White in 1900. Across from it on Massachusetts Avenue, Horticultural Hall opened in 1901. It now houses the library of the Museum of Fine Arts.

A few blocks down from the BSO on Huntington Avenue was The Boston Opera House. It opened in 1909 in a building designed by Edmund M. Wheelwright. It was demolished in 1958 and the site was rebuilt as part of the campus of Northeastern University. It was an elegant theatre and I recall attending the Ballet Russe as well as the final performance of the road company of *Oklahoma*. Boston has struggled to establish a viable opera company.

In 1897, Boston built America's first subway system. As Douglass Shand Tucci documented in his 1978 book *Built in Boston: City and Suburb* that led to the gradual demise of the Back Bay as businessmen and financiers commuted from mansions in South Brookline, Chestnut Hill, Newton, Wellesley, Lexington, and Lincoln.

Property in the Back Bay devolved into rooming houses and apartments.

From 1870 to the Great Depression there were thriving cultural/educational/medical institutions. After that were many factors for atrophy and decline. Boston's ability to compete with the financial and cultural resources of New York City lapsed. By the time I came of age in Boston during the 1950s, it had become a conservative, provincial, second-class city.

By the late 1960s there was a revival, which I recount in my book *Counterculture in Boston: 1968 to 1980s*. Part of that was the formation and activism of "The Studio Coalition" in 1969, the first ever instance of open studios. This occurred at the same time as the revitalization of the ICA under Andrew C. Hyde.

The decline reversed in the 1980s with the condo movement that transformed the Back Bay as well as nearby South End. Today, there is a real estate boom. Boston again is a vibrant, expanding, and culturally endowed community.

In 1978 friends of mine bought a 1,800 square foot condo on Commonwealth Avenue and Hereford Street. They paid $50,000 and sold it in 1981 for $160,000. A unit half the size in an adjacent building is listed (2021) for $1.25 million. Checking Zillow, prices in the Back Bay and South End range from $349,000 to $8,955,000

Building the Collections

During its first decades, the MFA took advantage of unprecedented opportunities to create world-class collections. Agents of the museum were often unchallenged in purchasing the best classical objects that came to market. Individuals living in Japan, for a variety of reasons, built an unsurpassed collection. For decades curator George Andrew Reisner sent home masterpieces excavated in Egypt. Bostonians collected and later donated choice works of French Impressionism and Post Impressionism. Prominent families donated portraits by John Singleton Copley and later John Singer Sargent, as well as a trove of silver, decorative arts, and furniture.

The great opportunities for acquisitions slowed down with the move to Huntington Avenue in 1907. Resources went toward construction. The museum organized its first fundraising drive during its centennial year. The trustees identified a need of $20 million that was adjusted to $13.4 as urgently needed by 1970.

The MFA is the 14th largest art museum in the world measured by public gallery area. It contains approximately 500,000 works of art, making it one of the most comprehensive collections in the Americas. Until the pandemic, annual attendance exceeded a million visitors.

Its collection of Japanese art is the largest in the world outside of Japan. There are some 100,000 total items including 4,000 Japanese paintings, 5,000 ceramic pieces, and over 30,000 ukiyo-e prints.

For American art, in addition to Colonial portraits, the strength of 18th and 19th century furniture, decorative art, painting and drawings came from collectors Martha C. and Maxim Karolik. For 20th century American art and photography there was the generosity of William and Saundra Lane.

Forsyth Wickes (1876–1964) was an attorney and collector who lived in France where he purchased a chateau to house a vast collection of fine art, decorative arts and furniture. He eventually returned with residences in New York and a "cottage" Starboard House in Newport, Rhode Island.

In Newport for a lunch engagement, by chance, MFA director, Perry T. Rathbone, was introduced to him. Rathbone and the museum's trustees were invited to visit. While Wickes was not present, the staff was instructed to provide lunch and the run of the house.

Wickes, a bachelor, died not long after and executors informed the museum that he had bequeathed his home and its collection of some 800 pieces. The museum undertook remodeling to install the objects much as they had been displayed in Newport. The museum also did this, for an extended but limited period, to show intact the Karolik collection.

This is a not uncommon demand of great collectors. It is often difficult, if not impossible, to make such accommodations. That has resulted in mega collectors creating private museums.

The Whitehill history records many highlights as well as acquisitions and incidents that today would be regarded as questionable, if not outright illegal.

Within a decade of its founding the MFA began to display and acquire Japanese art. In 1880 Dr. Williams Sturgis Bigelow loaned works, which by the following year, numbered 509. For a variety of reasons several Bostonians with ties to the museum resided in Japan.

The museum's website states that "The extraordinary strength of the MFA's Japanese collection is attributed to the foresight and enterprise of Edward Sylvester Morse, Ernest Francisco Fenollosa, William Sturgis Bigelow, and Okakura Kakuz (also known as Okakura Tenshin). Bigelow became the department's greatest benefactor, donating the majority of the Museum's 4,000 Japanese paintings and more than 30,000 ukiyo-e prints—one of the largest collections of its type in the world. Morse, Fenollosa, and Okakura all served as MFA curators, and Bigelow was a MFA Trustee. While residing in Japan during the late 19th century, they assembled examples of the highest artistic achievements in art, both religious and secular, ranging from the eighth century to modern times. Noteworthy among these holdings are the eighth-century Hokked konpon mandara, one of the earliest extant landscape paintings in East Asia; the 1189 image of Miroku; the earliest dated work by the master sculptor Kaikei; the mid-13th-century Heiji monogatari emaki, which chronicles the burning of the Sanjo Palace in vivid detail; and the Four Sages of Mount Shang, a pair of whimsical screens by the 18th-century eccentric painter Soga Sh haku. In addition, the MFA holds important examples of lacquer, ceramics, swords and sword fittings, and a large group of Noh robes and masks."

These acquisitions occurred during a period of transition for Japanese culture. Treasures were affordable and available. There were no restrictions for such acquisitions. Global laws would come later. Notably, the museum has been an ethical and transparent custodian including cordial relations with Japanese museums, curators, and scholars.

The collectors, however, had misgivings. Whitehill quotes Morse (page 109) "Many fine things of Japanese art are now on the market, like these we are buying. It is like the lifeblood of Japan is seeping through a hidden wound. They do not know how sad it is to let their beautiful treasures leave their country," Morse said.

His words went like a sword into the heart of the young Japanese sitting in the shadows. In that moment Okakura conceived a mission. On his return to Tokyo, he went to officials and important citizens and never rested until they, too, recognized the situation. Morse's words were the seed, flowering in the mind of Okakura, that produced the law of Kokuho (National Treasures) by which, by 1884, all remaining objects of ancient art were registered and restricted from export.

Whitehill published an 1884 letter from Fenollosa in Tokyo to Morse in Salem (page 112). It states in part "Already people here are saying that my collection must be kept here in Japan for the Japanese. I have bought a number of the very greatest treasures secretly. The Japanese as yet do not know that I have them. I wish I could see them all safely housed forever in the Boston Art Museum. And yet, if the Emperor or the Mombusho should want to buy my collection, wouldn't it be my duty to humanity, all things considered, to let them have it? What do you think?"

That came to pass when Dr. Charles Goddard Weld (1857–1911) purchased the Fenollosa collection of paintings. He soon loaned it to the museum from then officially known as the Fenollosa-Weld collection. Upon his death Weld gave the museum 2,072 objects, of which 1,099 were paintings. That same year Bigelow gave the museum 14,939 objects of which 3,634 were Chinese and Japanese paintings. This did not include his vast donation of prints.

While the assembly of the Japanese collection was unique for the museum field there were great accomplishments in other departments. The classical collection owes much to Edward Perry Warren (1860–1928). After Harvard, he read classics at New College, Oxford. He established a base on High Street of Lewes in Sussex. While gradually filled with antiquities, the dwelling had few creature comforts.

With an associate, John Marshall, they visited auction houses and private collections. Their group expanded to include Richard Fisher, G.V. Harding, and Matthew Stewart Prichard. Warren's brother, Samuel D. Warren, became a trustee of the museum. The museum's in-house classical curator was Edward Robinson (1858–1931). He was with the museum for 20 years while Warren remained an agent in the field. Because they were cheap, the museum acquired a number of plaster casts through the belief that original works were not affordable.

The Warren brothers proposed that their family provide a thousand pounds annually for the museum to match. Edward was given authority to make purchases as they became available and not have to pass through an acquisitions committee. Objects began to flow to the museum. There was resistance from Martin Brimmer the board president.

Whitehill (page 151) quotes from Edward Perry Warren's response to Brimmer. "First, a general exclusion of vases seems to me neither practicable nor desirable: not practicable because they constitute a chief means whereby a connexion (sic) with dealers and archaeologists is opened and maintained; not desirable, since they satisfy the needs of students, the Museum must eventually have a good-sized collection. This kind of purchase could be more or less held in check; but not, I think to the extent which the committee desires."

The standard for the MFA was to acquire objects comparable to those on display at The British Museum, Louvre, or Berlin. Great acquisitions included the long-disputed *Boston Throne*, a three-sided relief circa 470-460 B.C., the *Bartlett Aphrodite*, 4th century B.C., *Head from Chios*, 4th century B.C., *Head of a Patrician*, Roman, late 1st century B.C., *Limestone Lion from Parachora*,

Archaic Greek circa 550 B.C., and *Nike Driving Her Chariot*, a Greek gold earring, early 4th century B.C.

My friend Jim Jacobs, today a private dealer in contemporary art, was a part of the team which recovered the earring which were stolen in 1962. He recalled, "I was a freshman at Boston University in fall 1962 taking a course in Greek and Roman art with Emily Townsend Vermeule, the wife of the curator Cornelius Clarkson Vermeule of the Classical Art department. Emily was a can-do person. She heard that the thief, then in a mental hospital, said that he had buried the earrings near the museum. She formed an archeological dig to try to locate them.

"There was a $5,000 reward, which was a lot of money in 1962. Of course, everyone in the class volunteered to be part of the dig. Every weekend for close to 2 months the entire class came to the Fenway at the rear of the museum where Emily had set up grids. We all brought knives and spoons and proceeded to go over every inch of the grid.

"On the sixth weekend one of the female students came upon a crushed Coke can lying in a small pool of water. Looking inside the can she spotted something shiny and brought it to Emily's attention. The can was immediately brought to the museum's conservation laboratory. There the earring was extracted. Miraculously there was only a slight dent that was easily repaired.

"Imagine the energy that passed through the class when this happened. We all went a little bit crazy. The department hosted a party. The woman who found the earring was awarded $2,500. We each received a check for $100.

"At the party Cornelius came up to me and said, 'Jim, how does it feel to be a hero and get a fat check in the bargain.' I said, 'It was special event. Thanks for the party and check, but what I really need is a job.' Cornelius immediately said, 'Come in on Monday.' He hired me on the spot and I worked at the museum part time for the next four years. The Classical office adjoined the Egyptian office where Charles was an intern. *Life Magazine* picked up on the story, which went national. That was the highlight of my archeological career, as I later went into contemporary art."

The purchase of land in the Fenway entailed a reallocation of limited resources for collecting. Sir John Beazley, the authority on Greek vases published an essay "Warren as a Collector" which Whitehill quoted (page 160):

"He thought that the trustees would have been wise to defer building and spend their money on increasing the classical collection while they had the opportunity. As the result of many years' effort, he had obtained complete control of the market in classical antiquities. Almost everything that was good, whether a new find or an old (one), came to him for the first refusal. Competition had all but ceased. The chief private collectors in Europe were dead or had withdrawn from the field. The museums were comparatively sluggish. The British Museum could do nothing. Building could be done at any time; but this organization, allowed to decline, could not be reconstructed, and the market, once lost, could never be recovered."

The MFA, particularly for its Old Kingdom objects, houses one of the finest collections of Ancient Egyptian Art outside of Cairo. This resulted from the efforts of the archaeologist George Andrew Reisner, Jr. (1867–1942). He was an MFA curator but remained in the field and only occasionally returned to Boston. The administrative work was handled by Dows Dunham, who became curator. Dunham resigned to work on publishing the many excavations, and another Reisner associate, William Stevenson Smith, became curator.

When the pyramids of Giza were excavated, four international teams drew lots for the location of their dig. Boston excavated the area of the necropolis surrounding the pyramid of King Mycerinus. As luck would have it, this was the section of Giza that proved to be richest in objects. Reisner proved to be an astute horse trader when the find was divided at the end of the year with Egyptian authorities. He would hold back objects in the shed looking for the most opportune moment to trade.

That resulted in the acquisition of the polychrome, limestone bust of Prince Ankh Haf. With its remarkable naturalism, arguably, it is the finest object of Old Kingdom art. Reisner also excavated the greatest works of Nubian art. This great collection, however, has languished in storage. In 2021 it was installed in new Ancient Egyptian galleries.

In 2019 the museum presented 400 objects in *Ancient Nubia Now*. The greatest work in the Nubian collection, the enormous stone *Sarcophagus of King Aspelta*, used to be displayed in the lower rotunda. It was put in storage some years ago to make more room for the Ladies Committee to serve afternoon tea. The sarcophagus would be the pride of any museum.

There is a plan to install the Nubian collection as part of the galleries for the ancient world.

Works were acquired by Reisner, fair and square. Egypt, then too poor to excavate, issued permits and shared in what was found. In the event of a royal tomb, such as that of King Tutankhamun, all of the material was acquired by the Cairo Museum. In recent years, Egypt no longer shares the finds of excavations. A collection like that of the MFA is no longer possible.

Even for its day, the museum's 1921 acquisition of *The Apse of Santa Maria de Mur*, Catalan Romanesque, 12th century, was outrageous. The murals in small mountain churches in the region of Catalunya were studied and published in 1907 by the Institut d'Estudis Catalans. Money was offered to the very poor parish and its murals were removed.

Legend has it that the chapel was disassembled and packed in crates marked "Parmesan Cheese." They went by mules to port, then were shipped to Boston. When the theft was discovered, to prevent another occurrence, all of the chapels were stripped of their murals. They were installed in the Museu Nacional d'Art de Catalunya. That's where I saw them some years ago. Boston has the only one that slipped away.

Whitehill comments (page 339) "Publicity of any kind about valuable works of art is bound to attract thieves, miscreants, and art dealers. If improperly safeguarded objects are not stolen, they are likely to be bought and spirited away from the places where they belong." Responding to their removal and installation in the museum, Whitehill churlishly wrote, "The door was locked after only one had escaped and this one came to Boston."

Organization, Growth, and Finances

The MFA was incorporated by the Massachusetts Legislature on 4 February 1870. Twelve men were named to the Board. Of these three each were to be named annually by Harvard University, The Boston Athenaeum, and MIT. Ex officio trustees included the Mayor of Boston, the President of Trustees of the Boston Public Library, the Superintendent of Public Schools, the Secretary of the Board of Education, and the Trustees of the Lowell Institute. Martin Brimmer (1829–1926) was named president, a position he held for the next twenty-five years. When Perry T. Rathbone was director (1955–1972), through the state legislature, the makeup of the board was amended to one board member each for those founding institutions. The board was expanded to 35.

When George Seybolt (1915–1993) became president in the late 1960s, he tried to run the museum on a business model. Until then, Whitehill reports that once appointed, trustees served for life or until they retired. Seybolt conducted monthly rather than annual meetings and charged board members with more responsibility for fundraising. He thought of his position as equal to that of the director and broke precedent by interfering with curatorial matters. Seybolt demanded office space and two secretaries.

By 1877 annual attendance was 158,446. This increased steadily: 217,643 in 1891 and 301,315 in 1895. The endowment was some $1,706,453. With the move to Huntington Avenue, attendance grew to 496,883 in 1925, 526,378 in 1934, with a decline to 463,768 in 1945. During the era of "blockbusters," a benchmark was 500,000 for major exhibitions and, until the pandemic year of 2020, a norm of more than a million annual visitors.

Boston compares itself to New York, not only in sports, but also in culture. The MFA and the Metropolitan Museum of Art were both founded in 1870 on land granted by their cities, Boston opened in Copley Square in 1876, and the Met on Fifth Avenue with a footprint that extends into Central Park in 1880.

A crucial difference is that, from the beginning, the Met continued to receive annual funding from the city of New York. When the MFA sold its Copley Square plot that was the end of city money. There have only been small amounts to fund admission and education of school groups. The original museum structure was razed and replaced by the Copley Plaza Hotel. The sale raised $975,000 toward the move to the Fenway.

Compared to other major museums the MFA has always been cash strapped. While Malcolm Rogers raised $504 million, of which $345 million was for construction, he left a debt of $140 million, which by 2021 was reduced to $105 million. The 2021 endowment is $608 million. Compare that to an endowment of $3 billion for the Met or a staggering $10.1 billion (2017) for the J. Paul Getty Trust, which was founded in 1982. The Solomon R. Guggenheim Museum reported an endowment of $85 million in 2018, but a revenue shortfall of $10 million in 2020. The 2020 endowment of MoMA was $1.2 billion.

The Evolving Culture

John Francis "Honey Fitz" Fitzgerald (1863–1950) was Boston's first Mayor of Irish heritage in 1906. He was the father of Rose Kennedy and scion of a political dynasty. James Michael Curley (1874–1958), also of Irish heritage, served three terms as Mayor of Boston starting in 1914, and one as Governor of Massachusetts

(1936–1937).

That marked a social and political shift that had a major impact on cultural and educational institutions. In their private clubs (Algonquin, Somerset, The Harvard Club, St. Botolph Club, Club of Odd Volumes, The College Club of Boston, The Women's City Club, The Union Club of Boston), the old money, Yankees and Brahmins closed ranks.

When, in 1972, at a private club, an MFA trustee encountered a *Boston Globe* reporter who was then on a team investigating the museum, he stated, "You can't do that to my museum."

That remark reflected the elitism of the museum and its trustees. It signified decades of anti-Semitism, exclusion, isolationism, class struggle, and racism. That erupted in 2019 when the museum responded to a widely reported instance of racism targeting visiting students. That was underscored by the George Floyd demonstrations and Black Lives Matter movement. Calls for social justice have occurred during the Covid-19 pandemic and its consequences.

The MFA is hardly alone facing accusations of white supremacy and institutional racism. All cultural institutions are addressing demands for diversity and inclusion. The instrument for change is centered in boards and administrators.

Because the elitist MFA received no taxpayer-funded revenue, it felt no need for accountability to the general public. Museums have been described as "Palaces for the People" which has never been true, and now that concept is being deconstructed.

The MFA elected its first Jewish trustee, Sidney Rabb, in 1962. A decade later, in 1972, Phyllis Ann Wallace (1921–1993), an African American faculty member of MIT Sloan School of Management, became a trustee. An economist and activist, she was the first woman to receive a doctorate of economics at Yale University. In 2020 Edward Greene became the first black president of the MFA. While Maxim Karolik, a Russian-born Jew, was designated a Great Benefactor, he was never nominated to the board of the museum.

Asked about the Wallace appointment by a *Globe* reporter, the trustee Walter Muir Whitehill, was adversarial. He commented that the responsibility of a trustee is fiduciary, and as such, he did not support community-based appointments. Whitehill (1905–1978) was Director and Librarian of the Boston Athenaeum from 1946 to 1973. He was a leading scholar and author. He was commissioned to write *Museum of Fine Arts Boston: A Centennial History* (two volumes, 888 pages, illustrated, with bibliography, notes and illustrations, The Belknap Press of Harvard University Press, Cambridge, Mass. 1970).

Staunchly conservative, Whitehill was old school and resistant to change. His history, however, reminds us what is owed to the "Brahmin" founders, for their vision and philanthropy. Much as one might resent their mantra of "our museum," without their contributions there would not be a social justice transition to an MFA committed to all of the citizens of Boston.

Modern and Contemporary Art

An ambivalent aspect of the museum is its relationship to modern and contemporary art.

In particular, to the living artists of Boston. While still in Copley Square the artist Emil Otto Grundmann (born 1844 in Meissen–died 27 August 1890 in Dresden) was hired as the first director of the School of the Museum of Fine Arts. Initially, instruction was in the museum, but eventually, the school had its own building next to the museum. The relationship between the school and museum has long been problematic. Today, through Tufts University it offers BFA and MFA degrees. MFA director Malcolm Rogers once told me that the museum's greatest commitment to Boston artists was the Museum School.

While not a Boston artist, John Singer Sargent (born 1856 Florence, died 1925 London) was regarded as one. He was a great friend of Isabella Stewart Gardner, who invited him to use her home as a studio to paint portraits of wealthy citizens. There was gossip when he painted her then-provocative portrait. Her husband, the proper Bostonian, Jack Gardner, was less than pleased.

Sargent created murals for the MFA, Boston Public Library, and Harvard's Widener Library. In 1917, he began the MFA project starting with models created by Thomas A. Fox. The work was complete in the winter of 1924–25. The artist died in his sleep not long after, on 15 April 1925.

On the negative side, what the MFA did not accomplish in its first hundred years was a significant collection of modern and contemporary art. The reasons why, to be discussed further in this book, are indeed complex.

When, by the 1930s, the leading Boston artists were Jewish immigrants, or children of immigrants, the indifference of the MFA to their work was rooted in anti-Semitism. Beyond the Museum School, there was no commitment to the fine arts community of the city. Directors and curators did not support, with a few exceptions, Boston's collectors and galleries that represented local artists. The few serious collectors, for the most part, pursued acquisitions in New York, and in more recent decades, the network of national and global art fairs.

Mario Diacono, the Italian born gallerist who showed single works by blue-chip contemporary artists, told me that he made only a few sales to Boston collectors, but they all came to look. He said Ted Stebbins, then curator of painting, "bought for the museum a big Ross Bleckner painting in 1986. The museum also bought a work by Sherrie Levine in, I believe, 1988.... At the opening of the Philip Taaffe show, Alan Shestack (then director of the MFA) stayed for an hour. He told me 'I am waiting for Trevor Fairbrother (MFA curator) who is coming to decide if we want to buy a painting from you.' Trevor Fairbrother didn't show up. Alan Shestack went away and never came back. I sold all the paintings to Switzerland."

Despite that missed opportunity, Diacono said, "We were quite friendly. I even made a deal with Trevor Fairbrother. In 1990, he told me, 'Mario I would like you to make a donation of a work in my name to the MFA. It's important to me if people make donations to the Museum's collection.' I gave to the museum my certificate of being a living artwork from Piero Manzoni. Today it could be worth $100,000. I donated it, and didn't even ask for a tax break."

The founders of the museum expressed a commitment to supporting Boston's artists. It helped that they were primarily from the same social strata. As late as the administration of George Harold Edgell, the museum organized eclectic group shows of these genteel artists. When Perry T. Rathbone became the next director in 1955, those largely amateurish efforts ended. Regarded as a reformer, Rathbone acquired a few but significant examples of modern art and courted major collectors including Peggy Guggenheim and Susan Morse Hilles. They both donated a few works but their collections went elsewhere.

From 1952 to 1964, the privately funded annual Boston Art Festival was exhibited in tents on the Boston Public Garden. There was a stage for performances of music and theatre. I recall seeing the ballerina Maria Tallchief, a play by William Saroyan, and legendary, Bostonian baritone sax, jazz artist Serge Chaloff with the Herb Pomeroy Orchestra. There were lively debates about traditional, realist artists vs. progressive contemporary ones. I marveled at the prize-winning, life-size, welded-metal sculpture of John the Baptist by Kahlil Gibran. In later years, I became friends with Kahlil and his wife Jean.

Just before Rathbone arrived at the MFA, there had been discussion of a merger with the struggling Institute of Contemporary Art. A venture in an inadequate structure on the Charles River in Brighton had failed. It was inaccessible to public transportation. In desperation, the ICA returned there temporarily when it was evicted from Newbury Street in 1968. For three years the ICA occupied the second floor of the Museum School and there were negotiations for its director, Thomas Messer, to form a department of modern and contemporary art for the MFA. That didn't happen, and in 1961 Messer became director of the Solomon R. Guggenheim Museum in New York.

The MFA's mantra ever since has been that it did not want to compete with the ICA. Part of that problem is that, as a kunsthalle, the ICA, did not collect. That changed fairly recently. The argument was that a small ICA lacked resources to collect and without one remained intuitive.

At the end of the Rathbone administration, in 1972, Kenworth Moffett was appointed to head a contemporary program that should have started a generation earlier. Under Moffett, the museum collected within the narrow confines of Greenbergian formalism.

The argument for encyclopedic museums like MFA not to display and acquire works by living artists was the subject of an essay by the curator of Asiatic art, Ananda K. Coomarswamy. Whitehill (page 507) excerpts from a speech he delivered to the American Association of Museums in May 1941:

"It is unnecessary for museums to exhibit the work of living artists, which are not in imminent danger of destruction; or at least, if such works are exhibited, it should be understood that the museum is really advertising the artist and acting on behalf of the art dealer or middleman whose business it is to find a market for the artist; the only difference being that while the Museum does the same kind of work as the art dealer, it makes no profit. On the other hand, that a living artist should wish to be "hung" or "shown" in a museum can only be due to his need or his vanity. For things are made normally for certain purposes and certain places to which they are appropriate, and not simply "for exhibition"; and whatever is thus custom made, i.e., made by an artist for a consumer, is controlled by certain requirements and kept in order. Whereas, as Mr. Steinfels has recently remarked, 'Art which is only intended to be hung on the walls of a Museum is one kind of art that need not consider its relationship to its ultimate surroundings. The artist can paint anything he wishes, and if Curators and Trustees like it well enough they will line it up on the wall with all the other curiosities.'

Coomaraswamy was widely respected in the art world. One of his friends was the artist Georgia O'Keeffe. She gave him a set of 27 prints by her husband, Alfred Stieglitz. They were nude studies of her. While the curator accepted the gift, he did not appear to value and respect it. They disappeared for decades.

The art historian and photographer, Carl Chiarenza, told me the adventure of their rediscovery: "In the mid-1960s, I edited a little magazine called *Contemporary Photographer*. It was started in the very early 1960s with its first editor, Tim Hill. The second editor was D.W. Patterson; then Lee Lockwood, and then I became editor. While I was editor, Nick Dean and I discovered that Boston's MFA owned some Stieglitz prints. We went there one day to see them. They were surprised and didn't know where they were. Later we got a call that they found them and asked if we wanted to see them. So Nick and I went to see these prints. They took us down to the basement. There they opened a drawer in a dresser. In that drawer were the Stieglitz prints. Nick wrote an article about them which I published in *Contemporary Photographer*."

Saundra and William Lane donated their collection of photography. "That was a really important happening," Chiarenza said. "The curator of the Lane Collection, Karen Haas, continues as its curator at Boston's MFA. She was a graduate student in our department at Boston University. MFA curator Cliff Ackley, when we began to raise hell, did act forcefully. Since then the staff has increased considerably."

The MFA website states: "The photography program at the MFA dates to 1924 when Alfred Stieglitz gave 27 of his photographs. The Museum's first photographic purchases were made in the 1960s when Clifford Ackley joined the curatorial staff. In 2001 the Museum established the first curator dedicated to photography, Anne Havinga. She had been a curator of Prints, Drawings, and Photographs. Karen Haas, Lane Curator of Photographs, joined the department at the same time. The department grew with the additions of Kristen Gresh, Estrellita and Yousuf Karsh Curator of Photography. The Friends of Photography group was created. Through the Herb Ritts Foundation the MFA established a gallery for photography in 2008. Exhibitions range from historically based to those that are thematically diverse. Major acquisitions include early French and British photographs, turn-of-the-century photographs, the Lane Collection of more than 6,000 photographs including Edward Weston, Charles Sheeler, Ansel Adams, and Imogene Cunningham. The collection includes European postwar abstraction,

Bruce Davidson's original East 100th Street, Nicholas Nixon's complete suite of the *Brown Sisters*, archives of the work of Yousuf Karsh and Herb Ritts, and contemporary photography by Nan Goldin, Marco Breuer, Dawoud Bey, The Starn Twins, and Hiroshi Sugimoto, among others."

Museum of Fine Arts, Copley Square, 1900s. Courtesy of Museum of Fine Arts, Boston.

Asiatic Curator Ananda Coomoraswamy believed that work by living artists did not belong in the MFA. Courtesy of Museum of Fine Arts, Boston.

Walter Muir Whitehill with stroller walking on Boston Common. Courtesy of the Boston Athenaeum.

Walter Muir Whitehill in the Athenaeum with unidentified woman. Courtesy of the Boston Athenaeum.

The Rathbone Years

In 1955, Perry Townsend Rathbone (1911–2000) became the sixth director of the MFA. It was a position he held with great energy, flair, and distinction until 1972. Tall and handsome, he had a great eye and sense of style.

That was exemplified by his choice of vehicle. Out and about in a Ford convertible, a 1936 Ford Phaeton, even the car he drove was a work of art and museum piece. He purchased the car, then quite affordable, while working in Detroit. The vintage vehicle is slowly being restored by his son.

Until his arrival the museum was static and moribund. It was more a mausoleum than a vibrant museum. The elitist, Brahmin-endowed institution completely lacked any sense of community outreach. Board members routinely served for decades.

Like Miss Havisham's decayed wedding feast, galleries were allowed to become dank and shabby. When I first visited as a child, floors creaked and elderly guards passed their day sleepwalking. The collections of mummies and samurai swords in clunky, ancient vitrines, however, ignited what proved to be a lifelong passion.

In fall 1963, I walked into Rathbone's office where his secretary asked what I wanted? I replied that I would like to work for the museum. "Guards and custodians apply in the basement," she told me. "Actually, I'm looking for a curatorial position," I answered. Told that it was hopeless, I asked if she would object to my speaking to a curator?

Assured that it was futile but permissible, I hastily decided what department to query. I thought of all of the galleries I had viewed through my years of haunting the museum.

Perhaps I might learn more about Ancient Egyptian Art. I was a recent graduate of Brandeis University with a major in fine arts. Other than a lecture or two in its survey course, Brandeis offered nothing in that field. The department secretary, Mary Cairns, was less than receptive and loudly stated that she would call security.

From his office, the curator Dr. William Stevenson Smith emerged and asked, "Mary, what seems to be the problem?" She replied, "Bill, this young man wants to work for us."

He invited me into his office. After shuffling a stack of papers, he offered me a seat. Several more meetings ensued, and eventually, I was hired. Some two and a half years passed organizing the vast, dusty basement which was filled with shelves of objects and unopened crates. George Andrew Reisner (1867–1942) had sent them home from decades of excavations in Egypt.

In that sense, I worked for Rathbone and came to know the museum from the ground up. During lunch breaks, I roamed galleries and studied the collections. In particular, I enjoyed asking the guard to let me into the locked, dimly-lit gallery of ancient Buddhist sculpture.

The presence of Rathbone was palpable in all aspects of my time at the museum. He was gracious and welcoming to all staff, including me. While I was at my bench restoring Old Kingdom stone vessels, a guard came to the basement and said, "Mr. Rathbone requests that you turn down your radio." Alone all day I listened to the soul station WILD.

Years later, when I became a critic for *Boston After Dark/Phoenix* I had a different, rather adversarial relationship with Mr. Rathbone. Representing the interests of a vibrant generation of emerging artists, I harangued him about the museum's apathy to modern and contemporary art.

That came to a head when a group of artists organized a guerrilla exhibition, *Flush with the Walls*, in the museum's spacious, marble-walled, elegant basement men's room. Works and refreshments were smuggled in and there was a lively vernissage. Then administrator Diggory Venn walked in, freaked out, and called security.

Soon after, Rathbone was invited to speak to artists at the nearby, spacious Parker 470 Gallery. It was part of a series of organizational meetings that resulted in forming the Boston Visual Artists Union. The artist Tony Thompson moderated. Rathbone was visibly edgy facing a room packed with concerned artists. The tone was respectful and orderly until Joan Trachtman, the wife of protest artist Arnold Trachtman, asked the question that was on everyone's mind, "Mr. Rathbone, when will you appoint a curator of contemporary art?"

Not long after, he called me at the *Boston Herald Traveler* to say, "I want you to be the first to know that Kenworth Moffett has been appointed curator of contemporary art."

As a prelude, the museum had mounted an avant-garde exhibition curated by Virginia Gunter. With a focus on conceptualism, art, science, and technology, then and now, it was the most sensational, provocative and controversial exhibition ever organized by the MFA. During the press opening, I asked Rathbone when the museum would appoint a contemporary curator.

As Rathbone told Paul Cummings, in a series of interviews for Archives of American Art (Belinda told me that the family paid to have the AAA interviews transcribed), "We did a (1971) show called *Earth, Air, Fire, and Water: Elements of Art*. I mean, you really wouldn't believe the Boston Museum of Fine Arts, would put on this kind of a show. For example, in the biggest exhibition gallery, there was a kind of maze made up of plastic tubing, into which were deposited 100 eels, who swam. The idea was that they would swim up and down and roundabout, in this maze, to the entertainment of our visitors. Well, the sad thing about that was, of course we had to have lights playing on this maze of plastic. The lights created such a heat, that the eels were brought to an absolute standstill; they didn't move, turned over on their bellies and looked as if they were dead.

"It was only at night, when the night watchmen were going around and the lights were off, and they'd flash the light on the thing and they were swimming around like mad. [They laugh.] Oh yes, and we had gas balloons going up and down, the gas being heated by a fire below that would send the thing up or down. And we had fire raging inside of cubes of ice. We had a whole room that was a kind of artificial garden, sprouted with artificial light. We had water dropping into a great circular basin; just creating one marvelous circle of water after the other, you know, diminishing or expanding rings of water. Visitors came in great numbers and overall, nobody really went up in smoke over it, although I guess some thought the museum might go up in smoke before it was over. I used to wonder myself.

"Do you know the artist Otto Piene? His was the most spectacular exhibit of all, and that was setup in the rotunda. There were great big inflated tubes that sort of sprouted into points at the end, like some weird growth which would inflate and deflate over and over again by air pumps. They made a hell of a racket. But it was a most spectacular sight, when these things were swollen to their full size and pointing outwards. There was a red one and a white one and a black one or something. They were really spectacular. Well, that was an antidote to the (Andrew) Wyeth exhibition all right, you know, trying to please everybody."

(The Wyeth retrospective was a crowd-pleasing feature of the Centennial year. Later, years after Rathbone's departure, *Andrew Wyeth: The Helga Pictures*, was a 1987 exhibition of 107 drawings and watercolors. Executed during a 15-year span from 1971 to 1985 it entailed nudes of Wyeth's neighbor Helga Testorf of Chadds Ford, Pennsylvania. There was extensive media coverage when the artist revealed that he had worked secretly with the model. The works sold at the time for $10 million. The exhibition was a blockbuster for the MFA. On the watch of Malcolm Rogers, in 2014, the museum offered a well-attended exhibition of work by Jamie Wyeth, the son of Andrew.)

For the *New York Times*, Hilton Kramer reported positively on *Elements*. "BOSTON, Feb. 3—The Museum of Fine Arts, which has long been under attack in Boston art circles for its traditional policy of paying little or no attention to contemporary art, has suddenly upstaged its critics by mounting an extremely audacious exhibition of new art—an exhibition that includes the use of real fire, some wildlife, lots of water, and sundry other natural and technological phenomena. Entitled *Earth, Air, Fire, Water: Elements of Art* and consisting for the most part of very large and highly unorthodox constructions, tableaus and happenings, the exhibition is the final event of the museum's centennial program…

"What, you may well ask, do these disparate conceptions have in common other than their use of the four classical "elements"? I am not at all sure."

Artists in the exhibition included: Rachel Bas-Cohain, William Bollinger, Stan Brain, Richard Budelis *Eel Track*, Lowry Burgess, Geny Dignac, Edward Franklin, John Goodyear, Dan Graham, Laura Grisi, Hans Haacke, Newton Harrison, Gerald Hayes, Michael Heizer, Douglas Huebler, Peter Hutchinson, Jay

Jaroslav, Neil Jenney, Allan Kaprow, Gyula Kosice, (Joshua Neustein, Georgette Batile, and Gerard Marx), Dennis Oppenheim, Otto Piene, Ravio Puusemp, Gary Rieveschi, Charles Ross, Richard Serra, Vera Simons, Robert Smithson, Alan Sonfist, Christopher Sproat & Elizabeth Clark, Marvin Torfield, Uriburu, John van Saun, Andy Warhol, William Wegman, and Scott Wixon.

While there were indications that Rathbone was willing to initiate change, it was too late. By then he was mired in controversy. I was invited to interview him at that time. In the presence of PR director, Clementine Brown, however, I was informed that he would only take questions related to an exhibition of work by Paul Cezanne. Upon his resignation I wrote an overview of his tenure for *Boston Magazine*.

His position ended prematurely resulting from mishandling of an acquisition, alleged to be a small Raphael portrait of the young Eleanora Gonzaga, daughter of the Duchess of Mantua, which was subsequently returned to Italy. Extensive media coverage reflected badly on the museum and Rathbone in particular. From several offers he eventually became the director of the New York branch of Christie's, the London auction house. He crossed over from acquiring collections to selling them.

While the Raphael incident was alleged to be the reason for Rathbone's resignation from the museum, the true story is more complex. The museum never officially acknowledged that Rathbone had been fired.

"Because he wasn't," his daughter Belinda told me. "He agreed to leave taking his own sweet time. That allowed long enough to organize the exhibition, *The Rathbone Years*."

The Raphael incident occurred with drama and media attention in 1970. The director stayed on until June 1972. There were loose ends to tie up.

His 2000 *New York Times* obituary reported, "Curators at the museum paid tribute to Mr. Rathbone, who had always been most proud of his acquisitions, by organizing an exhibition of them in the unheard-of period of eight weeks. Called *The Rathbone Years*, it showcased 170 acquisitions made during his 17-year tenure as director and included a pair of portraits by Rembrandt, a Greek youth on horseback (circa 500 B.C.), a German Gothic tapestry titled *Wild Men and Moors*, and *La Japonaise* by Monet."

Acquired in 1969, the Raphael portrait was intended to be the highlight of the Centennial celebration and exhibition. The incident might have been finessed with diplomacy. It was mishandled by board president George Seybolt, who had been in conflict with Rathbone. Seybolt was the president of William Underwood Company. Its best-known product was Underwood Deviled Ham. He was attempting to run the MFA as a business. He insisted on office space in the museum and two secretaries.

Seeing his role as president as equal to that of the director became ever more problematic for Rathbone. There were constant memos to respond to. While Seybolt is described as abrupt and uncouth, the reforms he was initiating proved to be prescient for museum administration.

Rathbone represented the norm of museum directors wielding autonomous power over their institutions. Their role eroded to chief curator in charge of curatorial staff, acquisitions and exhibitions. Museums started appointing associate directors for administration and finance. This became particularly necessary as museums expanded and offered more diverse functions and services. Philippe de Montebello was unique in fighting this off as director and CEO of the Metropolitan Museum of Art from 1977 to 2008. Like Rathbone before him, he was the last of old-school museum directors.

In 2014, Belinda Rathbone published *The Boston Raphael: A Mysterious Painting, an Embattled Museum in an Era of Change and a Daughter's Search for the Truth* (Boston: David R. Godine). It is a thorough and insightful account of the forensic circus that spun out of control. One of the most stunning passages was an account of her visit to the storage area of the Uffizi Museum in Florence to view the small painting, which then repatriated, is not exhibited. The book about her father has brought balance to his remarkable career and reputation.

As Belinda Rathbone told me in 2015, "What you describe is a tipping point in the scale of operations that museums were reaching. There was a need to raise money and grow the staff, to grow the plant, everything. That's where we moved forward. Other museums realized a need for a two-headed administration. That continues today. My father found himself in an awkward situation.

"I don't think I'm too hard on Seybolt. People can read the book and believe that he was innovative and an agent of change. Maybe he was seeing things in a way that stodgy old Brahmins couldn't see. That's very clear.

"As to his personality I characterized him as others characterized him. I quoted other people, and I quoted him a lot. The most revealing document was his own interview with the *Archives of American Art*. It's very long and he tells a lot of lies. It's very self-serving. He's very insulting to others, and I quoted some of these things in the book. I almost didn't want to quote him because it was so mean to these other people. But I did because you have to know just what kind of a person he was. Toward the end of the book, I did give him credit for being helpful and instrumental in Washington for policy innovations, which helped museums, such as The Indemnity Act, which helped with international loans which were too expensive to insure privately. I wanted to give him credit for that. It was his strength, throwing his weight around in Washington.

"But I don't think I was hard on him. I run into people who knew him and they say, yeah, that's the kind of guy he was… It's an interesting exercise to work on my own parent, to put him under the microscope as a biographer. You try to put yourself inside their skin and feel what they felt. Suddenly you have a completely different relationship."

In Boston Rathbone formed the first "Ladies Committee" for the museum with Frances Weeks Hallowell. It was a successful strategy for helping to increase membership, and broadening the MFA's base of support. Rathbone staged unprecedented loan exhibitions such as *European Art of Our Time* and *The Age of Rembrandt*. He renovated more than fifty galleries, and increased the annual sale of publications by 1000 percent. From galleries and a studio in the museum, he introduced broadcasts, *Invitations to Art*, hosted by Brian O'Doherty. The museum increased education and community outreach.

As acting curator he collected Rosso Fiorentino's *Dead Christ with Angels*, Claude Monet's *La Japonaise*, Giovanni Battista Tiepolo's *Time Unveiling Truth*, and the anonymous fifteenth-century Flemish *Martyrdom of Saint Hippolytus*. He acquired the museum's first Picasso oil, *Standing Figure*, 1908. In 1962, after he and curator Hanns Swarzenski had lunch with the artist, they acquired Picasso's *Rape of the Sabine Women* directly from his studio. The MFA bought its first painting by Edvard Munch, *The Voice* and Rathbone donated to the museum his portrait by Max Beckmann. With help from the Ladies Committee, membership reached 15,000, raising annual revenue of $500,000.

Rathbone was born in Germantown, Pennsylvania, the son of a salesman. His mother was a school nurse. He graduated from Harvard University, with a major of fine arts, in 1933. That was followed by a year of graduate study with Paul Sachs in the program "Museum Work and Museum Problems."

The training at Harvard was notable for its focus on connoisseurship. That often entailed the study of objects in the small, but superb, Fogg Art Museum. A number of museum directors emerged from this program. Rathbone was not a scholar or curator as we would currently define those professions.

Michael Conforti, the former director the Clark Art Institute, discussed his study as a Harvard graduate student. "The early 1970s were a time of transition that continued through the 1980s with an even stronger change. At that point the Paul Sachs museum course had certainly evolved. Agnes Mongan was still around as an emeritus curator of prints and drawings.

"There was a traditional Sachs link but John Coolidge was not so much a connoisseur. Shall we say, there was a closeness to objects in various departments. But the strong connoisseurship-oriented course that Sachs had started in the 1920s had not petered out, but evolved. It was not as strong as it once was, but there were always possibilities of internships with departments, and there was closeness with the conservation lab. There was always closeness with it and connoisseurship. There was always the opportunity for closeness with objects. Particularly, if you took courses which were specifically focused on them. While Sydney Freedberg was viewed as a connoisseur, his courses were more oriented to theories of style than to objects themselves. There were opportunities to work with him in an almost informal way looking closely at objects.

"The most connoisseurship-oriented course I took was with Hanns Swarzenski at the MFA. There was a quite direct conversation around objects. In my experience, it wasn't as closely oriented to working with objects as it had been."

Upon completing the museum course in 1934, Rathbone's first job was as a lecturer in the education department of the Detroit Institute of Arts. In 1936 he was appointed curator of Alger House, a branch museum in Grosse Point, Michigan, where he lived with DIA director William Valentiner. They took a cross-country drive in Rathbone's car. In 1939 he assisted Valentiner in organizing the *Masterpieces of Art* exhibition at the World's Fair in New York.

In 1940, Rathbone was appointed director of the St. Louis Art Museum (then the City Art Museum). At age 29, he was the youngest museum director in America. From 1943–45 he served in the U.S. Navy in Washington D.C. as head of combat artists, and in New Caledonia as an officer. He lobbied to go to Europe as part of the team of "Monuments Men" charged with returning works looted by the Nazis to their rightful owners. The military, however, was unwilling to fly him from the South Pacific to Europe. Upon his discharge he married Euretta de Cosson, a British ski champion, on February 10, 1945.

Rathbone had been instrumental in helping the German artist Max Beckmann move to America in 1948 by securing him a teaching position at Washington University. The artist died December 27, 1950 (aged 66). Rathbone organized his first American exhibition at the St. Louis Museum. As museum director, he was a champion of modern art, and along with Joseph Pulitzer, Jr., and Morton May, stimulated collectors of modern art in St. Louis. Later, in Boston, there were no comparable collectors to nurture. Boston proved to be conservative compared to more-progressive St. Louis.

There he mounted popular exhibitions, some of regional interest, such as *Mississippi Panorama and Westward the Way*, others international, such as the 1949 blockbuster *Treasures from Berlin*, which attracted an average of 12,634 visitors per day.

In St. Louis, he had a flair for marketing and publicity that attracted national attention and the invitation to become director of the MFA. He had already accepted when he was approached to become director of the Met.

"We did quite a few stunts in St. Louis," Rathbone told Paul Cummings. "One of them, at the opening of *Westward the Way*, I was casting about for something to dramatize that moment, and just as good luck would have it, somebody told me that there was a band of Comanche Indians coming to St. Louis for some purpose or other, and they were able to do war dances and war groups and everything else. So, I managed to get in touch with this troupe, there were about six or eight, and asked if they would come and perform amongst the guests at the opening of the *Westward the Way* exhibition, as a symbol of the Indian life that we were celebrating after all, and they were delighted. And they came in at the proper moment in the evening—I don't know, whenever the largest crowd was there—and they just came in amongst the guests and asked them to stand back and they let go with a blood curdling war cry, you never heard anything like it, and they all had bells on their ankles, you know, and rattles in their hands, and drums, and they danced around, a sort of snake dance, in that big hall, shouting and whooping and hollering. You could never forget it. It just thrilled everybody, you know, to be that close to Indian life, with this historic evidence all around them."

He soon applied that showmanship in Boston. One of the shows he inherited was a traveling exhibition, *Sports in Art*. The museum at the time was exhibiting packaged shows and Rathbone helped the MFA curators to create their own projects ushering in the era of "blockbusters."

Special exhibitions at that time were installed in a large gallery at the top of the grand staircase from the Huntington Avenue entrance. The Ladies Committee made that ascent colorful with brilliantly imaginative floral arrangements. Guests gathered in the rotunda, under the Sargent murals, and were served refreshments in the adjoining tapestry gallery. It was a perk of membership to attend free gala openings. That gradually changed as membership grew. Eventually, a major exhibition might have a week of openings from VIP nights to member previews. During the Rathbone era it was fun to attend opening night and rub shoulders with proper Bostonians.

To perk up the pedestrian *Sport in Art*, Rathbone arranged to have a performance by Olympics Gold Medal figure skater Tenley Albright. To pay for the circle of ice he secured a promotional sponsorship with Filene's, the department store. Guests were appropriately dazzled, and Rathbone put Boston on notice that there was a new gun in town.

It was a dramatic departure from the administration of Harold Edgell (1887–1954 MFA director from 1935–1954).

As Rathbone told Cummings in 1975, "My predecessor, Harold Edgell, while a very attractive and charming man himself, felt no obligation or no desire to be sociable with his staff or his trustees at all. Now Paul Sachs, who had been, you know, at Harvard since, I think 1918 or something, told me that he had never been in Harold Edgell's house, and this is really astonishing. And I remember he was admonishing me, he said, 'Now see as much of your trustees as you can and do have them at home for dinner,' and so on, he said, 'That is a very important thing for you to remember.'

"First of all, let me say that my predecessor, Howard Edgell, this genial man, this charming man. Genial, I'm not so sure, but he certainly had an enormous amount of personal charm, but really, I think knew nothing about running a museum, never had any feeling for it. He had been a professor almost all his mature days, since his student years in Rome and Florence.

"He was in love with Italian painting, it's true, but he really was a scholar up to a point and a teacher, and he was a brilliant lecturer. A little bit superficial, you understand, but most entertaining, and he would say to anyone who was listening, 'You know, I really don't have to run the Boston Museum because I have the best staff in the world. I have, without question the best staff, and they just run the place.' Well, and that was literally true, because it was known.

"Everybody told me, who didn't know it already, that he was there and he left weekends, often Thursdays and always Fridays, and went off to a shooting preserve in New Hampshire, in a place called Newport, New Hampshire, where he owned thousands of acres with his wife…He had some little pied-a-terre in New York and would spend as much time away from his office as possible. And during office hours, he had his spaniels under his desk.

"He would come, have these rather abbreviated hours, and then he would walk around the museum, to the various curatorial offices, tell a few jokes in a very charming way, because he was very good at telling stories, loved that kind of humor, and then ask his curators if they had any letters that he could answer. Can you imagine?"

As Belinda told me, curators and visiting dignitaries were frequent dinner guests at their Cambridge home. Rathbone had particularly close relationships with curators. He would visit Classical Curator Cornelius Vermeule and his wife Emily on their digs. He was particularly close to Hanns Swarzenski head of the department of European decorative art and sculpture. In that position, he succeeded his father Georg Swarzenski. Perry and Hanns would explore European collections, visit dealers and auction houses. Swarzenski was masterful in sniffing out major acquisitions from medieval to modern art. One from 1957 was *The Golden Fish* by Constantin Brancusi. The piece was stolen and melted down for the value of its metal. Unfortunately, the insurance money was not applied to another modern acquisition.

W.G. Constable (1887–1976) left as director of London's Courtauld Institute to become curator of European painting in 1936. During the Depression years, there were great acquisitions, including the Paul Gauguin masterpiece *D'où venons-nous? Que sommes-nous? Où allons-nous?* When Constable retired, Rathbone took over that position, as was common for museum directors of his generation.

Day-to-day operation of the department was handled by Thomas Maythem, Lucrecia Giese, and Laura Lucky. In 1972 Lucky told me, "My BA is from William and Mary. Initially, I worked under Tom Maythem. At the end of ten years here, he was appointed assistant curator. Currently, he is director of the Denver Art Museum. Even before Constable came, there was a long gap in which there was no curator of painting. There is a history of directors assuming the post as Mr. Rathbone did. He functioned as a curator during his term…

"Many of the painting galleries are badly in need of painting and refurbishing. No major work has been done in the main painting galleries since the skylights were repaired in 1957…

"We both have the rank of curatorial assistant. Our positions are frozen until a curator is appointed. We have struggled to do things and organized a successful exhibition, *The Boston Painters* (1972). We fought for funds for an opening. Later we had a show of works by A. C. Goodwin (Boston artist, 1864–1929)."

I asked, "Is it true, Laura, that Mr. Rathbone would not allow you to attend graduate school when you requested it?" She replied, "Yes, that's true, but as you know, I am now pursuing a degree program (at Boston University). The department was small and I can partly understand why he didn't want me away from the museum."

Other curators were pursuing degrees, so why not her? She responded, "Perhaps that's partly because they are men and I am a woman."

Even the venerable curator of prints and drawings, Eleanor Sayre (1916–2001), experienced chauvinism. She was not welcome in the male domain of the curator's private dining room. That changed only with a move to a larger facility.

While Rathbone appreciated modern art, much more might have been accomplished. From 1956–1959 the Institute of Contemporary Art was housed on the second floor of the Museum School. Its director, Thomas Messer, advised the museum on the acquisition of works *Rowboat*, 1958, by David Park, and *Willem Sandberg*, 1956, by Dutch COBRA artist Karel Appel.

There was discussion of a merger, which Messer confirmed when I asked him about it during a press event related to the ICA's 50th anniversary.

"I have no personal recollection of Perry ever speaking of a merger of the ICA with the MFA." Belinda told me. "I know of him loving the ICA and having a lively relationship with it. Through my research, I know that he was a great admirer of Tom Messer. He considered them to be good friends."

Rathbone pursued the great modern collections of Peggy Guggenheim and Susan Morse Hilles. He organized a special exhibition of the Hilles collection. They both gave the MFA a few works, but their collections went elsewhere. In both cases, there are rumored, but undocumented, incidents of anti-Semitic comments. An individual who was in the room told me, off the record, what was said by a representative of the MFA to Guggenheim in Venice. The mishandling of Hilles occurred on the watch of director Merrill Rueppel.

When asked about it, Belinda Rathbone knew no details of either incident. To the best of her knowledge, her father remained a friend of Peggy Guggenheim despite not securing her collection.

Belinda Rathbone wrote a book about her father. Giuliano photo.

Classical curator Cornelius Vermeule was interim director after Rathbone. Giuliano photo.

Curator Hanns Swarzenski and Perry in Greece. Courtesy of Belinda Rathbone.

Rathbone and artist Dimitri Hadzi. Giuliano photo.

Christo and Otto Piene who Rathbone admired for inflatables in Elements. Giuliano photo.

Centennial Introspection

The occasion of the MFA Centennial was a time to celebrate great accomplishments. Trustee Walter Muir Whitehill was commissioned to write a history of the museum.

There was an exhibition, *Centennial Acquisitions: Art Treasures for Tomorrow, Museum of Fine Arts Boston*. Director Rathbone noted that the works were acquired over the previous three years by a range of departments. Notably the Raphael portrait was included in the catalogue but not the exhibition.

There were numerous highlights throughout the year. The museum acquired fine examples of classical and Asiatic art, paintings by Mary Cassatt, Edgar Degas, and Edouard Manet. Most significantly, there was progress in the acquisition of modern and contemporary art, with several works by Pablo Picasso, Alberto Giacometti, Andrew Wyeth, Pierre Soulages, Franz Kline (from Susan Morse Hilles), Morris Louis, and David Smith. Some of these works were included in the hastily organized exhibition, *The Rathbone Years*, in 1972.

The museum was, at that time, about to lose one of its greatest directors. He was on the wrong end of a power struggle with board president George Seybolt. As a businessman, Seybolt represented a new approach to the museum's administration and mandate.

The Centennial delineated a transition of the museum from a conservative but remarkable past to internal turbulence and a daunting transition to new challenges.

To get its house in order and plan for the future, the board formed the ad hoc policy review committee which reported its findings in November 1970. It was prefaced by the quotation, "No society can make…a perpetual law. The earth belongs to the living generation." (Thomas Jefferson, 1789)

The Committee included: Erwin D. Canham, chairman, John Coolidge, vice chairman, Nelson W. Aldrich, James B. Ames, Mrs. Paul Bernat, Lewis P. Cabot, John L. Gardner, Perry T. Rathbone, George C. Seybolt, Jeptha H. Wade, and Walter M. Whitehill.

The overview of the report stated, "The trustees of the Museum of Fine Arts in Boston have very large responsibilities. This institution, like most others in these changing and challenging times, face problems so serious that they could be crippling, as well as opportunities that are continuing and heartening.

"The museum has much of which to be proud, although this is no time for self-congratulation. As the very formation of this Ad Hoc Committee attests, it needs to re-examine its stewardship and make sure it is fulfilling its mission.

"The museum today has an "image." As far as we can see—and we have not talked with as many severe critics as we would have wished—the image is largely that of a rich, austere, acquisitive, dignified, and not particularly welcoming institution deeply representative of the Boston "establishment" culturally, financially, and socially. It is also, we know, a wonderful place to many people in all walks of life, where great beauty is enjoyed and understood and individual cultural horizons are profoundly extended.

"There is no escaping the Museum's basic obligation to preserve and conserve the wide range of great art in its possession. It sometimes needs to obtain more. There are some fields—notably that of primitive and contemporary art—where we are inadequately represented.

"But along with 'preservation' as stipulated in our charter, goes 'exhibition' and 'affording instruction in the fine arts.' Thus from the beginning we have been mandated to reach out and bring the reality of fine arts into the minds and emotions of people.

"In terms of this outreach, which will either greatly serve and strengthen the museum or greatly harm and hinder it in the last third of the twentieth century.

"We believe that while the outreach will be carried out through programs, its terms will be best determined by attitudes. We believe that the attitude of the Museum, both within its walls and in the community, should be that of openness. It should welcome. It should serve. It should cooperate in community affairs. It should apply its cultural resources, when it can, to the betterment of community problems. Particularly, it should help individuals and ethnic communities in their search for meaning and identity.

"Our black neighbors, a few hundred yards to the south in Roxbury, should feel that the Museum already has much, and can have more that relates directly to their own search for identity and heritage. Other ethnic groups can also feel an enlarged sense of cultural kinship with their many ancestral treasures in the Museum.

"But more widely still, millions of other people whose cultural experience is still narrowly constricted and barren should be helped to find their way into richer awareness of the beauty and meaning of life as expressed in the fine arts.

"The Museum has already done much to open better channels of communication with the wasteland of human unawareness. We have pioneered in television. Our lectures are well attended, well given. Programs for children are actively pursued. Many of our exhibitions, especially some recent ones, have had an unprecedented popular appeal.

"And yet, the demands of the 1970s are more insistent than anything we have seen yet. The Museum, like other institutions, must justify itself by giving proof of its meaning and value in the lives of its constituency, which is potentially very wide. This is what is meant by the overused word relevance.

"In the acceptance of such responsibilities, the Museum must build upon its strengths. Its collections are unequaled in some areas, very strong in others, weak or non-existent in a few. Its staff is a tower of strength and dedication, an asset of great value second only to the treasures they preserve and present. We have greatest respect for the Director and his strong corps of curators. We know they deserve support and greater resources with which to fulfill the large responsibilities, which they alone can meet.

"Thus it is to this splendid staff, safeguarding and articulating such treasures, that we urge confidently a still greater attitude of openness and responsiveness to the total community we must all serve. We urge close coordination and communication within. Attitude and morale are the keys to the success of any institution. They result from and they buttress leadership. We think the Museum is potentially equipped with the capacity to meet the challenges of the 1970s.

"We believe the trustees, perhaps more than anybody else, must be aware or the changing times and needs as they zealously preserve what is in their hands. Our report urges action and commitment upon the trustees themselves with a better grace than it does on any others. The trustees can set a tone which will directly affect attitudes and morale. We know we have tried to do so but we believe we can do it more responsibly and adequately than ever before.

"In this report we make specific recommendations about housekeeping, business and financial affairs, organizational reform, the safe-guarding and enlarging of resources. These are all of essence.

"(We should mention that in this report we make no attempt to study the problems of the Museum School, although we are well aware that it has many needs an is an important part of the total Museum function.)

"We come back to attitude-morale-leadership. We believe that all of us, Staff, Curators, Director, Trustees, who so profoundly believe in the Museum's place in the modern world, must move from intuitional aloofness to awareness and response."

The report made a number of specific recommendations from expansion and fundraising goals, climate control renovation, outreach to the diverse community, an improved management and accounting system, and the creation of a department for 20th century art.

To accomplish its objectives there was recognition of need for greater diversity of the board as well as community outreach. It stated, "But even before these proposals for increasing the staff have been carried through, the Museum must be developing new programs for exposition. These programs must not be motivated by a sense of guilt, a desire to justify accumulated treasure by putting it to immediate social use. Rather, as Miss Elma Lewis eloquently told us, they should start by a recognition of community needs, after which comes an analysis of what the Museum is best qualified to do to meet those needs. Community is certainly an ill-defined word, with local, national and international implications. We believe that as a beginning the Museum staff must make an increased effort toward two groups: the students in neighboring universities and professional schools, and people hitherto not attracted to the Museum."

An immediate action was the creation of a relationship with the National Center for Afro American Artists with financial and programming support. Its director, Edmund Barry Gaither, as an adjunct curator, initiated exhibitions for the museum.

The museum had a working plan for moving forward. It came to a decision to hire a new director charged with executing the template of the ad hoc report. How different the museum would be today had they stuck to the plan. They might have avoided the charges of institutional racism that surfaced with so much negative media in 2019.

The best-made plans were disrupted when George Seybolt preempted what should have been an orderly search for a new director. There were a number of qualified candidates. That included the museum's classical curator, Cornelius Vermeule, who was serving as interim director when Rathbone left in 1972.

There are varying accounts of how Seybolt hired Merrill Rueppel then director of the mid-level, regional Dallas Museum of Art. From the beginning, things did not go well and further deteriorated. The curators, leading scholars in their fields, felt that the director was simply not on their level.

Things fell apart, resulting in leaks to the *Boston Globe*, likely from curators. A team was assembled to investigate the museum.

When we spoke on August 3, 1976, Patrick McGilligan had left the *Globe*. He was part of the investigative team.

Patrick McGilligan: The word came down from (Tom) Winship to get on the story. To put Pat McGilligan and Otile McManus on the investigation full time. The story was that the curators were freely leaking their grievances to the *Globe* staff, particularly Bob Taylor. It seemed that nobody liked the director, who was an outsider. The story was then a conflict with curators.

As Otile and I investigated, we had the feeling that it was just a silly little story about some dirty laundry at the MFA. It was just a silly spat between the director and his curators. After a month of digging, we found that the story was much bigger than we had anticipated. At this point Bob Phelps took over the story and we became directly answerable to him.

Only four of the articles were ever printed. As we got into the story there were pressures on the *Globe* from the MFA.

The first installment of the story was run off the front page and announced the setting of the conflict between the curators and director. This was really bullshit as it wasn't really the problem at all. The real issue was that the MFA served nobody but itself. It was an institution founded by and intended for the blue bloods in their ivory towers and had no relationship to the people of the city, including the impoverished and disenfranchised. Otile and I didn't think that this was newsworthy but the *Globe* higher ups seemed to think that it was.

The second installment covered the ad hoc report and the resulting conflicts in the board of trustees. The fact that there was an ad hoc report and nothing was being done about it. The MFA was doing poorly financially because of its traditional reliance on old money. The MFA was essentially a private institution and the old money was drying up.

The fourth point covered the fact that some members of the board of trustees collect and traffic in art. Lewis Cabot, in particular, is a dealer…This was dropped from the story by the *Globe*.

The second installment of the series was on Rueppel himself and the waves he was causing that resulted in having him thrown out. If you know anything about the guy he was clearly not the people's choice. He didn't really try to get in there and open up the institution. Rather, he was trying to build up his own power.

It was really a story about the old line and old power vs. the new one. The most powerful members of the board are emeritus ones. They don't even have to attend meetings but can change things by sending in their votes on key issues. It is a question of old Brahmin powers like Coolidge, Whitehill, and Gardner vs. the newer more progressive trustees.

Otile was sent to Dallas and seems to have found something. Nothing illegal, but shenanigans about inflating the value of donations to the museum by wealthy collectors. Rueppel was the only American museum director to vote against the censure of American institutions for taking objects from other countries clandestinely and showing them in museums. We had him nailed as a conservative right winger.

This is what the *Globe* was after, to get Rueppel because he was an outsider. He was an arrogant man with a poor PR image. In my opinion that was not the real story. The only story that mattered was the composition of the trustees themselves and their interlocking power through a network of banks and corporations and older trustees who just send their opinions to meetings…

According to their own ad hoc report, they were pledged to open up the MFA and make it more responsive to all aspects of the community. There is one interesting statement about all this. One priority of the report was to specifically get blacks and minorities active in the MFA. Seybolt made a blundering statement that there was only one person in Boston qualified to be an MFA trustee. He apparently wined and dined Elma Lewis but then she turned him down. This was used to explain why the MFA does not have a black trustee…

I personally wrote the third installment. I took it to Phelps several times. He kept making me rewrite it in *NY Times* style. We were to tone it down and imply rather than directly state a number of things. He liked it very much and praised me. We were all set to go. It was Friday afternoon and the story was set to run on Sunday. We even had the graphics commissioned. The MFA was rendered as a huge cash register full of art works. Somehow Winship caught wind of the story and wanted to see it before it went to press.

Up till then we had been getting regular memos from Winship saying "Great Stuff." This is very unusual as ordinarily he never sends memos to the arts department. This time it seemed that Winship was under considerable pressure from the MFA. It was felt that we had done our job in nailing Rueppel and now we should just step aside. Winship called Otile and me and said that he was going to kill the story. Then he changed his mind and said that he would personally edit it.

We demanded to be present when he edited the story. He became furious and threw us out of the office. Before we left, I demanded that my name be taken off the story as I could not identify with it. This got him even madder as this is just not done. This was to be the climactic piece of the investigation. All of this was incredible as he is not known for personally editing stories. He called us back at 6 p.m. and showed us the heavily blue-penciled copy. He had changed it completely and Taylor ended up having to rewrite it. A great deal of argument resulted and I insisted on not having my name on the story…

On Monday, after the story appeared, Winship called and said that he liked the story and he seemed apologetic about what happened…As far as the *Globe* is concerned the story was over. After months on the story and many hours of overtime it was just dropped like a hot potato although some stories later appeared that updated the events…

Charles Giuliano What was the *Globe*'s motivation in running the story?

PM Right from the beginning it was clear that the *Globe* was going after a Pulitzer Prize. They had no interest in the deep implications of the story. They kept feeding the word Pulitzer to us and from the start; we were enchanted. We were out to get

Rueppel and to knock Seybolt who hired him through unorthodox means without full committee approval. Seybolt acted like a one-man show.

CG Rueppel has denied the validity of that accusation.

PM He was furious about that aspect of the story. He called the *Globe* repeatedly demanding to get back the tape he made with me and Bob Taylor. But it is there on the tape. He just blurted it out. He threatened to sue over that…

Seybolt was symbolic of the changing scene. He was from the crude money end of the spectrum. John Coolidge was caught in the middle. Somebody had to be sacrificed, and one month after Rueppel was fired, Coolidge resigned as the president of the board of trustees. Overnight, with Rueppel and Coolidge out, things calmed down. He resigned to take the heat off of the MFA. But this didn't change anything. The key people you never hear anything about are the ones who virtually own the museum.

When we called the trustees for information, we couldn't get anything out of them. Those we did talk to, in no uncertain terms, told us to lay off "our museum" or "my museum." We heard this over-and-over.

In a private club Bob Taylor was physically assaulted by an irate trustee who emphatically told him to stay away from "my museum." We put this in the story but it was taken out by higher ups. The fact is that they run the museum like their own private club…

CG Where were the leaks coming from, curators, trustees?

PM Many of the curators were friendly with people at the *Globe*. The trustees, though, were like a private men's club. We had to ask them very blunt questions and they didn't offer much information. That's why the story was difficult to crack and took so much time…

CG What was the point of all this?

PM As I said, all that the *Globe* wanted was its Pulitzer. It didn't matter that they were completely blundering into the issues and that the stories were badly written and very confusing to follow. This is because they were written by committee. The whole thing was Mickey Mouse but they submitted it for a Pulitzer as well as other awards…

Centennial Introspection 57

Rathbone acquired an alleged portrait by Raphael as part of the Centennial celebration. Giuliano photo.

Curator Hanns Swarzenski often collaborated with Rathbone to make important acquisitions. Courtesy of Museum of Fine Arts, Boston.

The Brief and Turbulent Tenure of Merrill Rueppel

Merrill Rueppel (1925–2011) was MFA director from 1973 to 1975.

Education: Bachelor, Beloit College, 1949; Master of Arts, University of Wisconsin, 1952; Doctor of Philosophy, University of Wisconsin, 1955.

Career: Research assistant, Minneapolis Institute of Arts, 1956–1957; assistant to director, Minneapolis Institute of Arts, 1957–1959; assistant director, Minneapolis Institute of Arts, 1959–1961; assistant director, City Art Museum St. Louis, 1961–1964; director, Dallas Museum of Fine Arts, 1964–1973; director, Museum of Fine Arts, Boston, 1973–1975; director, Contemporary Museum, Honolulu, 1991–1995; retired, 1995. Consultant Ford Foundation, New York City, 1963–1976, Internal Revenue Service, Washington, 1970–1974, Rockefeller Brothers Fund, New York City, 1978. Associate professor art history Washington University, St. Louis, 1963.

As the *New York Times* reported March 16, 1973 "Mr. Ruepel (sic) was chosen from a field of contenders that included Joseph V. Noble, director of the Museum of The City of New York, and Cornelius Vermeule, the Boston Museum's acting director. He comes to the Boston Museum, one of the country's leading art institutions, at a time of growing concern over illicit traffic in art objects. Museums have been accused of encouraging the looting of archeological sites by creating a market for plundered objects.

"Asked if he had given any thought to this problem, Mr. Rueppel commented: 'This is certainly a very pressing issue. But I don't want to make any statement, because I do not know what the policy of the trustees here is. As soon as (I) have taken over, this is something I would to have a clear policy on.'

"At a reception today, George T. Seybolt, president of the board of trustees, described the new director as representing 'an extremely happy marriage' of the administrator and the art historian. Mr. Rueppel responded by saying that 'I am in great awe of this museum—I am overwhelmed at being invited to be director.'"

Having installed Rueppel, the position of board president was passed to John Coolidge. Seybolt focused on being a lobbyist for museums. Things might have been different had he stayed on to partner with Rueppel. Coolidge did not share Seybolt's vision. As the former director of Harvard's Fogg Art Museum, he had his own agenda.

Following the blueprint of the ad hoc report, Rueppel attempted to initiate changes.

He inherited an idea that the Board had been discussing to either move or divert the museum's grand staircase at the base of the Huntington Avenue entrance to the museum. There was a problem related to the flow of traffic through the museum. It was not his idea, but endorsing it evoked an outcry.

Early on when asked to attend a meeting of the acquisitions committee, he was instrumental in rejecting the seminal painting *Lavender Mist* by Jackson Pollock. It was a major blunder and the masterpiece was soon acquired by the National Gallery. The painting, which was offered to the museum for less than a million, is said to have sold for twice that and today might be valued at $100 million.

He initiated Seybolt's idea to professionalize the curatorial staff. Salaries were increased to that of professors at leading universities. But they were mandated to confine teaching to within the museum. With teaching and consulting positions for some of the curators the museum was where they hung their hats.

Traditionally curators were regarded as gentlemen with resources and social status independent of what they earned. Or, outside work, such as teaching, offset their low salaries. Messing with the curators resulted in a cabal and leaks to the *Globe* that brought down the director. It would not be the last such incident.

Given time and board support, Rueppel might have resolved differences.

The museum's curators were talking out of school. The action taken by the *Globe* may be described as a witch hunt. It caused damage to the institution which took a generation to recover from. What was lost was initiating social justice and community outreach aspects of the ad hoc report. The cabal against Rueppel came back to undermine the administration of Jan Fontein, who followed. An alleged coup ended when John Walsh left to become director of the mega rich J. Paul Getty Museum in Malibu, California.

August 6, 1976, by phone from Rueppel's Needham residence.

Charles Giuliano What has and has not come to light?

Merrill Rueppel It's true that a lot has not come to light. The trustees never made a clear statement about my removal. There were a lot of things that I tried to do, and the trustees that supported me, that met with fundamental resistance. There were those who didn't want the institution to change, whereas they knew that I was brought to the MFA with the understanding that I would bring about changes and make the museum more responsive to the public.

What wasn't seen by me, and my supporters, was that there wasn't the basis of any real support on the board of trustees.

CG What were some of the changes that you hoped to make?

MR These were the basic changes that were outlined by the museum's ad hoc report that was issued in 1970 and that was what I set out to do.

CG How did moving the staircase become such a volatile issue?

MR The staircase incident was just the first example of resistance. We didn't want to remove the staircase but just move it 90 degrees to the side to redirect the flow of traffic through the collection. This wasn't even my doing. The change was recommended by a committee, and I merely approved the plans and passed them on to the trustees, who turned them down flat. Somehow Guy Lowell's staircase became a very sacred issue and I managed to get saddled with it as though it had all been my idea. We were just trying to open up the museum and make it more accessible.

Like when a furor was touched off because I had some corridors painted white and paintings replaced by plants. I feel that a museum must have white space, some breathing room, and we had too much on display in areas where we couldn't provide adequate security. Besides, it wasn't possible to see the works in those places.

CG Isn't one key issue that you wanted the curators to in-house their teaching and use the museum as a teaching facility? Didn't this step on the toes of curators who receive notoriously low salaries but traditionally compensated for this by having teaching positions as well?

MR My purpose was to make the MFA into a great teaching institution and thereby to bring students and scholars into the museum. Here we have this great facility. For someone studying textiles, for example, they would have access to the collections and storage facilities that we have. This is a way to learn about art, not from slides in a darkened classroom where one had no sense of true color, scale, and surface texture.

One of the programs that I did succeed with was improving the salary scale throughout the museum. Depending on the length of tenure and other factors, the salary of full curators was upgraded to the range of $20,000 to $30,000. Added to this was another twenty percent in fringe benefits that I brought about. My feeling was that they were being very well paid and that they had a very good job. Therefore, it was my feeling that they could contribute more of their time to the MFA by teaching here rather than running all over and moonlighting. This is even more true of junior members of the curatorial staff. It is my belief that a number are still moonlighting.

I was even working on an arrangement whereby every four years they could take a one semester sabbatical which would allow them to go anywhere in the world to teach, but nothing came of this.

In certain cases, there were even exceptions. Ken Moffett the curator of contemporary art, for instance, was hired as a half-time curator as he is a full-time faculty member of Wellesley College. Similarly, the curator of Egyptian art, William Kelly Simpson, is paid on a half-time basis and has teaching obligations elsewhere (Yale University). In both of these cases these men worked really hard and gave us better than half of their time.

CG Is this one of the reasons that curators were opposed to you, because you were stepping on their toes?

MR Yes, but I think that is just one of the reasons. Since the departure of Perry Rathbone they were largely left to their own devices for a year. They were used to having their own way and someone had to be brought in who would bring them back together. This they resisted because it interfered with their status. As you know, there was a seminar program that is offered through the universities here. I was in favor of expanding this.

(The acting director during the interval between Rathbone and Rueppel was the classical curator, Cornelius Vermeule, who was also a candidate for director. He was popular with the curators but passed over for the position. While a graduate student at Boston University, I enrolled in his seminar, which was conducted at the museum.)

CG Was this the issue that caused trouble?

MR Not really, that was a private, internal issue, whereas the staircase became a public issue. It was all recommended by staff and committee and it wasn't really my doing.

CG The crux of the matter appears to lie with the trustees. Was it a matter of older, more conservative trustees resisting modernization?

MR Yes, I think that comes close to the issue. Mr. Seybolt, during his several years as president of the museum, had tried to clarify goals for the institution. He was trying to make the museum face up to future financial problems and commitments which were very pressing. For instance, the museum must raise $10 million for climate control.

When Mr. Rathbone resigned, (1955–1972) Seybolt led the search committee. The *Globe* has made it out that Mr. Seybolt handpicked me and hired me on the spot. That is simply not true. I was interviewed by the entire search committee and met with personnel before I was given the job. Somehow, though, I was linked to Seybolt, and there were those on the board who wished to see him step aside. I feel that attitude prevailed in firing me.

It was not necessarily older members of the board who resisted change, but there were conservative elements who resisted the intrusion of an outsider, which I was. There were trustees who backed the curators and sustained them in what they wanted to do. In essence, they were letting the staff run the museum, whereas, I thought the director was supposed to run it. A man must be master of his own home and similarly a man cannot serve two masters as some of the staff were trying to do. The problem with the MFA was that there was too much participation on the part of the trustees at the museum. It is one thing to be interested and involved, and it is another to be up to the elbows in matters that are beyond their scope. What they found was that there was a maverick from Texas coming in and telling them what to do.

CG Do you feel that they treated you as an outsider?

MR There is no question of that. Somehow my credentials were always questioned. I had my PhD from Wisconsin, for instance, instead of from the Fogg (Art Museum). Mr. Rathbone, for instance, did not hold an advanced degree in art history, but he was a graduate of the museum training program at the Fogg. This was somehow considered as right and proper, whereas my credentials from Wisconsin and a small museum in Texas were suspect. This is sad but true.

CG Although Mr. Rathbone had limited background as an art historian, he did insist on making a number of curatorial decisions. It is true, for example, that when William G. Constable retired as curator of painting when Rathbone came in, there was no attempt to replace him.

MR Yes, this is true. And look at the MFA today as a result of that. Modern art, for example, seems to stop five years before and after 1900. Now, of course, there is a contemporary curator but his job is defined as covering the period from 1945 to the present. He has no interest in collecting from 1900–1945.

CG How do you think the *Globe* got onto the story?

MR The *Globe* had direct access to one or more trustees and staff members who talked and gave a very prejudicial, one-sided opinion of what was happening. *Globe* reporters Robert Taylor and Patrick McGilligan interviewed me for an hour and a half on tape. I answered all of their questions and they then went back and seemed to write whatever appealed to them as a story, whether it has any bearing on the story or not. They simply could not be trusted with the facts.

CG What do you think was the motive for the *Globe* to do that series?

MR Somehow the *Globe* was set up to do a hatchet job and they did it. I don't think they did an honest job of reporting all of the facts. If they wanted to get me fired, they did a very good job of that. Then to turn around and publish all of that, and then on top of that to apply for a Pulitzer Prize, is absolutely preposterous. They only demonstrated that they are a joke as a newspaper. Their real goal was to sell newspapers, which they did by playing the story off the front page. They made a scandal of internal friction, which if left alone, could have resolved itself. We were making progress and moving forward. The story really came about because of the climate of Watergate. Every editor wanted to handle just such an investigative story. It is ironic that the story came to light because of the work of the reporter Jane Holtz Kay (author of *Lost Boston*). She invested considerable time and work into the story, only to conclude that there really was no story. The *Globe* caught wind of her work and decided to scoop the story even though there really was none. What they produced was sheer pyrotechnics. They should be ashamed for what they did.

CG Where does this leave you now?

MR I'm spending my time writing and enjoying life as a private citizen. I still look upon the museum with interest, but I have a limited involvement. I still go there occasionally to use the library.

CG What changes have occurred at the museum since your departure.

MR I haven't kept up with it and you probably know more about that than I do. But I get the sense that Dr. Fontein, who replaced me, has gone in the opposite direction.

CG How had it changed?

MR It's a shame to see a great museum wallow without direction. The standards for performance are not as high as they should be. They are not generating first-class exhibitions and top publications. For a museum of that scope, they are substandard.

CG Could you be more specific.

MR For instance the fact that there had been no curator of painting has worked very much against the collections. Many of the paintings are in very poor condition and only recently has a systematic survey of paintings taken place. Also, there are a number of inferior works on display. The MFA is showing too much and poorly. It is very difficult to find a good curator. However, I was on the brink of making the appointment when all of the controversy surfaced.

CG Will all of this effect the search for a new director?

MR At this point the museum has a difficult reputation. I had a very good job and reputation when I came here. In the past three years the trustees have in effect fired two directors and had two on a temporary basis. The job has a reputation of being something of a rattrap. After all, the trustees took me apart in less than two years. If they had left me alone, I could have organized the institution. Anyone coming to the job with less than carte blanche would only expect to hold the job for a year or two. Mr. Rathbone was a full trustee as well as director. He ran the place as a one-man act. I was clearly brought in with no such power. I was secured as a hired hand to do a job. The issue is, are you going to let the staff run the place, or is the director going to run the show? The trustees are confused as to whether they are going to live up to the guidelines of the ad hoc committee or not?

CG What was your reaction when it was alleged that the position was offered to John Pope-Hennessy? (Then retiring from the British Museum.)

MR That was utter nonsense. Why should he come in with less than a mandate to rule? They would have to issue him a blank check in order to induce him to come here. Unless the board has changed drastically, I do not see that happening. They have their vested interests and they are in this all too deeply for that.

CG Do you get the impression that Boston is a little backward?

MR Boston is, without doubt, the most provincial city I have been in in my life. In this sense, little Dallas, where I spent a number of years, is more progressive and international. People from Dallas with money have been all over the world. They have flown as far and wide as a jet plane can take them.

On the other hand, when Bostonians think of the West they usually don't mean beyond Needham. It's a shame that so many of the MFA curators have never been to the museums in Cleveland, Saint Louis, Dallas, Minneapolis, Cincinnati,

Chicago, Los Angeles and other cities.

They have no sense of what's going on in museums on a national and international basis. In order to be a truly great museum, the MFA must have a major change in the board of trustees, face up to the realities of the '70s, and to decide what are the real obligations of the MFA, to select goals, and get moving. We need a new board and a director they can stand behind one hundred percent through thick and thin.

CG Isn't it true that Perry Rathbone was brought here to do just that?

MR Don't sell Rathbone short. He completely renovated the museum and built two wings. He built the membership and ladies' committees. He transformed it from a stodgy and very uninteresting place into a very active one. In the long run he didn't move it as far as it might have gone. He made errors and it was time to move on. Perry ran the MFA single-handedly and that changed when I was brought in as a hired hand.

CG What changes would you envision for the trustees?

MR They seem to be involved in every activity except fundraising, which should be their first concern. There are some 35–40 trustees and they have various interests. Some of them are too involved with the arts and have their own ideas about how to run the show. Lewis Cabot, for instance, is an art dealer. Several members are architects or are involved with the arts on a professional basis. One, John Coolidge, is even a former museum director (Fogg Art Museum).

(In 1976 the board included: Nelson W. Aldrich, (architect), James Barr Ames, (senior partner Ropes & Gray), Mrs. E. Ross Anderson (her primary focus was the Museum School), Mrs. Paul Bernat (collector with her husband a Brockton business executive), Lewis P. Cabot (collector and consultant of contemporary art), Erwin D. Canham (retired editor-in-chief of *Christian Science Monitor*), Richard Chapman (former president of New England Merchants National Bank), Landon T. Clay (director of Vance Sanders, an investment firm and collector, donor of problematic Pre Columbian objects), John Coolidge (former director of the Fogg Art Museum), William Appleton Coolidge (senior partner of Ropes & Gray), Charles C. Cunningham (son of scholar Charles C. Cunningham of Sterling and Francine Clark Art Institute), John Peterson Elder (Dean of Harvard University Graduate School of Arts and Sciences), Dr. Henry L. Foster (president of Charles

River Breeding Laboratory, Inc. a supporter of contemporary art and the Rose Art Museum of Brandeis University), John L. Gardner (Staff treasurer, son of long standing trustee George Peabody Gardner), John Goelet, (real estate and B.&G. wine, through his mother, put up the money to purchase the alleged Raphael), Graham Gund (architect and collector, supporter of contemporary art), Paul F. Hellmuth (attorney and law partner in Hale & Dorr the firm of President Nixon's impeachment attorney, James St. Clair. He was named in a Jack Anderson column as a front man for the Central Intelligence Agency. He proposed to the board deaccessioning as a means of meeting the museum's deficit), Susan Morse Hilles (collector), Edward Crosby Johnson III (Fidelity Management and Research Co.), Howard W. Johnson (president of M.I.T.), James R. Killiam (honorary chairman of the board of M.I.T.), Williams J. Leary (ex officio, superintendent of Boston Public Schools), John Max Rosenfield (scholar of Japanese Art representing Harvard University), George Crossan Seybolt (president of William Underwood Company), Ellen Stillman (self-made businesswoman, serves on the board of Ocean Spray Cranberry Company, chair of the museum's Ladies' Committee), Katherine Stone White (special interest in film), Walter Muir Whitehill (author and scholar, brother-in-law of board member John Coolidge), John Wilhon (collector and State Street Bank and Trust).

CG It has been said by sources that the real reason you ran into difficulty was because you were lumped with Seybolt and that it was actually a move to unseat him disguised as an attack on you.

MR George Seybolt retired on his own volition. He stepped down with the understanding that he would head the development committee that had a goal of raising $10 million. The trustees basically made a mistake in electing John Coolidge to replace him. There are some that say that Coolidge wanted the job of director and that it was foolhardy for anyone to take the job with him as president of the board of trustees. At least I had to suffer under his tenure. I was fired last June and Coolidge resigned in August. Howard Johnson took over the trustees. It would have been a different ball game if I had served under Howard Johnson.

CG It is said that the *Globe* stories were considerably rewritten and modified prior to publication. Is there any truth in that?

MR The *Globe* was skating on thin ice in regard to libel. I am sure that their legal department made them moderate some statements. There is still room for a lawsuit on grounds of several quotes that they obtained in Texas. Again, they dispatched a reporter who came back and reported only on what they wanted to hear rather than the whole picture.

CG It would seem that you were set up as a patsy.

MR It was a witch hunt on the part of the *Globe*, and I don't to this day know why they wanted to do this. It was very clever, however, that they had contact with trustees and staff, as there were certain items in the story which could have only come from those sources. They came too quickly after certain events to have made the rounds through the usual rumor mills.

CG Did any good come from the articles and investigation?

MR It was a losing situation for everybody. It was ridiculous to put the MFA in that position. As an institution it is still recovering. It took more than two years to recover from the Rathbone incident and it will take another several years for the situation to stabilize at this point, unless they bring in someone with great prestige and absolute power at this point. Why should such an individual take such a chance?

At this point, even if by the process of elimination, Jan Fontein stays on as director, it will take 3–5 years for him to make progress. On a personal level, I have gone through a lot of sweat and sleepless nights over this. In this matter the *Globe* has proved itself to be so lousy that it couldn't sink to a much lower level than this.

CG Would it be any different for a new director?

MR A new director would have all the problems that I had and even more. Let me explain that I am not bitter or sad about all of this. There were sad and unhappy circumstances, but I came with an awareness that I was taking a risk. It was my responsibility to get something done, but given the board it was hopeless from the start. Certain characters made the job tough, if not impossible.

CG What were the goals that you set out when coming to the MFA?

MR I hoped to get the MFA back to a high level of performance in regard to:
    Preservation and conservation of the collection

Making the institution more accessible to the public

To appoint a curator for painting and the conservation of paintings

The storage facilities are in scandalous condition with no climate control. The entire building needs to be climate controlled and this is now a $10 million project

To push for a solid education program

To get the Museum School going on the right track

To beef up security

To increase salary and fringe benefits for the staff while avoiding union involvement. (A union was formed in 2020 with no apparent resistance from director Matthew Teitelbaum or the museum's trustees.)

I was just getting started on these priorities. At the end of my term I made a list of those accomplishments that ran to four pages. On paper it looks like something to be proud of.

Merrill C. Rueppel had a brief and troubled tenure at the MFA. Courtesy of the Dallas Museum of Art.

The Museum as a Business

A combination of the centennial and the simultaneous departure of Perry T. Rathbone caused the evaluation that resulted in the ad hoc report to the board in 1970. As board president and a businessman, George Seybolt proposed new models for the board and administration.

Rathbone represented the traditional approach as chief executive reporting to a supportive board and its committees. The departments and curators functioned as independent fiefdoms, which he dealt with as chief curator and through cordial, respectful, collegial diplomacy.

These plans were put forth in the ad hoc report, which is excerpted below. Accordingly, when Merrill Rueppel became director, it was understood that he would share administrative authority with business, fundraising, and marketing specialists.

As Rueppel told me, he came in as a "hired hand," never had true board support, and was sabotaged by a cabal of curators talking out of school to the *Boston Globe*. Administrators and curators I spoke with related that they had no issues working with Rueppel. Given more time and board support, differences may well have been resolved.

Even though it crashed and burned, the ad hoc template initiated by Seybolt and Rueppel became a paradigm for the MFA and other museums. With their departure, the organizational structure was modified by director, Dr. Jan Fontein, board president, Howard Johnson, and later, Robert Casselman, the associate director. That triumvirate provided checks and balances that stabilized management of the museum.

Ad Hoc Excerpts

We believe that avoiding deficits will increasingly become a responsibility shared by the Trustees and the Staff. We, therefore, urge four concurrent actions:

That the museum vigorously continues its efforts to adapt a modern system of accounting;

That it should distribute every year (at least to the Trustees and Senior Staff) a clear, comprehensive, and detailed statement of income and expenses;

That the Board of Trustees should decide upon investment strategies after considering alternatives recommended by the Investment Committee;

That appropriate members of the Staff and the Board prepare, early in 1971, a broad plan for fund raising and expenditure to cover at least the next five years. This would not necessarily be widely distributed, but would be recurrently revised.

Organization

The Museum's present table of organization developed gradually in response to the overriding desire, first to assemble collections and then to display them. Activities in education and preservation were afterthoughts. Slowly, they expanded to the point where they, too, required separate departments. Thus, the existing pattern of departments does not conform to what the museum is now doing; still less does it conform to what the Museum should be doing. Today, no aspect of this structure should be considered sacrosanct.

One staff member submitted to us a challenging proposal for comprehensive reorganization. Others have contributed valuable individual suggestions. We are particularly grateful to the Curators for their careful estimates of the needs of their respective departments and recommend that the heads of other departments make similar estimates for the Director. But though all these actions suggest a widespread recognition that there is a problem, they may not reach to its heart and result in an adequate solution.

The issue is urgent. The direction of the Museum's activities has changed under Perry Rathbone's leadership, but the basic structure has not. This has imposed strains. The requirements of fundraising, of arranging for physical expansion, of celebrating the centennial year have imposed further burdens. We are aware that under this accumulation of pressures, communications between the departments of the Museum has been attenuated. They must be strengthened.

But our ultimate concern is deeper yet. We are anxious that an organization which has proved itself sensitive, flexible, innovative, responsive, and disciplined in the pursuit, preservation, and publication directions should retain and increase exactly those qualities as it reverses its emphasis.

We are impressed that several major local institutions confronting parallel problems have set up committees to consider internal governance. We urge the Staff of the Museum to undertake something similar. We recommend that before the next annual meeting they present to the Trustees a comprehensive study of the desirable organization and staffing of the Museum.

The study should not be a mechanical compilation of desirable additions to the existing structure. It should:

Take as its point of departure the objectives outlined above;

Boldly recommend wholly new patterns of organization, including creating new departments, consolidating existing departments and, where appropriate, recommending trans-departments or non-departmental appointments;

Be attainable in the terms of the financial information which we have recommended that the Trustees provide to the Staff.

Trustees

The Board of Trustees should:

Be responsive to the needs of the community. This may be achieved if the Board is obviously, in reasonable measure, broadly diversified.

Include a careful balance of experimental collectors and connoisseur's in various fields of the arts, persons of learning, especially those connected with universities and colleges in the region; persons familiar with teaching and with various media of communication; persons of financial competence, who are able to handle investments and guide the business operations of the Museum; persons of national standing who can readily approach and command the respect of other organizations and individuals, both governmental and private, in order to assure continued effectiveness of the Museum; otherwise qualified persons from the ethnic minority communities in Boston, and indeed from the major communities which are still not adequately touched by the Museum. All these persons should have a particular interest in the museum.

Art Larson, Assistant Director for Administration, August 16, 1976

Charles Giuliano Could you discuss the details of the bank transfer from First National to New England Merchants?

Art Larson That happened in '71, slightly before I came here. We were working toward improving financial controls, including the reporting and the system of accounting. This would be the concern of any normal business. At that time, a number of things were looked at. The procedures for accounts and investments were looked at.

Much of our endowment is in procedural accounts, which involve care-taking stocks and securities which are kept in bank vaults. In these care-taking arrangements, we keep the stocks and bonds and the interest on them is deposited in our checking account.

The main thing that happened at this time was that we invited proposals from a number of different banks, including New England Merchants. You have to understand, though, that there are essentially two accounts. Whereas, one care-taking account is handled by New England Merchants, our main account is with First National, and this is how we pay our bills.

We disperse roughly $8 million annually. Operating expenses, including the Museum School, are $6 million, and we spend about $1.5 million on acquisitions. I would say that ninety-nine percent of the acquisition's funds come from restricted funds. Of the endowments for acquisitions, I would say that the majority are for painting. After that, prints and drawings, followed by Asiatic art. In general, painting is what you leave your money for.

CG How does New England Merchants function with the MFA account?

AL The money earned from the endowment is collected in New England Merchants and almost immediately transferred to First National.

CG What was the advantage of switching the account from State Street?

AL It seemed to make sense for the museum to be in a couple of different banks. As far as their advantage, for all of this service, they charge us a fee of $20,000.

CG Why go through so much trouble for a moderate advantage?

AL The MFA had an "asleep at the switch" kind of feeling. It was time for a change, and as part of the reassessment, the feeling was that State Street was not doing the job. Also, New England Merchants offers a ten percent discount on their fees to charitable institutions.

CG Does New England Merchants handle investments?

AL They act as an agent, but do not make the investment decisions. That is handled by the investments committee, headed by John Gardner and Preston Wallace. They were in charge of the Centennial Fund, which received some $8–10 million including the value of works of art donated and purchased. There, essentially, had been no funding campaign since then, until the recent NFA grant of $2 million toward a goal of $10 million for climate control.

CG How does the annual budget break down?

AL We have a $6.5 million operating overhead. Add to that $1.5 to 2 million for the Museum School.

CG Does the Museum School have an endowment?

AL It has about $1.6 million in endowment, mostly for scholarships. There are generous funds for traveling fellowships. In the last three to four years, we have leased space for the Museum School, which has increased costs.
    (Adjacent space from Wentworth Institute.)

CG How much of the operating expenses are covered by endowments?

AL Just 25 years ago at least ninety percent of expenses were covered by the endowment. Now it accounts for covering forty-five percent of operating expenses. Today the endowment provides $2,225,000 toward operating expenses.

CG What are the funding sources to cover the remaining costs?

AL It breaks down into the following sources.
    Annual appeal. (Last year $200,000 this year $350,000, handled by Walter

Robinson)

    Memberships provide $425,000

    In 1975 admissions provided $431,000

The museum shop makes money with $100,000 net, but this offsets the restaurant, which loses money as it only serves one meal a day. It operates only one night a week when the museum is open. A new restaurant will be a part of the new wing and auditorium, which can remain open at night when the rest of the museum is closed.

CG It appears that this is a new direction for the museum, as business administrators are in charge of aspects of the museum which were formerly handled by directors and trustees.

AL There was a great need to do this. We (Larson and Robinson) were brought in because we had experience as financial people used to controls and procedures. We were brought here largely through Mr. Seybolt. I don't set the goals. I don't know anything about art as such, and I don't want to interfere with the curators. It is up to the trustees to set our objectives.

CG What kind of relationship have you had with the museum?

AL You would have to ask the trustees that, but I have had a good relationship with Mr. Seybolt in particular.

CG What are the current goals for the museum?

AL Look, at the moment, you can find somebody to support any hair-brained scheme that you can think of. There are many ideas floating around and you can find advocates for anything. The point is that anything is worthy of being done, but it is up to the trustees to decide on our objectives. We have to realize that we can't do everything and we have to do some things well.

    We were the first museum in the country to establish a five-year projection of our needs. We have done a similar study for the Museum School. Now other museums are trying this. Everything can't be done and there is a tendency to do a little bit of everything.

CG One area in which the museum appears to be lagging is special exhibitions. Too many of the major touring shows aren't stopping in Boston. What does it cost to install a major exhibition?

AL Major shows get corporate support. We received a grant of $100,000 toward the exhibition *Paul Revere's Boston* which cost $200,000 to mount. (It was organized by MFA curators.) It is very difficult for us to compete with other institutions, as these shows are very expensive. The National Gallery is said to have spent $750,000 on their installation of the traveling Chinese exhibition. (*The Chinese Exhibition of Archaeological Finds of the People's Republic of China*, 1974, National Gallery of Art)

CG What did the Goya show cost? (In 1975 Eleanor Sayre curated 255 works called *The Changing Image: Prints by Francisco Goya*.)

AL That cost about $80,000 because of the many loans and insurance costs. There were curators flying as couriers with the works. That's not at all unusual.

CG How much did the Alfred Leslie show cost?

AL That was not an expensive show, and didn't entail costly shipping and insurance. The show cost about $8,000. On the other hand, the Anthony Caro sculpture show was very expensive. It was a cooperative effort between several museums (primarily MoMA). Our share of the rental fee was $12,000 and overall, that show cost $60,000. In terms of attendance, the Leslie and Caro shows drew about the same (10,000).

CG I understand that you run the personnel department. Traditionally, museum jobs pay poorly. In the past, curators relied on family money. It was a genteel profession. Like ambassadors they were expected to have independent means.

AL We are trying to change that. Under Merrill Rueppel, we came up with a job description and grading system for every staff position. We were trying to align salaries with comparable institutions like universities and libraries.

Based on experience, education, and other factors, an assistant curator with a certain grade would enjoy the same benefits as someone with the same grade in a library. We were trying to create some consistency within the museum. We wanted to keep pace with what was being offered to people in other jobs.

CG You mention education as a factor in grading.

(Traditionally, in museum work advanced degrees were not required. There were museum directors from Perry Rathbone to Kathy Halbreich and David Ross with B.A.s. Under Rathbone, the painting department was staffed by two women with B.A.s who worked for years as curatorial assistants rather than assistant curators.)

How many employees does the museum have?

AL There are 400 to 500 employees, including part-time help.

(During the 2020 pandemic the museum furloughed some 300 workers, or more than 40 percent of its 750-person workforce, in anticipation of losses of $12–$14 million, based on a projected closure through June 30. Through various means, the museum balanced the books for the fiscal year. When the museum was closed by mandate, the loss was quoted to me as some $250,000 a day. The loss for 2021 was projected at some $21 million.)

CG Of the MFA's employees, what percentage is represented by people of color?

AL I won't answer that question specifically. What we don't need is to provoke a government investigation. This is time-consuming and costly. We recently went through this with the Federal government. Let me just say that like any business or corporation we must comply with the guidelines established by the Federal Government, and we are making every effort to do this.

CG How well-endowed is the MFA compared to other major museums?

AL The endowment of the Met is roughly double that of the MFA. That's a drop in the bucket compared to the J. Paul Getty Museum. (In 1982 the Getty's bequest was $1.2 billion.) Compared to our $1.5 million annual acquisitions fund they have some $35 million to spend.

(That, however, was 112 years after the Met and MFA had assembled America's greatest museum collections.)

Walter Robinson at the MFA, August 16, 1976

Walter Robinson was originally from Bass River Savings Bank on Cape Cod. He moved to Minneapolis in 1960 to work for Museum of College of Art and Design. It was a holding company which later took on children's theatre.

He was brought to the MFA by Merrill Rueppel to head development and fundraising.

Charles Giuliano What was the response when a professional money-man took over in an area, which had traditionally been handled by trustees?

Walter Robinson To put it mildly eyebrows hit the ceiling. There were a number of museum directors I knew who wouldn't talk to me after that.

CG What were you doing in Minneapolis?

WR It's a much smaller city than Boston with an inner-city population of 500,000. It's a venturesome city and had more culture per acre that most other American cities. It can boast of a major museum as well as The Walker Art Center, a symphony orchestra, opera company, the Guthrie Theater, and a university. It's a lively community and just completed a $32 million complex including the College of Art and Design and a theater. I was president of the society but felt that it was time to step down.

CG Was it a demotion to come here as an assistant director?

WR The job in Minneapolis was done and the challenges here are great. The potential for the MFA is enormous. It's the number-two art museum in North America.

CG Let's quantify its status. What is the endowment, for instance?

WR Give or take fluctuations in the value of the portfolio, the endowment stands at approximately $55 million. That breaks down to sixty percent restricted funds and forty percent unrestricted funds. Most bequests are given for a specific purpose, for paintings, or oriental jade. For operating funds, we can only draw on forty percent of the endowment.

CG It took a hundred years to create a $55 million endowment. In that time there were great acquisitions but not a commensurate generosity from old money sources. What is the museum doing to recruit new funding sources?

(During 23 years with the Boston Symphony Orchestra, recently retired Mark Volpe, tripled the endowment to $456 million. Malcolm Rogers raised the MFA endowment from $180 million to $602 million. While $500 million was raised for the American Wing, Rogers left a debt of some $140 million. The endowment of the Metropolitan Museum of Art is $1.7 billion. In 2017 the Getty Museum endowment was $6.9 billion. In 2013 the MoMA endowment was $870 million.)

WR We are working on a number of approaches. One involves deferred giving or living trusts. This was first developed by Dartmouth College a few years ago. A widow, for example, is living on a trust. The trust can be transferred to the museum, which in turn guarantees an income for life. In this arrangement, there are no capital gains taxes, and through exemptions, she is paid almost twice the dividend the trust would normally earn. The transfer is final and the museum takes over the trust upon the death of the widow.

There are trusts that can be written which do not divert to the museum until the death of the children. This comes under the heading of long-range funding. The MFA, after all, built its endowment over a hundred years. We have to pursue bequests in order to provide for the future. Traditionally, nobody has approached individuals about this. The norm has been for individuals to volunteer their bequests.

The curse of museums is that in spite of the richness of collections, it's hard to get people to dig into their pockets for operating costs. As of June 1975, there was an operating deficit of $600,000, and this year's deficit is some $500,000. This has the adverse effect of decreasing the principle each year.

CG What funding is coming from the Jewish community?

WR The new auditorium was funded by Mr. and Mrs. HarryRemis. The Foster family funded the gallery for contemporary art.

CG Many potential donors feel disenfranchised from the elitist museum. Doesn't this hurt fundraising efforts?

WR My experience in Minneapolis wasn't much different. There is also the matter of some old families who have long faced their obligations to the community. Somehow people are not aware that we need money. They think that they can come to the museum free of charge. Our admission is just $1.50. The Science Museum and Aquarium charge more than that. Our operating costs are higher than theirs.

The MFA is unique among major American museums in having little regular state or city support. The state provides $90,000 in a program that allows children under 16 free admission. We received $10,000 from Boston University to cover free admission for their students. They suggested that to us and we would like to see similar programs with more schools and colleges in the area.

CG You were a Rueppel appointment. Has this caused problems for you?

WR I had known him for quite some time. He knew my work and what I was trying to do. I knew that I was in for a lot of flack when things began to go sour for him. When things collapsed for Mike, I said to him, "Do you really want me?" He said that he did.

CG Considering the enormous depth of the collection, are there ways to monetize it? There are a number of smaller and regional museums that might benefit from loans for a fee?

WR I am very much for outreach. We have already been doing that through loans to area museums. We have done several long-term exhibitions with the Brockton Art Museum. The participating museum would have to meet our criteria for insurance, security, and conservation.

CG Why is fundraising so difficult for the museum?

WR This is largely an image issue. Most museums do not articulate their needs very well. People regard the MFA as a great and rich institution and don't conceive that we need funding. We have to list priorities in a way that the public can understand them. Our costs have risen in recent years. It now costs $500,000 annually for security. Take fuel, for instance. In the first five months of 1975, we reduced heating by thirty-nine percent yet paid seventy-five percent more for fuel than the year before. That gives you some idea of cost increases.

We have to initiate outreach programs that bring people into the museum. That's why we have programs like a free week or *Art in Bloom*. We must meet funding goals. As we proceed with climate control installation we will change and refurbish most of the exhibition spaces.

CG There has been a decline in attendance figures.

WR The Bicentennial had us hopeful and excited. All over the country, however, the Bicentennial was a flop. We made a major commitment by providing exhibitions and programs geared to the celebration. Projected crowds never materialized.

CG What is the extent of the museum's commitment to the National Center for Afro American Artists?

WR We fund them to the extent of $35,000 a year. This pays the salary of adjunct curator Barry Gaither (director of NCAAA) and his assistant Harriet Kennedy as well as the costs of some special exhibitions.

CG Last year Gaither curated *Jubilee* for the MFA. There was outcry that there was no catalogue for the exhibition.

Clementine Brown (The museum's PR director sat in on the interview.) That has been misinterpreted. When we originally planned the show and provided funding, the curator was allowed to spend it as he saw fit. He very much wanted a cabaret opening, as he felt it was the spirit of the occasion. This was very successful but consumed funds for the show. There was no money left for a catalogue and that was his budgeting decision. Naturally, the artists all screamed because, to them, documentation was very important. We are, in fact, producing a catalogue. Not an elaborate one, but there will be documentation. This is taking from $6,000 to $7,000 more than we had originally budgeted for the show. This is how misunderstanding arises.

This is very much an era of accountability. We have nothing to hide.

WR The *Globe* article (Rueppel) alluded to taking us to account. What it actually was though, was a sick set of articles that made people in the business community very mad. We are a big, open target with a lot of visibility to anyone who wants to take a shot at us.

CG Has that made your job tough, if not impossible?

WR I've been a businessman for a very long time. I know as much as anybody about what goes on in this area. I am also a retired banker and that gives me a certain credibility. I'm coming back to where I was born and raised to do a job.

CG It is often said that Boston is a poor town for support of the arts.

WR That was one of the challenges in coming here. We had just got finished raising $44 million in Minneapolis and that is a town with smaller population and resources than Boston.

It is maddening to think of many businesses that have located here and recruited top executive talent by dangling in front of them the vast cultural resources of Boston. These same corporations don't then turn around and support the arts.

We solicited 90 corporations for contributions. Between all of them we were only able to raise a few thousand dollars. We would like to see more participation in the arts on the part of the business community. We have to tap into the business corridor along Route 128.

CG What about Polaroid for example?

WR Actually Polaroid is an exception. They have been very good to us, including providing funds to collect photography. The problem is that this museum, like so many, has a sense of elitism. We need more outreach like the BU grant. Given the vast number of students here (some 250,000) during their four years they will make several visits. We also need an educated membership that will be more cognizant of our needs.

The MFA as a private institution relied on its patrons, but by the 1970s needed new sources of revenue. Gary Lombard photo.

Board President George Seybolt Wanted to Manage the MFA Like a Business

George Crossan Seybolt (1915–1993) was president and chairman of the William Underwood Company, best known for its canned Deviled Ham. Raised in Hannibal, Missouri, he dramatically changed the tone and mandate of the board of the Museum of Fine Arts, which he joined in 1968.

He was recruited by director Perry T. Rathbone, whom he was then instrumental in ousting. That resulted from a bungled attempt to smuggle from Italy a small portrait of Eleonora Gonzaga alleged to be by Raphael, *Portrait of a Young Girl*, 1505. The acquisition, for some $800,000, was to have been the highlight of the museum's centennial celebrations in 1970.

The incident might have been handled with diplomacy. The ouster of Rathbone was extreme and may have been the opportunity Seybolt seized upon to initiate a broad agenda for change. These were articulated in an ad hoc policy report created when he was president of the Board of Trustees.

When Rathbone resigned in 1972, there was a transitional year with classical curator, Cornelius Vermeule, as acting director. A list of potential directors, including the architect I. M. Pei, was initiated. Given the turmoil of the museum at that time, it was alleged that top candidates were not anxious to assume the position.

Acting preemptively, Seybolt offered the position to Merrill Rueppel, a relatively unknown museum professional, then director of the small Dallas Museum of Art in Texas. Seybolt stepped down from the board and was replaced by former Fogg Art Museum director, John Coolidge. There was turmoil that resulted when Rueppel attempted to initiate the ad hoc directives. Internal conflicts with curators and staff were leaked to the *Boston Globe*. Investigative reporting led to Rueppel being fired. Coolidge also stepped down and was replaced by former MIT president, Howard Johnson. The Asiatic curator, Jan Fontein, became acting director, then a year later, director.

When Johnson and Fontein got the museum back on track, some of the initiatives of the ad hoc report were followed. They included climate control renovation, construction of I.M. Pei's West Wing, support for a contemporary art program under Kenworth Moffett, and the appointment of John Walsh as curator of painting. Broader mandates for diversity and community access were given token response.

Essentially, Seybolt attempted to run the museum as a business. Toward that end, he demanded an office and two secretaries. He barraged Rathbone with memos and expanded the role and authority of the president to at least equal to that of the director. During the Centennial he chaired the museum's first capital campaign. At the time, the museum's endowment was half that of the Metropolitan Museum. While ranked second for its collections, the museum was relatively poor. Decades of renovation, expansion, acquisitions, and blockbuster exhibitions would follow.

In 1974, Seybolt became president emeritus of the museum. In 1980, he retired from Underwood. Expanding on his work with the MFA, he became a lobbyist for museums. President Jimmy Carter appointed him the first chairman of the National Museum Services Board, an advisory group, and he was a founder of the Museum Trustees Association in Washington. That was the focus of our discussion in May 1977.

He had a reputation for being abrupt and uncouth. The curators were mandated to attend the screening of a promotional film for his company as a model for how he wanted to run the museum. That rankled the curators and staff, which carried over as resentment and opposition to his hand-picked director, Merrill Rueppel.

One might argue that Seybolt was a pioneer with a new vision for museums.

Charles Giuliano What is the status of your appointment to the Institute of Museum Services?

(IMLS was established by the Museum and Library Services Act [MLSA] on September 30, 1996, which includes the Library Services and Technology Act and the Museum Services Act. This act was reauthorized in 2003 and again in 2010. The law combined the Institute of Museum Services, which had been in existence since 1976, and the Library Programs Office, which had been part of the Department of Education since 1956. Lawmakers at that time saw "great potential in an Institute that is focused on the combined roles that libraries and museums play in our community life.")

George Seybolt The legal position is that the President nominates a board of fifteen. The Senate committee provides advice and consent. The President then nominates a chairman. So, it's a long way from an accomplished fact. I have not been pressing it. My position is that they ask if you will serve and you say yes. It takes time. Based on everything that I have seen, I suspect that, if the administration was established, it would have been done a long time ago.

CG It seems the Carter administration is still getting settled.

GS It's dealing with something that's just been created. Here is a whole new thing, so it is much harder than filling existing positions. I haven't met President Carter. He takes recommendations, but it's his decision.

CG Is this under HEW?

GS This is a separate organization.

CG Where does Califano fit in? (Joseph Anthony Califano Jr. is a former United States Secretary of Health, Education, and Welfare.)

GS He's enthusiastic about it. He sees art and education as parallel, and I think he's right about that. A new budget for IMS starts on October 1 with $3 million. Both House and Senate have recommended it. But they have differences, so they need to meet and come to a compromise. The total authorized for the first year was $15 million. When Congress creates a piece of legislation, particularly expenditure legislation, they put a ceiling on the authorization. They authorize it for three years. The ceiling for 1976, which starts on October 1, is $15 million.

This bill was created a year ago and went through both Houses, and President Ford signed it. He made no recommendation for funding. He was less than enthusiastic. Our best friends were Democrats in Congress: Pell, Javitz, and Brademas. It went through with the highest vote for any arts legislation that has been passed.

When Mr. Califano came in and had to go to the Office of Management and Budget (run by Bert Lance, a Georgia businessman, who resigned in his first year because of a scandal from which he was later cleared), he and the White House group said okay and authorized $3 million. It was the White House saying: We just want to spend $3 million on this and see how it goes.

CG Why do we need the IMS? How is it different from the National Endowments?

GS I was a member of the Endowment Council for three years, so I am in a good position to answer that. The Endowment is project oriented. It is supposed to take care of specific and particular one-time needs. These may be defined as a catalogue for an exhibition, or it may be six catalogues, but they are specific and separate things.

CG How is that defined in the charter and bylaws?

GS It is and embedded in its policy. There are exceptions to this. For instance, symphony orchestras, if they are a certain size, are given a certain amount of money each year. There are other things the Endowment does that are voted on every year. They have some uncertainty, but are accepted, and that's expected every year. As far as museums are concerned in the Endowments, they were never envisioned as being included when Roger Stevens and Livingston Biddle invented it, and wrote the legislation to a large part, and Biddle was deputy director under Stevens. Today, Stevens runs the Kennedy Center. He's a businessman who made a lot of money in construction. He became interested in the arts and became a producer and a backer. He got into this and helped to promote the Endowments, particularly the Arts Endowment. He served as the first chairman there and there have only been two, Stevens and Hanks. He's a producer and financier at the Kennedy Center. When Roger conceived of the Foundations, his only interest was in the performing arts. It wasn't until he retired, and Nancy Hanks came in eight years ago, that there was any museum program at all.

CG Didn't Brademas have a role in bringing about that program?

GS Claiborne Pell and John Brademas introduced legislation similar to the IMS. It was not the same, but had a similar principle. Perhaps the reaction was that it was a rival and could be taken care of in the Endowments. When that program was first brought in, it was about $1 million. It was for project work, perhaps a catalogue, but not for brick and mortar. It was not for purchases and endowment, but for operating things related to projects, perhaps a study of air conditioning and climate control, or the restoration of some paintings, perhaps funding a sabbatical for a curator.

CG What about the MFA's $2 million grant for climate control from the NEA? Isn't that bricks and mortar?

GS That came later. They went around the country and found, in the older museums like Philadelphia, Boston, and Chicago, that they never provided for climate control. The NEA set up one-time grants for that purpose. They tried to clear them all up and to give all those museums a turn at bat. I was advised that legally it was possible to do that.

CG So the NEA did not initially consider museums?

GS The cost of running museums is two to three times the cost of running all other performing arts: dance, theatre, and symphony. Despite this factor, supporting museums was never envisioned. We have gotten up to fifteen percent of the annual Endowment budget and now are down to eleven percent. While we're getting more money, the Endowment's budget has been going up so fast that we find ourselves with a smaller percentage, while the clear fact is that we should get a greater percentage because of the relationship between the fields of visual and performing arts and the cost of running them. I think that Pell and Brademas, House and Senate, felt that there would never be a proper shakeout there, as far as money is concerned. I would agree with them. No amount of fighting that I have done in the past two years has done much for us in terms of a percentage increase. They put the IMS into legislation, and there the thrust is different. It is money for straight, functional, housekeeping and maintenance, for salaries which are about two thirds of museums' budget on average. Take a look at museum job listings to see how low salaries are. You are better off teaching public school than to earn eight to ten thousand dollars a year as director of a small museum. That's not so true for the larger and better-funded museums like the MFA.

When I was president of the MFA, we instituted a policy where salaries were on a par with those at MIT and Harvard. There is a great difference in salary between working for a large or small institution. The result of that is that traffic has been to education, among art history majors, rather than to museums. Traditionally, it has been a profession for individuals with independent income. Today, I don't think that's true. People come to museums because they have a calling. I would hate to be a young married man and director of a small museum trying to raise a family. Fifty years ago, curators tended to be dilettantes with a collector's mind and inclinations.

(Rueppel did attempt to raise salaries for curators but at a cost. He mandated that they work full time for the museum and suspend outside income from consulting and teaching. They were to do any teaching at the museum. That happened to some extent. But they were not to hold university faculty positions. William Kelly Simpson chaired the Egyptian Department and was a professor at Yale. Ken Moffett had a half-time position as curator of contemporary art and was tenured at Wellesley College. Later, under Fontein, John Walsh was curator of European painting and a salaried curator of the William I. Koch Foundation. The arrangement doubled his compensation. Walsh left to head the Getty Museum just prior to my reporting his Koch salary, as a conflict of interest, for the *Patriot Ledger*.)

CG When you were president of the MFA, your reputation was that of a "brutal business type." How did this jibe with the attitudes of Brahmin trustees and their emphasis on attaching their names to labels of glamorous acquisitions? You were regarded as an intruder because you reminded them of the bottom line. How did you apply business practices to a museum?

GS A hundred and fifty years ago there were no museums. The few that existed did so to support egos and were the playthings of royalty. In their castles and estates, they had collections, which the public had no access to. The French Revolution changed that as the public regarded the former royal collections to be in their domain. That transition from private to public occurred in a variety of ways. Tax revenue financed armies to loot treasures and bring them home to national museums. In today's world, tax deductions for museum donations mean that we all pay for those works. I think the public has latent knowledge of this. They say, 'I have an interest and stake in this. I don't want to be shut out and want to enjoy it as well even though I lack an education in art history. It's a part of our life and I have a right to it.' My greatest difficulty at the MFA was espousing a viewpoint that the museum has a responsibility to the public.

It has to discharge that responsibility or someday the public will say, 'I don't like the way that they run museums and let's take them over and run them ourselves.' On this point, they have tremendous grassroots support. There is great belief in and a desire to be a part of them. There are awe-inspiring things in museums. When I was a young fellow, you went into railroad stations and great public buildings. Today it's different. There is not an impressive building that has been built in Boston recently. They have modest lobbies. Look at bus stations and airport terminals today. They are pretty utilitarian. Older museum buildings have the problem of not being inviting, seeming cold and repellant. That's one place to start. They are lovely buildings and there are all kinds of places to show art in. In the last generation, there has developed a problem of feeling at home in museums. People feel oppressed by their grandeur and scale. Then what happens when you are inside them? How does one get oriented? Who takes them through and says 'now this label will mean…' How do you install collections so that there is a sense of logical succession? Whether it's all art or organized into departments. You demonstrate the point about how early Italian Renaissance art had no linear perspective. There is a narrative and sequence developed to convey that. Or how art develops to today's abstract art where yet again there is no perspective. You convey how and why that happened and what it means to a viewer.

As trustees, I thought we had a responsibility as instruments of education to convey that in a manner which the public can grasp, to not just run museums for dilettantes and the occasional well-trained visitors. You have a dual purpose. That's not been the most popularly held viewpoint.

The job of trustees is to represent the public to the staff and work out some understanding of what the public needs. Some very distinguished museum directors had a panel discussion here when Mr. Brademas was holding hearings. I heard them say that by the year 2000, museums would be incorporated into the public education system of the United States and would no longer be independent institutions. Whether that becomes true or not, I won't be around to see.

CG You came to the museum, not through art, but as a money person. Was it your role on the board to apply business acumen?

GS I don't think so. It would have been a mistake, because they weren't ready for that, and I'm not sure they ever will be. As I saw it, I was coming in with a fresh mind and fresh approach with no preconceived notions. My job was to find out what a museum was in today's world and what it should be. I came to the MFA because I was interested in Brian O'Doherty's TV broadcasts (WGBH from the museum).

Since no country or museum has a monopoly on art, perhaps you put objects together in big exhibitions. But they have almost gone out of style because they are so expensive to produce. Despite the need and opportunities for them, there are now very few of these exhibitions in spite of support from the Endowments.

CG Did your experience at the MFA serve as a prototype of what museums need?

GS It started there. I took on the trustees of the American Association of Museums three years ago. Since then I have visited museums all over the country. I am astonished to see how many I visited in the past five years. In this manner I learned of museum problems.

CG The combined National Foundations for the Arts and Humanities this year has a budget of $250 million. It has taken time to get to that level.

(For 2020 the NEA has been funded at $162 million and the NEH for $162.25 million.)

What will the IMS need to be effective?

GS The museums need at least $150 million. The $3 million for next year is more than the Endowments started with years ago. At this point, we would waste money if we were appropriated $40 million. In the long run, though, we will need $150 million. This isn't to start new museums. There's a building and it needs to be lit and heated. There are guards and staff expenses. Doubling attendance doesn't cost that much. If you get 200,000 people to come to the museum for a successful exhibition, then everything comes to life. The restaurant and sales desk all do business. For an MFA, that can make or break the institution. If you can draw a million visitors a year, that solves all fiscal challenges. Currently annual attendance is half that. When a museum has financial struggles, it becomes intellectually and emotionally bankrupt. What gets peeled off the top are people that represent the real talent of the museum.

Museum Board President George Seybolt. Courtesy Museum of Fine Arts.

Seybolt was president of William Underwood Company, which was known for its Deviled Ham. Giuliano photo.

Jan Fontein, from Asiatic Curator to Museum Director

It is unclear what role Jan Fontein played in leaks to the *Globe* and the investigative reporting that led to the ouster of the director, Merrill Rueppel.

The Asiatic department, of which he was chief curator, was arguably the most prestigious and best endowed of the museum. Another curator, Cornelius Vermeule, had served as acting director in the period between the departure of Perry T. Rathbone and the preemptive appointment of Rueppel by Board President George Seybolt. Vermeule aspired to the position but was passed over.

It was assumed that Fontein would be a placeholder while the museum searched for a new director. But the post was less than enticing for the field of top candidates. The museum pressured Rathbone to resign, passed over Vermeule, and then fired Rueppel. That left the museum with a reputation for not supporting its directors.

The curators were notable for their independence and turf wars. All seats at the round table were not equal. There was competition for space, special exhibitions, and unrestricted funds for acquisitions. Elevated to the position of director entailed diplomacy in exerting authority over the strongly independent curators.

New to the position and on uncertain footing, he found an ally, partner, and mentor in board president, and former MIT president, Howard Johnson. On many levels Johnson took Fontein to school and groomed him into the position.

They raised $14 million for I.M. Pei's West Wing. While it was being built in the late 1970s, the museum opened a branch in the Faneuil Hall Marketplace curated by Kenworth Moffett.

In 1981, the West Wing opened and housed the Graham Gund Gallery, the Remis Auditorium, and a spacious gallery for traveling shows, as well as the wing's restaurant, café, gift shop, and auditorium. The museum initiated a film program curated by the critic Deac Rossell. More than $60 million was raised during his tenure for construction and endowment. Several blockbuster shows were staged on his watch, including *Pompeii*, *Pissarro*, and *Renoir*, which alone drew more than 500,000 visitors.

One might say that Fontein grew into the position, but then again, not really. He did not distribute the goodies evenly. The Asiatic department prospered with major renovations, special exhibitions, and other aspects of favoritisms.

As my relationship and interviews evolved, over time there was a change. He enjoyed and tended to abuse power. There were leaks of an internal power struggle, particularly with John Walsh, whom he appointed to head the Department of European Painting, a position that had remained unfilled since W.G. Constable resigned shortly after Rathbone arrived in 1955.

In turn, Walsh convinced Fontein to appoint Theodore E. Stebbins, Jr. as curator of American Painting. Resenting Fontein's abuse of resources (funds diverted from other departments to support his ambitions for the Asiatic Department), there were secret meetings of curators to unseat Fontein and replace him with Walsh.

That collapsed when Walsh left to become director of the J. Paul Getty Museum in Malibu. There was also an ouster of Moffett, who faced general dissatisfaction with his narrow vision for the collection. In this power vacuum, Stebbins took over the portfolios of Walsh and Moffett. With no expertise in this area, Fontein opted not to interfere.

In this complex balance of power, overall, Fontein oversaw ambitious expansion, renovation, and all-important climate control installation. There were blockbuster exhibitions. From the outside all seemed copasetic.

Other than some key bullet points, however, Fontein's administration drifted away from the mandates set forth in the 1970 ad hoc report. The museum supported Barry Gaither and the National Center for Afro-American Artists, but less than adequately. There were protests when a show that Stebbins organized of American masterpieces sent to Paris failed to include any African American Masters. Work by Henry Osawa Tanner was added at the last minute, but not added to the catalogue, which had been printed.

My liaison to the museum and Fontein was the director of publicity, Clementine Brown. As she told me, "When he visits Japan, he's treated like a Shogun."

August 1976 at the MFA

Charles Giuliano When Merrill Rueppel was forced out, you were appointed as acting director. You have been in that position for a year. Can you discuss that experience and thoughts about staying on as a candidate for the permanent position?

Jan Fontein I have enjoyed doing this job. Having returned from a long vacation, I am able to look at it with a fresh view. A year as director has taken its toll. The job tends to gobble you up, but I have enjoyed the endeavor. Every director has ideas of what they want to carry out, but they are frustrated in doing so. Overall, I have worked well with the trustees.

I came to the museum ten years ago, not as director, but as a curator. You think you know the museum. I have always talked to other curators and thought I knew what was going on.

I was quite surprised when I moved up here (offices in the administrative wing), which offers a different perspective of the museum.

CG It has been discussed that there are plans to diversify tasks and positions in the administration. Perry Rathbone presided over all aspects of the museum, and that is no longer the case. The era of centralized, high-profile directors like Rathbone and Thomas Hoving of the Met, appears to be over. As museums have expanded and become more complicated, it is no longer possible for a single individual to run them.

JF There is a slightly different concept today. On the whole the "one man show" concept is out of date. That model puts a lot of burden on that man's knowledge and experience. If you come from a scholarly field, you are aware that there are things that you don't know. We are looking at a very different organization to take maximum advantage of our staff. There is a great diversity of talent, and the intent is to use that to our advantage. The talent gets to do what it does best. I don't see that as breaking down the authority of the director. The director is responsible for fund raising, administration, supervising staff, and being responsible to trustees.

There are two ways of looking at the museum.

That there is a pecking order in which orders from the top filter down to the staff.

That it is an organization with some very good ideas present at the grass-roots level.

I have been in the museum field for some 25 years, and during that time, transition has occurred. The field has become more professional.

CG There have been comments that curators went to the media with their grievances against Merrill Rueppel. In essence, that he was encroaching on their domain and privileges in regard to travel and outside income through consulting on attributions and acquisitions by private collectors and dealers.

JF Personally, I had a good working relationship with Rueppel. I did not have any problems with him. Please understand that I am a curator at a museum. I was informed on how other curators felt, but I do not know that curators were crybabies who went to the press. I did not at any time go to the press, and to my knowledge, neither did my colleagues.

Bear in mind that there was a fairly serious crisis, and under the circumstances, people exercised a great deal of restraint. I did not speak one word to the press or the trustees. If I was asked an honest question, I did give answers. People who become curators, on the whole, are just interested in that kind of job. What I am doing (as acting director of the museum) is temporary.

CG Is it true that Rueppel restricted curatorial travel?

JF No, that is not true. Rueppel did not restrict travel. I was supposed to do an exhibition, and in the midst of it, an opportunity transpired to visit an area of the Orient, which I had never seen. He let me go on that trip.

CG Rueppel wanted to end "moonlighting" by curators, particularly regarding their university affiliations and appointments.

JF This issue doesn't exist anymore. We have a summer institute with Boston University. The BMFA is in an area densely populated with colleges and universities.

Most of the curators teach in the area and work with colleges and other museums. We are working on a program with the departments to benefit schools.

If a student is doing a paper on a certain painting, for instance, they just go to the department with the name of the artist, title of the painting, and accession number. A staff person can look up the work and find a file card that summarizes the bibliography of the object. This should be a great benefit to students.

We are trying to come up with interesting programs. I teach a course every two years at Harvard. I like to use the university to stimulate students. By this manner, you get students to come to the museum to look at objects. Some of them become involved with departments in cataloguing and some students have worked on exhibitions.

We are trying to open up the museum. The new wing and auditorium complex will help that. (The West Wing designed by I.M. Pei) We are initiating free admission on Tuesday evenings. I had much hope of reducing general admission fees. We did not have the result I had hoped for.

CG During this time of transition, attendance is off. Is part of that the fact that there have been no blockbuster exhibitions that draw large crowds?

JF Those big shows seem to solve statistics on paper but haven't solved a single problem of the museum itself. For a museum like the Brockton Art Museum, special exhibitions are the only way out, as they don't have a permanent collection.

(The museum did have a collection that occupied the central corridor as one entered the museum. Faced with debt, the director, Katherine Graboys, sold work to stay afloat. This was broadly condemned. She died young of cancer and was followed by Jennifer Atkinson, who also died of cancer. The museum organized important exhibitions including *The Brockton Triennial*. An exhibition of the 19th century Boston visionary William Rimmer was curated by director Marilyn Hoffman. Dorothy Thompson curated a Hyman Bloom show, and there was also a retrospective for Boston expressionist Henry Schwartz. Several years ago, the museum was reorganized as the Fuller Craft Museum.)

We would be in the same position if we were arousing interest only through exhibitions. We would enjoy them, but what must we do to make our collections more exciting for the general public?

CG Is the lack of climate control a factor in why the museum is not getting major traveling exhibitions?

JF No, it is not climate control. I have never been refused an exhibition for that reason. Major shows like the China show want to hit a certain number of geographically dispersed institutions. They choose, for example, Washington DC, Kansas City, and San Francisco. Why is that?

Major exhibitions come from countries that want to deal with museums on a government-to-government basis. It would be unthinkable, for instance, that such shows not come to Washington DC with its many embassies. These enormous shows are beyond the financial reach of almost all museums.

The National Endowment often provides funds for these exhibitions. They want to place the shows in a couple of East Coast museums and then spot them around the country. The lending nation and museums are looking for the broadest exposure. After Washington DC, they look to the vast audience of New York and its Metropolitan Museum of Art. In that equation, Boston, Philadelphia, and Baltimore are in the same boat.

CG Because of climate control renovation, the museum is closing galleries. That is impacting attendance and visibility. Is that an issue in view of the fundraising entailed for major brick and mortar projects?

JF There will be some big shows despite climate control renovation. The installation problem will be minimized by doing it in stages. Obviously, you can't pursue climate control and exhibitions at the same time. We expect to spend a lot of this downtime working the collections themselves.

CG How many Japanese prints, for instance, are there in the collection?

JF There are some 60,000 prints.

CG What percentage of the Asiatic Collection is on view?

JF At any given time, some three to four percent of the collection is on view. This is very desirable for the Asiatic Collection. They are not intended to be on permanent display like Western oil paintings. If you put Oriental works on permanent display, they would be destroyed in a matter of time.

The following interview occurred in April 1983.

Charles Giuliano The last time we spoke was just before climate control renovations were announced.

Jan Fontein I didn't realize it had been that long. I've been doing this now (been director) and there were several things, which we set out to do. Much has been done with much yet to do. It's always good to look back after several years. What haven't we yet done, and what could have been done differently? That's a useful exercise for me and the trustees.

You have been around this museum since you worked here in the Egyptian Department (1963–1966). I don't have to remind you that the museum has changed. You know that, so it makes it easier for us to talk about that.

My appointment as director of the museum, and that of Howard Johnson (president of MIT) as president of the museum, practically coincided. He came on in September, and I was appointed as actual director, having served as acting director. In 1975 I became acting director and director in 1976. At that time, we discussed what we wanted to achieve. One thing was climate control. That's not finished, but very soon we will resume that process with the Evans Wing (of Painting). We have finished projects and want to pause and see what we have done.

In the past year, the country was in such an economic state that the museum had to be prudent. Policy required that we look and see before moving full steam ahead during a time of recession. I am sure that within a reasonably short period of time we will go full ahead with the Evans Wing. Once we start it will be a year and a half until it is finished. It's much less complicated than new construction or rebuilding the Asiatic collection.

The Asiatic Collection entails an enormous diversity of objects: pots, paintings, textiles, screens and scrolls. Compared to which, with the Evans Wing, you are looking for clean galleries with open walls. You then hang pictures and it's a much less-complicated operation.

The Evans Wing, which was constructed several years after the initial museum (designed by Guy Lowell), is slightly different. There is sufficient space behind the walls for the necessary ductwork. When we initially talked, we were not discussing a new building (the wing designed by I.M. Pei). There had been a previous trustee decision not to go beyond the perimeter of the existing building. Later, very wisely, the trustees decided to abandon that decision. I.M. Pei then polled all involved of our hopes, ambitions, and requirements.

CG When did Pei become involved?

JF I remember very well standing on the top floor in the library on the other side. There were windows, which are still there. They now look down on the glass dome of the galleria. I looked outside and recognized Pei. I had met him a number of times. He was circling the building with a notebook in hand. He came up with the idea of a new wing and everything that's in it.

CG Which makes perfect sense.

JF Of course, but it's his job to draw up the plans. Our job is to list our needs. We have now been using the building, which has not yet performed all of its functions, as a loop connector. That will not occur until the Evans Wing is renovated. In every other sense, the building has been everything we hoped for.

(The design of Pei changed the main entrance away from Huntington Avenue and its grand staircase flanked at the top by special exhibition galleries. Entering from the parking lot, allows for loops on two floors. There are amenities such as dining, bookstore, auditorium, and special exhibition galleries. That space is now assigned to modern and contemporary art. The former Gund special exhibition gallery is now in the basement of the American Wing designed by Lord Norman Foster.)

CG What was the cost of the West Wing?

JF It's difficult to say exactly. There are many ways of looking at the total cost. The primary cost has been climate control. The plant for that is below the West Wing and was some $10 million. That's about a third to half of the construction cost. The entire cost is difficult to calculate. It's the same with (the renovation of) the Asiatic Wing. How much of the total cost of the project do you assign to climate control? You can kind of calculate on a square-foot cost basis.

CG How much did you have to raise, and how much of that came from the National Endowments?

JF The total money raised is $25 million, and of that, the Endowments gave $2 million. That was a challenge grant for climate control. We had another grant for installing the education department in the West Wing (basement area near the cafeteria).

CG Compared to $25 million overall, the NEA money of $2 million seems relatively small.

JF We got the Endowments money at a time when the credibility of the museum was low. We had never undertaken a large project like this. As you know, the museum was in a lot of trouble. There are institutions that go through this during the duration of an institution over a long period of time. We were regarded as a museum that had been in a lot of trouble.

CG When you came to the museum, did you ever imagine becoming director?

JF If I was told that years ago, I never would have believed it. I can tell you a few things because most of those problems are now far behind us. In a short period of time, we had seen one director go, a short time with an acting director (Vermeule), then a new director (Rueppel) not long after that. In order to get the museum back on track, you need time. From the beginning, I felt that I could achieve that only by doing certain things. We got a bit sidetracked when we undertook climate control because we were already under consideration for a grant initiated by my predecessor. It was an issue that had to be dealt with at an early stage of my becoming director. There were a number of other things we wanted to achieve.

People think that it's just a matter of appointing the new man to get things right. To put together a major exhibition, for example, you need a lead time of at least two years. When you go past initial projections, people get impatient and say, "They don't know what they're doing."

There were two problems that I saw as the most immediate. The first was that we had a horrendous deficit. At that time, it was some $600,000 a year. That drains all of your resources. It eats up unrestricted endowment. You can change that in a year but that does great harm. You can take an institution and say let's chop off $600,000 from the annual budget.

In the past five years, gradually, we reduced the deficit. Last year, for the first time, we operated in the black. I went to a large foundation and was told, "Don't bother to come if you have an operating deficit. Institutions with operating deficits are losing propositions." It is important for museums to put their houses in order, to operate within your means. So that was our first priority.

Also, I wanted to create a friendlier and more hospitable atmosphere. For that, you need the help of everyone. You need the help of staff, and to change a lot. For example, the museum has traditionally had a guard force of relatively advanced age. This is not unusual for museums. It's not a job that pays well. You tend to get people who have had other jobs for a long time. They are generally middle-aged or past that. This causes friction between generations.

One of my sons had red hair down to here (gesturing to his waist). Lots of people in the museum didn't know he was my son. When he visited, he got flack and nasty remarks from the guards. It's useful to get the feedback he gave me. We have older guards who are loved by the public. But, when there was turnover, we replaced them with younger guards. We hired artists and students from the Museum School. Each summer we have a staff show at the Museum School. These artist guards have a more friendly interaction with unconventional visitors.

Another idea was to make the museum free to all in December. That brought people in who haven't been here in a long time. That resulted in a change and drop in the age of our average visitors.

CG You appear to enjoy these changes. On busy Saturdays, I have seen you at the information booth directing traffic and handing out brochures. You like directing visitors to special exhibitions.

JF I'm here at least one day on weekends for a variety of reasons. A large percentage of visitors come on weekends. It's as high as fifty percent on those two days, particularly because of free admission on Saturday mornings. That's been a great success.

CG That's when I come with my students. The guards all know me, and some are quite interested in my comments. If I start a tour with 50 students there may be 150 as people in the galleries join in. At times I feel like the Pied Piper.

JF The best way to keep in touch is to walk around with people and see what they are interested in. There have been very busy weeks, particularly after the opening of the West Wing.

When the Asiatic Wing reopened, we had a special exhibition *Living National Treasures of Japan*.

CG I much enjoyed the demonstration of master sword making. (There was a hut/workshop set up in a courtyard.)

JF (A staff member tended to a ficus tree in his office.) Plants and flowers make the museum much more humanistic. The women's committee has done a fantastic job, and they raised funds to endow their work. We have special programs *Free for All* and *Art in Bloom*. It's important to know what's going on here. Two hours in the information booth on Saturday, I assure you Charles, will tell you a lot about the public.

CG In the era of war and colonialism, museums were where nations put their loot. Lord Elgin stole the sculptures from the Parthenon that ended up in the British Museum. The army of Napoleon took what was left, as well as other classical treasures for the Louvre. In Whitehill's history of the MFA, he refers to the acquisition of *Burning of the Sanjo Palace*, one of the national treasures of Japan. He talks about a letter in which, if the Emperor asked for the scroll, they (Ernest F.) Fenollosa (1853–1908) and (William Sturgis) Bigelow (1850–1926) would be obligated to hand it over.

JF Yes, of course, I know the letter. It is very interesting.

(*The Burning of Sanjo Palace*, Heiji Monogatari Emaki, Kamakura period. 16.25in x 22ft 9in, 13th Century. Provenance: Before 1878, Honda family, Japan. Acquired in Japan by Fenollosa in 1886, sold with the Fenollosa collection to Charles Goddard Weld (1857–1911), bequest of Weld to the MFA. Accession Date: December 7, 1911.)

CG There is also the matter of the Catalonian Chapel.

(Removed from a small, rural, Romanesque, Spanish church. It was dismantled and shipped to Boston in crates marked parmesan cheese.)

JF Let me start by saying that times have changed. Personally, I'm not sorry that times have changed. We have made progress rather than taking a step back. I would be happy to say how I came to that realization. When I was a curator here, I bought a very fine statue from India.

CG The *Shiva*?

JF Yes. Someone hinted that it had been stolen. I started an investigation. I found that, indeed, the piece is mentioned in a few books in which it had been published, including an article by (Ananda Kentish Muthu) Coomaraswamy (1877–1947 former MFA curator of Asiatic Art). By doing that research, I found that the piece had been owned by a museum in India.

Pieces can leave museums under all kinds of circumstances. There is a lot of semantic confusion when you speak of a stolen work of art. The definition of stolen often depends on the nationality of the person who uses that word. Perhaps, in the most extreme example, the government of Sri Lanka takes the following position. Sri Lanka, the former Ceylon, gained its independence in 1947. Look here, they have the right to their opinion and I'm not quarreling with that.

They maintain that any piece that left the country before 1947 is stolen because it left without the permission of the government of Sri Lanka, because it did not have a voice in those decisions. They sent an art expert to all the major museums in the world to catalogue all works from Ceylon, and later Sri Lanka. When that was done, that went to UNESCO. They said that all of the works were stolen, and they asked that they be returned.

Coomaraswamy was from Ceylon. They would claim that anything he brought with him in 1918, since it was before 1947, could rightfully belong to them. They would feel that they had a claim to that. This is something that I would question.

If, however it was stolen, as you and I understand the word stolen here in the United States, I think then that there would be nothing standing in the way of returning the object to the country that it comes from. I do not want to have in my museum something that was stolen from someplace else. You wouldn't handle stolen goods as a private person. I wouldn't handle stolen goods as a museum person.

I went myself to the museum in India to verify the account. I visited with a group of tourists and asked to see the objects of a particular excavation. I was informed by the director that they had been stolen from the museum. There were newspaper accounts of the theft.

CG Did you identify yourself during that visit?

JF No, I did not. I wanted to form an impartial opinion. But, look here, I was only a curator at that time, and I wanted to present the issue to the museum. This was a clear-cut instance of theft. The museum is located in Calcutta. There is such a level of human misery that it is difficult to blame the thieves. I was profoundly moved that we had a piece that was stolen in that way.

I came home and proposed to the director, Merrill Rueppel, and he was most cooperative in this matter. We returned the piece to India. They were enormously grateful. We were the first to know and brought it to their attention. I really felt that this was a piece that I could no longer enjoy having.

As museum director, I have been involved in returning pieces on two occasions. How could we have known that a piece we had acquired, a head, was chopped off a statue in Rome's Capitoline Museum? The piece was not published. This is something that is discussed a lot in the enabling legislation. At this moment, the United States is implementing the legal framework of the UNESCO convention.

One of the points is, that if you have had a piece in the basement for twenty-five years, then bring it up and say, look here, this happened twenty-five years ago, that's not considered to be fair. And I agree.

If you publish a piece as soon as it is acquired, you don't hide it, it's published in an annual report and a catalogue—if there is anything wrong about the piece, you will soon hear about it. We published the Roman head in a catalogue. The director of the Capitoline Museum wrote to us. I responded, "Fine, we will be happy to return the piece to you."

CG Isn't it true that other than the Raphael incident (of Perry Rathbone) that has been the standard practice of your predecessors?

JF Forget about the Raphael incident. Times have changed. I'm not going into that Raphael business.

CG Well then, what is your position on returning the Catalonian Chapel to Spain or Sanjo Palace to Japan?

JF Well, okay, I was coming to that. With the Chinese and Japanese, for totally different reasons, the issue is no longer a real issue. With the Chinese, everyone knows that during the period of political unrest in China, basically during the end of the Imperial era and the Ching dynasty, let us say from 1870 on, China was in turmoil. Foreigners were all over the place. All kinds of objects that would never leave today left at that time. Those who were engaged with this at that time felt that it was perfectly all right.

I can give an example of how that mentality has changed. A French orientalist, Paul Pelliot, went to Dunhuang, China, which had a cave in the desert which had been bricked up. It contained a huge library of Buddhist scrolls, texts, and other writing. The works had been placed there around 1000 A.D. The library was discovered early in the 20th century. This material was acquired by the Bibliothèque Nationale in Paris.

(When the Library Cave, known as Cave 17 from the Mogao Cave Complex at Dunhuang, China, was opened in 1900, several tons of an estimated 50,000 manuscripts, scrolls, booklets, and paintings on silk, hemp, and paper were found literally stuffed into it. This treasure trove of writings was collected between the 9th and 10th centuries CE, by Tang and Song dynasty Buddhist monks who carved the cave and then filled it with ancient and current manuscripts on topics ranging from religion and philosophy, history and mathematics, folk songs and dance.)

He was later asked if he had regrets about this after the War. He said, "There was one book, that after all the foreigners had left." It was a very rare book of which the first five pages were missing. Although he was a brilliant linguist, he failed to recognize it. A Chinese scholar published about the book. Pelliot then said, "I regret that I didn't take that book." That was the mentality of that time. My teacher published his remark, but not in any way as a criticism. They had absolutely no regret about this.

CG That was the robber barons era of museums.

JF Well, in a way. There has been very thoughtful writing about this by Arthur Waley. He says that what contributed to this was that many of the things taken in Asia, scholars who did that saw a certain justification. These Buddhist treasures came from an area that is now Islamic. The Islamic tribes that live there have no respect for ancient Buddhist treasures. They chopped out wall paintings and took them to Berlin. In turn they were destroyed during the bombing of WWII. What happened was very bad.

(Arthur David Waley CH CBE, born Arthur David Schloss, 19 August 1889– 27 June 1966, was an English orientalist and sinologist who achieved both popular and scholarly acclaim for his translations of Chinese and Japanese poetry.)

What is the difference between China and Japan? Since 1945 and 1950, with the establishment of the People's Republic of China, there have been great discoveries of treasures that completely outclass anything discovered previously. For the Chinese, the question of looted treasures had become moot.

For the Japanese, it is different. In this respect, I must say that the Japanese are among the most enlightened people in the world. If you must establish a law that states that nothing may be exported, that makes of any dealer who sends important works abroad, a criminal. It drives legitimate art dealers underground. You must give an art dealer a chance to make a legitimate living within the law, and, arguably, making a larger amount, illegitimate. Those laws mean being forever a person who may go to jail and may even be hanged in some countries. That is still done.

CG Do you know of instances where art dealers have been executed?

JF I know that in China they have executed art dealers. Yes, they have. I understand that they have done this. Especially in the beginning, when they wanted to establish their authority. If they have a choice, most art dealers will settle for a compromise. They are reasonable beings. One of the good things about the Japanese system is that, rather than seeing the art dealer as a criminal, they regard them as people with whom they have to cooperate with for the protection of property.

The Japanese see collections of work outside their nation as cultural ambassadors. I am personally very grateful for this. It would seem, and Whitehill quotes a letter to the same, that Fenollosa and Bigelow were genuinely fond of Japan and the Japanese. In no way did they want to hurt that country. They exercised a considerable amount of restraint. They probably could have carted off anything. But they were much more aware of the role of art in traditional Japanese life than Pelliot was in China. When you think of his remark about the book, it is quite different.

They (Fenollosa and Bigelow) lived in Japan for a very long time. They are both buried in Japan. They felt that what they were doing was the right thing. That restraint means that we do not have *The Elgin Marbles* of Japan. We don't have *The Elgin Marbles* in our Japanese collection. In other words, a piece without which that country believes it cannot honorably live. If you see what I mean.

When the Greek actress Melina Mercouri was asked about *The Elgin Marbles* she said, "I do not call them *The Elgin Marbles*, I call them *The Acropolis Marbles*." The acropolis, of course, stands at the very heart of Greek culture. I can understand her point of view. I am extremely grateful that, although we have extremely important works of art, we have nothing that I would call, you know, in the category of what you are calling *The Elgin Marbles*.

CG Yes, but isn't it a fact that the MFA owns works that are regarded among the greatest national treasures of Japan?

JF Do you know where *Sanjo Palace* is at this time?

CG Japan.

(Until fairly recently, it was displayed in a long horizontal vitrine. It was covered by a cloth which a visitor had to push back to view the work. Most visitors likely passed by with hardly a glance at one of Japan's greatest national treasures. Despite the importance of the collection the Asiatic galleries get far less traffic than European painting or the American Wing.)

JF It's currently in Tokyo as part of a special exhibition. I have felt from the beginning that this is one of the ways in which we are respectful custodians of these pieces. The Chinese were always very much against the Pelliot collection in the Bibliothèque Nationale. But why? In France, libraries are for librarians. Other people find it very tough to get in. That's a concept that doesn't exist in this country. There is a joke that Pelliot couldn't get in to see the Pelliot collection once it was in the Bibliothèque Nationale. Of course, that's an exaggeration.

CG There was a recent incident when a Mexican national stole an Aztec Codex from the Bibliothèque Nationale. When he brought it home, he was celebrated as a hero.

JF What I am saying is that, if you want the nation from which the pieces originate to be persuaded that it is a good thing to have them, rule one is: The works have to be accessible to scholars of the country of origin within reason of course, but you have to give them access. That's one thing. Another is that you share it with the nation of origin as much as possible.

Perhaps you don't know what's special about the current exhibition in Tokyo. I was overwhelmed when I first found out about it.

The Japanese donated a large sum of money toward our project to climate control the Asiatic galleries. They wanted us to preserve that collection here for future generations. The Japanese government came through with that money. There are few things in life I have been as happy with as that. I felt that we had to do something special for them after they had done that. There was one thing that had never been done. I will explain to you exactly how it happened, as it is important for you to understand.

The museum accepts a collection as a donation or a gift. There was a gift with certain restrictions. When the donor dies it is very bad to break their rules. I have confidence that when we negotiate with people who are giving us things that they do not attach conditions. Once we accept a gift, we must abide by those terms. Even though they are no longer alive, we can't change them.

Dr. William Sturgis Bigelow gave his collection to the museum in 1899. He had promised Weld, who bought the Fenollosa Collection, that if he would give it to the museum, he would give the Bigelow collection. When 1911 came, and Dr. Weld died, the collection was actually given to the museum. Dr. Bigelow felt that he had to act right away so that nothing prevented the collection from going to the museum.

People often assume that things are given to museums as tax deductions. The income tax was established in 1912 or 1913. (In 1913, the 16th Amendment to the Constitution made the income tax a permanent fixture in the U.S. tax system.) The Bigelow collection was given before then. I believe that tax deductions were put in place in 1917.

Bigelow could have used a tax deduction, I can assure you. He gave the collection to the museum, and later, a considerable sum of money. He did this free of any restrictions. He was a trustee. It was clear to him that if you appoint the right trustees, you don't have to set restrictions that might later work against your own best interests.

In 1928, two years after Bigelow died, a friend of Bigelow's, gave pieces to the museum with the restriction that they never be exhibited outside the museum. He requested at that time that the trustees rule in a similar manner regarding the Bigelow collection. So, as of 1928, the Bigelow collection could not leave the building.

(In 1921, the brothers William S. and John T. Spaulding donated their collection of Japanese prints to the Museum of Fine Arts, Boston, but with an unusual condition. In order to preserve the delicate colors of the woodblock prints, which fade rapidly when exposed to light, they specified that the prints must never be exhibited in the galleries. Fontein did not identify the collector making the 1928 request of the trustees. But it may have been one of the brothers.)

The first exception was made at my request when I discovered that Bigelow himself had sent his sword collection back and forth to Japan to have it polished.

The rule was well established that anything that we can't repair or restore here can be sent to conservators in Japan. A number of pieces from the Bigelow collection had been sent back including the *Kibi Scroll*. They were shown in the Tokyo and Kyoto national museums.

(*The Scroll of Kibi's Adventures in China*, Heian period, 12th century. Provenance: By 1441, Oshio Hachiman Shrine, Wakasa Province (now Fukui Prefecture); probably acquired from the shrine by the Sakai family, Lords of Wakasa Province, and passed to Sakai Tadamichi (d. 1920); to his son, Sakai Tadatae (1883–1939); 1923, sold by Sakai Tadatae at auction, Tokyo Art Club, to Toda Yashichi, 2nd (1867–1930), Osaka; to his son, Toda Yashichi, 3rd (Toda Rosui; dealer, 1892–1942), Osaka; 1932, sold by Toda Rosui, through Yamanaka and Co., New York, to the MFA. Accession Date: July 7, 1932 by exchange.)

Other than individual pieces, the Bigelow collection itself had never been back in Japan.

A few years ago, I was in Kyoto for the opening of an exhibition of ours. At that time Boston's Sister City Committee, led by Mayor Kevin White's wife, Katherine, was in Kyoto for the opening. The following day on the program was a visit to the Hymyo-in temple where Fenollosa and Bigelow are both buried. They died here, but were cremated and their ashes sent there. That's where they had spent the happiest days of their lives.

I went with the group to the cemetery. Their graves are well kept in beautiful surroundings. While standing by their graves I thought, "If you put in your wills that your ashes be sent to Japan, I cannot imagine that you would not want your collections to return at least once." I honestly felt it was something we should do one day.

When we considered an appropriate time to reciprocate, this was it. This was the first gift by the Japanese government to a foreign museum. They have since given money to other museums: The Metropolitan Museum, Asia House, The Smithsonian. Ours was the first ever gift to a foreign museum. I felt that we had to do something, so I went to the trustees. There is a letter, which Bigelow wrote in 1902, twenty-four years before he died, that states that he wasn't so keen on exhibitions.

You have to realize that international exhibitions in 1902 were very different from today when they are common. That, and that his ashes were sent to Japan, were important considerations for me. That's what I conveyed to the trustees, and they immediately agreed. If this was a restriction that Bigelow imposed, I am the first to agree, and uphold what the trustees had voted on. But I feel that this was a matter of honor, especially with someone who had been as generous to the museum as Dr. Bigelow. In this case, I felt that the restrictions had been imposed by trustees themselves, so the contemporary trustees could lift them if they chose to do so. With that request, I went to them, and they lifted the restriction. That's why, for the very first time, pieces from the Bigelow collection are on view in Tokyo.

CG How long was this project in the works?

JF The idea first came to me four years ago when I visited the graves. I officially took it to the trustees about a year and a half ago. After a vote by the trustees, I approached the National Museum in Tokyo. I think the trustees were wise. They did not lift restrictions to the Bigelow collection, but they made an exception. The only exception is for Tokyo and Kyoto national museums, just this one time, and that's it. It's very exceptional. Of course, other trustees and my successors may think differently.

CG How many pieces were sent?

JF Eighty.

CG What was the insurance set for such priceless works?

JF It's a figure in Yen. We worked that out with colleagues, and a Japanese firm is covering that cost. The figure looked like (laughing) such that I didn't know what it was. I had to use a calculator to figure it out. The Japanese, Chinese, and Koreans count large numbers in units of 10,000 rather than 1,000. The result is that back and forth you constantly have to write down the numbers. There are many zeros to figure out. As with any large exhibition, the evaluations are in the millions.

CG If *Burning of the Sanjo Palace*, hypothetically, came to market what would it be worth?

JF Last year there was a similar one available in Japan. It was a work very similar to *Sanjo Palace* and the value was in the range of $5 million to $8 million, In other words, as expensive as the most expensive Western paintings. One had to bear in mind, however, that Japan is now a very affluent country. They now have collectors willing and capable to put up very large amounts of money. Were something as significant as *Sanjo Palace* on the market, I don't know of a Western museum that would be willing to outbid the Japanese.

CG Except, perhaps, the Getty Museum.

JF (laughing) You will have to ask John Walsh about that.

CG Thank you for a complete and adequate answer to my question.

JF The basic points are: Make it accessible to the country of origin. Show it as much as possible. Take care of the works of art in such a manner that the country of origin has no complaint. Our works now in Tokyo have been superbly preserved. Our chief conservator, Noguchi and his staff, have worked on this for years.

CG What was the response to the exhibition? There was a new item in the *Globe*.

JF I was very pleased by that. If I start sending out press releases from here, we are just blowing our own horn. To see it datelined Tokyo, particularly pleased me. The day prior to the opening there was a visit scheduled for the Prime Minister of Japan. It turned out that he was very knowledgeable. I spoke with him, and it was wonderful to see that. Having him come provided a certain quality of publicity. There are 5,000 to 6,000 daily visitors to the exhibition.

Now with the UNESCO convention, and enabling legislation going into effect very soon, that's the end of acquiring great archaeological treasures for Africa, South, and Middle America.

CG Turkey.

JF The countries of the Mediterranean, all those countries, it's just going to stop. Once that happens, it's no longer our job to smoke out the last masterpieces and grab what hasn't yet been picked up. I am fully aware that there are other museums which do not have the great collections that we have. So, this might sound arrogant. I am fully aware that other people do not agree with me on this issue. But I feel that exhibitions, conservation, and research of works of art in our collections will take priority over acquisitions.

CG In your opinion should the British Museum return its *Elgin Marbles* to Greece?

JF It's not fair for a museum director to go to another museum director and point to pieces that should be returned. The British have a responsibility to make up their own mind.

CG There is sustained and mounting pressure to make that happen.

JF During WWII it seemed that Rommel was about to take Egypt. The Germans were preparing for that eventuality. Through back channels, there was contact with the Egyptians. They stated that they would be in Cairo in a matter of months. They wanted to sit down and work out details before their arrival, something like that. Do you know how the Egyptians answered?

They were unwilling to talk with the Germans for as long as the head of *Queen Nefertiti* remained in Berlin. I just give you this as an example.

CG The Germans were excavating at Amarna at that time, and a lot of strange things occurred before they pulled out. Many works were looted and ended up in the art market. That's how a couple of pieces came to the MFA. I was there when a dealer brought a piece of relief that matched perfectly with one in the MFA.

(In 1999 the MFA mounted *Pharoahs of the Sun: Akhenaten, Nefertiti, & Tutankhamen* curated by Rita Freed. It surveyed the unique Amarna period and style of Egyptian art.)

JF Those kinds of things happen. If that's what we are getting into, there are things that I can tell you that must be returned. But I will only give examples of things that must be returned. It's not the place of a major museum director to say what must be returned by other museums.

CG Although you agree in general that there are many things that should be returned.

JF In the 19th century when the British conquered Mandalay, in Burma, they carted off the royal treasures which were shown for many years in the Victoria and Albert Museum. In 1947, Burma regained independence. In order for a free Burmese government to have legitimacy, the crown jewels had to be returned. They were taken during a punitive expedition and belonged to the royal family of Burma. So, the British decided to return the treasures. The Burmese were so overwhelmed by the gesture that they donated one of the finest pieces to the V&A.

Around 1903 the Dutch launched a punitive expedition next to Bali. A rare piece was found in the palace of the sultan. It is a unique manuscript and rare example of Indonesian literature. They took the crown jewels of the sultan, large diamonds. It was glittery stuff but not of great aesthetic value. I was a young curator in the (Dutch) museum and argued for the return of the treasure to Indonesia. I felt that during a time of independence that ought to be done. There was much bitterness between the two countries. It was not possible at that time and a great opportunity was lost.

The Indonesians later demanded and got the treasure back. It would have been more elegant if that happened in a better manner. A group of sculptures from the temple of Singosari in Eastern Java were taken to Holland in two ships in 1819. One of the ships perished in a storm at sea. It lies at the bottom near the Cape of Good Hope. The pieces on the other ship were shown for many years at the National Ethnographic Museum in Leyden. One statue represents a royal person in the guise of the goddess of wisdom.

To have a royal person in divine form is the kind of piece that belongs to a nation which has become independent. It's the kind of a piece that a nation must feel strongly about. When I went to their museum in earlier years, there as a plaster cast of that object as a reminder of what was missing. Now the plaster cast has been replaced by the original. I am pleased by that even though it was no longer in my museum. It is difficult to accept, however, that a country has the right to everything that was produced in it. That, I think, goes too far. But there are particular works that have historic, sentimental, and symbolic significance that are the essence of the identity of a nation. If you have such objects in your museum it is difficult to justify that.

CG (Pulling out of my pocket a one-dollar bill with the head of George Washington on it.) You mean like this?

JF (laughing) I have always taken a neutral position on that (joint ownership of Gilbert Stuart's Washington portraits with The National Portrait Gallery). I came to this country seventeen years ago. I liked the paintings. But the people you would expect to be very keen to keep them here, apparently, were not. And people you wouldn't expect, surprisingly, were. The wish to have them here was not shared by all Bostonians. But you can't find a Greek citizen who doesn't want back *The Elgin Marbles*.

CG You say there are areas of great strength in the collections and accordingly a shift away from acquisitions. But there are areas for which this is not true.

JF Yeah, yeah, contemporary art.

CG That glaring need continues to be controversial. During his tenure, Perry T. Rathbone never appointed a curator of painting. Now there are three curators covering the former domain of Rathbone and Hanns Swarzenski (curator of medieval and decorative art). As evidence of your significant appointments, John Walsh (curator of European painting) has now been made director of the J. Paul Getty Museum, which has one of the nation's greatest endowments. Ted Stebbins for American art, and Kenworth Moffett for contemporary art, are renowned scholars. The collection of American art is one of the best in the nation. But after 1900 American and European art in the MFA is not on a par with major American museums.

JF You will see a sensational change with the recent acquisition of the (William and Saundra) Lane Collection. But let me respond, as I know what you are talking about. First, I do not blame my predecessors. Two predecessors did not appoint a curator of painting.

As you have gathered from my remarks on importation of works of art from abroad, since I am myself an orientalist, I was involved in a lot of importations. My personal interest, and not as a museum director—the things I have alluded to, like giving back to an Indian museum, and seeing the poor devils there being robbed (even I was surprised at not being robbed when I was there)— does change your attitude toward acquisitions. I am now having more opportunities to be in Asia than I had in the first twenty years of my career. Through that experience I have come to appreciate works in their own habitat.

I really don't see the job of a museum director to be sitting with art dealers, drinking coffee, and smoking out the last remaining masterpieces. I recognize that colleagues might have a different view of that.

Acquisitions take research and enormous amounts of time. A director should leave that to curators. I am interested in painting, but have no expertise. If I had to do the buying, there would be mistakes. Though perhaps I might have bought a few nice pieces, I wouldn't be any better than another amateur.

For a large museum with painting as a large part of what attracts an intelligent audience, I felt that we had to have a good painting department. An active painting department has to be the core of the museum. I did my best to attract the best people. That has led to the success and quality of the department. I see my task as helping them to get funds. Occasionally, I act as an arbitrator, because there are competing demands on limited funds. I get involved when there are complicated issues, as there often are. We now have three curators of painting.

The museum had to start from scratch with contemporary art in 1970. There are advocates that want as wide a net as possible to gather as much as possible. For a museum with limited resources, it made sense to collect in depth in a relatively limited area. As you know a frequent criticism is that the contemporary department is too one-sided. You have heard this. People have to realize that. I'm not saying that we should stay forever in this limited area.

CG The exhibitions policy for contemporary art has also been narrow.

JF We have been looking at that and lately there have been a few changes.

CG It has been pointed out by Boston dealers and collectors, that when representative works of art are offered to the museum, they are not accepted by the museum unless they conform to aspects of formalism—even as gifts.

(Phil Guston at the time commuted from New York to teach weekly at Boston University. He was then creating figurative expressionist works that are now prized by museums and collectors. He offered the pick of his studio to the MFA. Moffett asked for an earlier abstract expressionist painting. The artist declined. The MFA subsequently acquired a Guston of the later style, which is not the best example of that period. The MFA was slated to take part in a traveling Guston show. The project was postponed by the National Gallery because controversy that some works depicted Ku Klux Klansman in a satirical manner. After much media coverage the project has been rescheduled to 2022, with MFA as the first venue.)

A prominent collector sent a letter to the board of the MFA that he will not give works to the museum because of its narrow acquisitions policy. There was an article in the *Globe* last week by Christine Temin about that issue. Did you read that?

JF I was away last week and didn't see it.

CG It was a review of a Danforth Museum exhibition that Moffett curated.

JF Oh sorry. Yes, it did see that article.

CG In the ten-plus years of the Contemporary Department it has collected in a narrow frame of reference.

JF Well, I can see that, but look here, I know very little about contemporary art and I have undertaken my own education. One of the aspects of being director is that you have to address issues you are not familiar with. I do not think that many people are aware of how limited are the resources of the museum.

CG Well then, why refuse gifts?

JF You sometimes hear that, but it is more talk than reality. I don't know of any major gifts that have been rejected. Funds for acquisitions are limited and must be shared by all departments including European, American, and contemporary. When we started the contemporary department in 1970 there were a lot of expenses entailed in getting it up and running. There were staff, office space, and storage, as well as establishing an exhibitions policy. That's where a lot of money went.

My predecessor (Rathbone) decided that we had to start somewhere. There was a decision to limit acquisitions to color field painting and realism. At the time this decision served a good purpose. Now, however, it is a good time to see if you have achieved your ten-year objectives, and to look to the future. We're looking at everything, and there is a lot of room for improvement.

The very nature of contemporary art is such that we shouldn't avoid controversy. Dead artists can't speak for themselves, and they aren't disturbed by discourse. On the other hand, if we had started out on a broad front, we wouldn't be where we are today. I'm not saying that we should follow the same course for the next twenty years. Any curator with certain ideas has an impact that is felt for many years. Overall, we will retain a balance. Over a long period of time the idiosyncrasies are unavoidable. When there is a fifty-year span, it is likely to have a number of curators setting a unique character to the collection. The museum is in the business of taking a long view.

I honestly believe in and admire the work of David Ross who is doing a splendid job for the ICA. We work with the ICA on a very cordial basis, but we don't try to duplicate what they are doing. They, for their part, shouldn't try to do things that we are better at. As you well know, there are serious gaps in our 20th century collection. We would love to acquire a Leger or a Mondrian. But those lacunae are the most expensive ones to try to fill.

CG It's costly to play catch-up.

JF You pay through the nose. The cubist work that we own by Picasso cost well over a million dollars. That purchase has tied up acquisition funds for a number of years. As a matter of fact, Charlie, I bought the Picasso about a month after our last interview. It was behind you as we talked but you never saw it or asked me about it. You haven't made that mistake today, noting and discussing the work by Dove hanging in my office.

As I recall at the time (laughing) you were kind of grumpy, saying that the museum wasn't doing anything about modern art. When you came in and sat down, your back was to the Picasso. It was hanging in my office for me to have a chance to get used to it, and prior to making a commitment for its purchase. You didn't notice it. I was rather nervous about it because negotiations were then in a sensitive stage.

A few hours later, during another appointment, Robert Hughes of *Newsweek* walked in and right away said, "Oh, so you've got this Picasso." (laughs) I must look up the date of our meeting in my appointment book. I will get it to you.

(Pablo Picasso, *Portrait of a Woman*, 1910, was acquired in 1977.)

CG How is the MFA different today from what it was before you became director?

JF Gradually our constituency has become more solid among the people of Boston. Our attendance is now twice what it was. People come in larger numbers and more often.

CG Given that there is a large audience for modern art hasn't it been costly to neglect that area?

JF You pay through the nose for being late. If you want to show people that you are a serious museum you must set an example. I thought that Picasso was a good picture. It also signified that we were making an effort to get into modern art. I agree that our collection of modern and contemporary art is weak. But if you put it together with the holdings of the American department, prints and drawings, you begin to scrape it together.

Also, do you notice the large (Frank) Stella that hangs in the galleria? That painting is on loan to us from Graham Gund. That painting belongs there, and Gund has been agreeable to lend it to us. Through loans and acquisitions we are building a collection. There will be many surprises when we reopen the Evans Wing. I may assure you of that.

(*Private Vision: The Graham Gund Collection* MFA exhibition was a 1982 project of Kathy Halbreich in the brief time when she was curator after leaving the MIT List Museum and before becoming director of the Walker Art Center. Gund, an architect and MFA trustee, provided funds for the special exhibitions gallery and with his sister, Ann, endows the position of Director. He was also a supporter of the ICA when Gabrielle Jepson was director taking over from Sydney Rockefeller in 1975.)

CG In the 1970s the MFA missed out on the international tour of *Treasures of Tutankhamun*. It was rumored that Boston initiated the project. This was a particular snub considering the importance of the museum's renowned collection of Egyptian art. There was an unfortunate pattern regarding touring blockbuster shows. The reason given was that Boston lacked climate control. Where does the MFA now stand in regard to being included in these major touring exhibitions?

JF The government and endowments that underwrite these large shows are looking for a regional spread. New York, for example, offers more resources to do these shows. In that sense the East Coast with New York and DC is spoken for, and there is the issue of relative proximity to New York which works against us.

As much as six or seven years of planning go into those major exhibitions. Regarding the Tut show, we couldn't have handled it because of the expense and security involved. Even the Pompeii show drained our resources. Our greatest success was that show, which drew some 450,000 visitors. That finally outnumbered our Andrew Wyeth exhibition. Even the income from that many visitors doesn't cover the cost. But we don't look at shows just in terms of attendance. For our exhibitions of (Jean-Baptiste-Siméon) Chardin and (Camille) Pissaro, for example, we had the highest level of quality. The (Thomas) Eakins show that we mounted was named "The Show of the Year" by the *New York Times*.

CG May I ask your age and when you plan to retire?

JF I will be 56 this year and not seriously looking into long-range planning. I enjoy what I do, but haven't made long-range plans. There are projects which I must first see to completion, such as climate control. We have finished the Asiatic Wing and now must start work on the Evans Wing of Painting. There are things I want to do and can't postpone until I retire.

(From 1966 to 1992 Fontein served as curator of Asiatic art at the MFA. He was director from 1975 to 1987. From 1945 to 1953 he studied Far Eastern languages and Indonesian archaeology at Leiden University.)

CG The museum's Asiatic Collection is regarded as the world's most comprehensive. As curator, that would make you one of the foremost in the field. As such, isn't it difficult to give up research and teaching to assume the responsibilities of director? To what extent do you miss your role as a curator?

JF When feasible, I do some scholarly work and teaching. But teaching requires that you have a fixed schedule, and that's not possible given the demands of my position. Doing research, however, is more independent. As the museum's director I recently participated in a survey. It stated that there have been some 237 doctorates in Asiatic art awarded since 1945. The survey asked how much of what I do now is what I was trained for?

Today I deal with administration, budgets, public relations, arbitrating disputes between curators, and making executive decisions. I derive a great deal of satisfaction from doing this.

Perhaps I am different from other museum directors, because at heart, I am basically a populist. On the other hand, my predecessors had backgrounds in painting. But the museum has other great collections: Classical, Egyptian, and Asiatic.

People have accepted me for who I am. I chat with people and have contact with the public. That way I find out what's going on from the time I put into that. When there is an open curatorial position, I try to get the best person available. That influences what we collect. Gradually, the institution changes. I find it necessary to have colleagues who see the museum as more than a job. The best people on our staff understand that. From 1947 to 1955, I served as a part-time assistant in a museum, and the pay was very low.

CG Today you earn $75,000 a year as director.

JF I didn't go into this profession to make money or to be director. It was like taking a vow of poverty when I started, and I was willing to do that. It was not a sacrifice. As to my salary, there is an obligation to publish that information as director of a nonprofit institution. *Boston Magazine* obtained that through the

Freedom of Information Act. I am all for freedom of information, and in that sense, must pay the price for full disclosure.

(Salaries are stated in annual tax reports which are available to the public through the charity desk of the office the Attorney General. That's how I discovered, for example, that MFA curator of European Painting, John Walsh, was paid an annual stipend of $25,000 by the foundation of the collector William I. Koch. That was a third of Fontein's annual salary, which was considerable for the time. I asked Fontein for a comment when we published that information with editor Jon Lehman in the *Patriot Ledger*. Fontein said that he was aware of the arrangement. Walsh, who was speculated to succeed Fontein, had just departed to become director of the J. Paul Getty Museum. Works that Walsh acquired for Koch were briefly exhibited at the MFA, including paintings by Cezanne and Manet. MFA director, Malcolm Rogers, later mounted a major exhibition of the eclectic Koch collection. That included displaying two of his America's Cup racing vessels in front of the museum's Fenway entrance.)

CG Thanks for your time and one last question. What do you do when not at the museum?

JF I am often here until 8 p.m. and have a late evening supper. I take off at least one day a week. So, I get by.

Curator Ted Stebbins, ICA Director David Ross, and Jan Fontein. Giuliano photo.

Jan Fontein at his desk. Giuliano photo.

Former MIT President Howard Johnson Chaired the MFA Board

At the MFA September 22, 1976

Howard Wesley Johnson (July 2, 1922–December 12, 2009) served as dean of the MIT Sloan School of Management between 1959 and 1966, president of MIT between 1966 and 1971, and chairman of the MIT Corporation (the university's board of trustees) from 1971 to 1983. He became board president of the MFA in 1976, bringing much needed stability. Forming a good working relationship with then acting director, Dr. Jan Fontein, who, after a search of some twenty candidates, became full director a year later. It was a time of brick and mortar: climate control installation, gallery renovations, and major curatorial appointments. Johnson launched a $21.5 million capital drive. By all accounts, he was an outstanding board president.

Charles Giuliano Your predecessor, George Seybolt, attempted to make the trustees aware of money issues and other priorities. His means of appointing Merrill Rueppel was regarded as unorthodox. With a director in place, Seybolt left the board to focus on a role as Washington lobbyist for museums. There was friction between Rueppel and John Coolidge, who followed Seybolt. They were both ousted prior to your becoming board president. How do you view those events?

Howard Johnson That is substantially correct, but not quite accurate. There are a couple of things wrong. As far as my coming to the museum, I do not believe in the theory of "the man." I do feel that leadership is necessary, but no one man can do it all. George Seybolt did the MFA a great service in putting focus on the financial forces that must be aligned for the future in regard to general funding and the budget. He decided not to remain as president as Rueppel and Coolidge were congruent appointments. Rueppel resigned in the summer of 1975, and at that time, John Coolidge withdrew his name from consideration for reelection. This was a tough time for the museum for various reasons.

CG It was my understanding that Coolidge was sacrificed along with Rueppel, as there had been fractional infighting. Essentially, that there was a conflict between conservative and progressive forces on the board.

HJ I can't comment on Mr. Coolidge, but I sat on the board through that period of time. I was a trustee from 1971. It is not true that there were just two factions on the board, as there were many shadings of points of view.

CG In becoming president, how did you view the situation given the confusion at that time? What did you think you could bring to the museum?

HJ How it looked from my point of view was that these are complicated times. At that time, I was not in the center of the museum, and I had no central role. In 1975, the situation was that the director was leaving under strained circumstances. The MFA was a great museum, which had undergone several years with an indistinct set of purposes.

The nominating committee came to me to have me stand for election. I thought that I needed another job like I needed a hole in the head. I had turned down their offer before, but I began to feel that here was this remarkable museum and that it was not coming together. I asked for some time to think it over, and I realized that I should. My own impression is that I don't feel it is a leader sort of thing.

Rather, I view my job as discussing the issues and clearing away the smoke. This has, to a large extent, happened on the board. They are now discussing the issues, and we have recently had a very good discourse on policy. Dr. Fontein deserves a great deal of credit for this. For all of the factions, each trustee has come at least half way on the issues.

CG Are the terms of the 1970 ad hoc report still valid?

HJ The report is just as valid today as it was then. But it is not complete, and it was addressed to the issues of the time. Now we should put it in another dimension, as there are other needs and interests. We now have additional priorities in terms of the financial structure of the museum's relationship to the (Boston public) school system, the surrounding college systems, needs of general viewers who use the museum, as well as our role in a national and international sense in the world of other art institutions.

CG Can we discuss money? Beyond $10 million for climate control, what additional funding does the museum need?

HJ In addition to the money for conservation, we need at least an additional half million dollars a year in new money in order to offset the deficit for operating expenses. There are a lot more things that we would like to do.
    (Quotes Mayor Cobb from the first annual report, July 3, 1876, "This is one of the great general museums in the world among people who know.")

CG In terms of collections, the MFA is second only to the Metropolitan Museum in the United States, but where does the MFA stand in terms of endowment? How does it rank behind the Getty Museum with $800 million, or the Metropolitan Museum?

HJ With $70 million (market value, not book value) the MFA ranks about fifth among American museums. We are not as well off as Cleveland and Philadelphia.

CG The point has been made that the trustees of the MFA are not doing their job regarding recruiting new money. The old money has dried up, and because of traditional stances, they have not encouraged new money to participate in the museum's fabric.

HJ The days are over when the trustees could write a check to offset operating deficits. We are now in the phase where we need the support of all of the people. We do have the old families, and they have made a great contribution. The problem is not with them, but elsewhere. Compare the MFA to the Met for example. The funding that we receive from the city of Boston is just two percent of our overall budget. ($90,000 for museum visits by every fifth-grade student in the Boston public schools.) On the other hand, the Met receives $3.5 million annually from New York City, as well as $1 million from New York State. That's $4.5 million annually for the Met compared to our $90,000 from the City of Boston.

This is not an ideal time to ask for more money from the city and state. We have to make people realize that the museum is a net plus for the city as it enriches the life of Boston, and that it must be supported. I would personally welcome a sum from my tax money being given toward that end. As taxpayers we should pay some money to support the museum.

CG One of the problems in seeking broad-based support for the MFA is the long-felt notion that the MFA is a Brahmin enclave that answers only to its own needs. In particular, it has a bad reputation for representation among Jews and minorities. Historically, trustees have been opposed to those who don't represent their own point of view. Maxim Karolik, for example, was voted a Great Benefactor of the museum, but was not appointed to the board.

HJ There are ethnic problems on the board, but I wasn't there in the beginning, so I cannot comment on that. I won't talk about the past. I will guarantee for the future, though, that we will choose trustees on the basis of their interest in the museum and their qualifications, without regard to their ethnic background or social position.

CG Have you elected a black trustee?

HJ We have, as of the most recent meeting (the week prior). She is one of three new trustees: Lawrence Richard Fouraker (Dean of Harvard Business School, followed Johnson as board president), Richard Devereux Hill (CEO of First National Bank of Boston, also a former president of the MFA), and Phyllis Ann Wallace (faculty member of MIT Sloan School of Management).

CG How well does Professor Wallace know the museum? Does she have background in museum work?

(Phyllis A. Wallace [1921–1993], an economist and activist, was the first woman to receive a doctorate of economics at Yale University. Her work focused on racial and gender discrimination in the workplace.)

HJ She knows the museum well, as a visitor. She is one of the nation's leading experts on equal opportunity. I see Professor Wallace, though, as not representing any group. I want the trustees to call the shots as they see them, and not try to act as representatives of any specific interest group. We are looking for people from diverse backgrounds and points of view to bring their expertise to the board. I personally work with a lot of boards and I always tell them to call the shots as they see them.

Keep in mind that our board is a small board. Once you take away the number of ex officio members, you are left with a small number of active trustees. That provides a limited number we can appoint. We are preparing a report on it. What we are looking for is a method of finding a broader-based policy change.

Take the Ladies' Committee for example. A number of these women have had a very deep involvement with the museum over a range of years. I can think of at least thirty of those individuals who could be a great asset to the museum. It was also my thinking that it would be desirable to have a person on the trustees with a Spanish surname.

In a year of financial crunch, we need more business people on the board, especially with our funding problems. We need more industrial and business representation on the board.

CG Let us address the issue of accountability. It has been reported that the Raphael incident focused on clandestine dealings of the MFA, but that the MFA is not the only museum to be so involved. What guidelines have been established regarding acquisitions?

HJ It is difficult at this time to make a firm statement because of a lot of as yet unsettled variables to define. For instance, the Mexican government has enacted a law in which they set a retroactive policy going back some eighty years. The law states that any art object taken from Mexico during that time period belongs to Mexico. It is smart not to say anything at this time.

CG The great museums of Europe, the Louvre, British Museum, and others, were established to stash the loot from an era of war and colonialism. Lord Elgin, for example, removed the Parthenon sculptures now in the British Museum. The MFA and Met were formed in the 1870s, and primarily derived their collections through excavations, purchase, and donations. They were however, not innocent of making acquisitions through illicit means.

HJ I assure you that such circumstances cannot happen in the future because of the new awareness that objects with questionable backgrounds had already been turned down for acquisition by the MFA.

(When we spoke in 1976, the museum's alleged Raphael portrait of Eleonora Gonzaga had been returned to Italy. In 1972, the Met paid $1 million for the Euphronios Krater, which it returned through litigation. In 2018, the Getty Museum was ordered to return a life-size, classical bronze sculpture, *The Victorious Youth*, which had been looted from Italy.

The collection of billionaire William I. Koch was shown at the MFA by Malcolm Rogers. Koch acquired illicit Athenian decadrahms. A hoard was discovered in Antalya in 1984. It comprised some 2000 ancient silver coins. It included rare Athenian decadrahms which were produced as a commemorative 10-drachma coin. There were only seven previously known examples. The Elmali Hoard contained 14 of them and became known as the "The Hoard of the Century." The first one sold for $600,000 dollars, breaking the old record. Koch bought 1,800 of the coins for $3.5 million dollars. The Turkish Government started legal proceedings in Boston. The judge gave an interim judgment in Turkey's favor. Koch lost the hoard to Turkey.)

CG Controversial acquisitions are a part of the MFA collections dating from when international law was lax or non-existent. The most flagrant example is the Catalan Chapel, which was removed, disassembled, and allegedly shipped in crates labeled "cheese."

(Consider the 12th century, apse of Santa Maria de Mur, Lérida, Spain. In 1919, its frescoes were sold by the rector of the church to Ignasi Pollak, and removed from the church. They were sold by Pollak to Luís Plandiura, 1921, then sold through Rafael J. Bosch, New York, to the MFA for $92,100 on May 5, 1921.)

HJ This past summer I spent time with the director of Museu Nacional d'Art de Catalunya, where all the remaining Romanesque chapels were removed and reassembled. When the MFA's apse was removed, that resulted in the Spanish taking steps to preserve the remaining work, which might have been lost through neglect.

(While Johnson made clear that he was aware of questionable acquisitions, he avoided making a policy statement regarding them.)

CG A recent example would be a Turkish Hoard (Koch's) of classical Greek coins.

Is it a coincidence that it occurred at a time when five of the museum's trustees are alleged to have CIA connections?

HJ It was a long-standing practice of the art world to go through all kinds of back room deals. This is now out. Our notion of collecting has changed. The era of the robber barons and their great pieces has ended.

CG How do you respond to historical precedents like the Catalan Chapel?

HJ It would never happen again. In Egypt, The Soviet Union, Europe, and other places as I travel around, I realize that if we act in a responsible manner, we will have good relations with governments and other museums. The future is in traveling exhibitions in which we trade our resources with other governments and institutions. We hope to have major exhibitions in exchange with Cairo, the Hermitage, and Mexico City. We are establishing the policy that, in order to enjoy great art, you don't necessarily have to own it.

CG The museum is about to undertake installing climate control. I understand that this will occur in several phases. The first step is for the auditorium and some galleries. The system for this will be installed below the new West Wing. Once work for climate control of the West Wing is completed, the museum will be able to keep the auditorium, gift shop, and restaurants open if it has to close some, or all, of the museum.

HJ That is substantially correct. The contemporary gallery will be gutted, below which the climate control system will be installed. We started off thinking we could do this in stages and keep the museum open during the four years required for this work. Essentially, we are planning five phases for this operation. The more that we get into this, however, we are tantalized that there may be a more efficient way to do this. It might be more effective to start phase one on a trial basis, and see how we manage. Or is it better to literally close for a year?

    Philadelphia did this, but not very successfully. Their people were not prepared, and their public was not prepared. We should not do this without alternate galleries and alternate plans. That is something that we would hate to see. We are planning about three or four months of study of this problem. We must decide whether we save money, and if, in the long run, is it more efficient to do it in this way. This is a good time to reshuffle the deck.

(With much of the museum closed for renovation there was an annex gallery in Boston's Quincy Market.)

CG What is the status of the search for a new director and a curator of painting?

HJ I'm surprised that you didn't ask that sooner. It is difficult to answer your question. We have a very good search committee. For the moment we are considering a pool of some twenty candidates.

CG It is said that the museum is having difficulty finding a director because of its reputation resulting from having four directors over five years.

HJ In the process of talking with potential candidates, a number have expressed great interest in serving as director of the MFA. As one person put it, "The MFA is a sleeping giant waiting to be aroused." Regarding a curator of painting, we have asked Dr. Fontein to create that appointment as soon as possible.

(John Walsh was appointed by Fontein as curator of European Painting, but left for the Getty Museum in 1983, where he served as director until 2000. Ken Moffett, appointed by Perry T. Rathbone, was curator of contemporary art from 1971 to 1984. He was director of the Fort Lauderdale Museum of Art 1989–1997. Theodore E. Stebbins, Jr. was John Moors Cabot curator of American Art from 1977 to 1999. He then founded the American Art Department for the Harvard Art Museums.)

CG One gets the impression that the museum is not waiting for a new director to decide on matters of long-range policy. To a large extent, the trustees are moving forward with new long-range planning quite independently.

HJ To a large extent, that is true.

CG I'm not satisfied with your answer about funding. Through sources, I have learned about ambitious plans for the Museum School, the Contemporary Department, education, conservation, exhibitions, and other projects. How much money is needed overall? Beyond $10 million for climate control, how much more must be raised?

HJ In real terms, over and above $10 million for climate control, we need to raise another $10 million for our additional needs. (Johnson launched a drive to raise $21.5 million.)

CG Can you reach that goal? Doubt has been raised about the museum's fundraising potential.

HJ Yes, I think so. The money is there. It becomes a public relations job in selling this to a broad spectrum of people. We must make people aware of our needs and that we have to be responsible.

MIT and MFA president, Howard Johnson. Courtesy of MIT.

Board Member Lewis Cabot Was Also a Private Art Consultant

Points taken on by the *Boston Globe* team that investigated the museum and its director, Merrill Rueppel, were trustees with conflict of interest as associates of banks and investment firms handling the museum's accounts. It explored, but abandoned, reporting on connections between trustees and the CIA. That was a part of the Cold War era and would be a part of any board at that time. It might have been regarded as patriotism.

During the Vietnam War, when radical protesters and members of SDS occupied administrative offices of MIT and Harvard, documents were revealed and published in the underground press of direct ties between the universities and the military industrial complex. There were demonstrations against MIT for its role in the development of weapons of mass destruction. As a source told me, he was recruited as a doctoral student at MIT to become a covert operative of the CIA. He related to me that it was common at the time.

It is interesting as background, but had no direct relationship to the cultural activity of the MFA. An area of investigation with direct relevance was the role of trustees as collectors. It was a conduit for Pre-Columbian and classical objects of questionable provenance and disputed authenticity to make their way into the collection. In some instances, objects were returned to their nations of origin either voluntarily or through diplomacy and litigation. These circumstances resulted in high profile and even criminal charges for the Getty Trust and Metropolitan Museum, and other institutions.

A lingering issue for the MFA was its lack of initiative in the field of modern and contemporary art. Arguably in favor of personal and commercial interests, Lewis Cabot was influential in the appointment of Kenworth Moffett as the museum's founding curator of contemporary art. That resulted in a narrow focus on abstract art and formalism. The MFA missed the boat on Pop art, minimal art, realism and figurative expressionism, feminist art, conceptualism, and other movements when they were still affordable.

Lewis Pickering Cabot, 1937–2019 was a collector, businessman, and manufacturing executive. He was a collector of Color Field painting and contemporary sculpture. Cabot was a founding trustee of Storm King Art Center in New Windsor, New York, where he introduced founder Ralph Ogden to the work of sculptor David Smith. His trusteeships included the MFA, the Museum of American Folk Art (New York), the Portland Museum of Art, the Maine College of Art, the Society of Arts and Crafts of Boston, the Philadelphia Maritime Museum, the Maine Maritime Museum, and the Maine State Music Theater.

Born in The Hague, the Netherlands, Cabot was educated at the Groton School (Class of 1956), Harvard College (Class of 1961), and Harvard Business School (Class of 1964). Cabot purchased the Southworth Machine Company of Portland, Maine, in 1977. It is now a multinational corporation. He was also a director of the Material Handling Institute Roundtable from 1988 to 2007. In 2017, he was awarded the Norman L. Cahners Industry Award for lifetime contributions to the material handling industry.

August 24, 1975 at the Museum of Fine Arts

Lewis Cabot The first steps I took in 1968, when I came on the board, was to talk with McKinsey & Company and get them to undertake a study of the museum. (They are a management consulting firm.) They gave us $100,000 worth of free advice. They did a study to get the trustees to reconsider their priorities. This was incorporated, voted on, and approved by the trustees as an ad hoc report. It discussed background and the need for the study and analysis of what happened prior to it.

During the 1920s they were some of the top men and board chairmen in the country. That was a golden age for Boston and they were riding high. Harvard was the top educational institution in the country. The MFA was the second oldest and greatest museum in the country. (The Met was also founded in 1870.)

We had the great Boston Symphony Orchestra (founded in 1881) and outstanding hospitals, like Massachusetts General, and a top technical institution in MIT. That was through the war years. After that, all of us woke up and said maybe we are not what we thought we were. Our standards had changed. A lot of places were just plain doing a better job. We didn't keep up the old standards. Now if you need heart surgery, you go to Texas. Look at how much the Getty Museum has in its endowment.

(The museum was founded in 1982 when J. Paul Getty endowed it with $1.2 billion. In 2017 the endowment stood at $6.9 billion. In 2017 the MFA endowment was $585 million. When Malcolm Rogers arrived in 1994, the budget was about $77 million; today, it is more than $101 million. The number of visitors was 864,179 in 1994, and it hit 1,227,163 in fiscal year 2015. The endowment grew from $180.6 million to $623.7 million today. When Rogers arrived, the debt was $35 million; today, it stands at $140 million, which is down from a peak of $189 million.)

The Sterling and Francine Clark Art Institute has a larger endowment than we do.

(Founded as a private museum, it is a center for research and conservation with programming connected to nearby Williams College. Under former director, Michael Conforti, the endowment grew from $128 million to $357 million.)

We began to realize that we are not living in that period (1920s) and that we are trying to play catch up.

Universities like Harvard, MIT, and Brandeis are growing on national money and not just local funds. The BSO and MFA, however, were entirely locally supported. The Museum of Science receives a lot of corporate money, and has fared well for that reason.

The problems we faced started in the 1940s and accelerated through the 1950s and 1960s. During the 1940s the trustees were riding high. All of the finances of the museum resided in the mind of one man (Baldwin). Today that job is more complex than it was twenty years ago.

Perry Rathbone had been very successful in running the museum (1955–1972). He had to pull together many different energies to get the trustees to agree on what had to be done. In the old days the museum had been run like a country club. All of a sudden, the museum became so complicated that it was beyond the limits of a single man. The problem was how to get Rathbone to delegate some of his authority.

CG The version that I have is that Rathbone was doing well until the Raphael incident exposed the museum to criticism.

LC That's not at all how I see it. Essentially, the Raphael incident was a sideshow. The real problem was that he wasn't bending on the other issues. Otherwise the trustees would never have knocked him just over the incident involving the painting.

I went to Perry and said that we had to have a show of this guy Morris Louis. We proved to be the first major institution to devote this attention to Louis (1973). This later led to a gift of his work worth some $1 million. The contemporary department has done well because it has done well, if you know what I mean. We have tried to do first class shows and to get the best pictures and sculptures that we can find.

We did the Anthony Caro show (1975 MoMA retrospective traveled to Boston), for instance, and he is one of the best sculptors alive today. That show was done jointly with MoMA. It was the first time that the British Arts Council awarded money to American museums for an exhibition of British art. In the sphere of contemporary art, the museum has done well in the past few years. (Ken Moffett curated Caro's *York Series* of large-scale metal sculptures. It was installed on the lawn in front of the Christian Science Church on Massachusetts Avenue diagonally across from Symphony Hall.)

It is a matter of ambitious people doing good things. They cause the updraft, and one place in the museum which is doing well right now is contemporary art.

CG That may be, but critics feel that Moffett's taste is narrow and Greenbergian (a disciple of Clement Greenberg).

LC Perry said, "I have just the person, Dorothy Miller of MoMA. She is one of the seasoned people there." When I heard that, I said that I would have to vote against contemporary art if it meant having her as a curator. By that appointment, all we would be doing is becoming an outpost of MoMA, and we had to do something different than duplicating the effort of another institution. We had to do something different, and get people charged up to make it go. What we needed, specifically, was Ken Moffett and a strong contemporary art department.

(He showed me a document regarding funding the contemporary department. It indicated an annual budget of $32,000. Moffett was paid as a part-time curator at half salary or $8,000. When I spoke with Cabot, four years later, it had been raised to $9,000. There was a full-time curatorial assistant at $7,500. The commitment to the contemporary department was roughly that to Barry Gaither and the National Center for Afro-American Artists in liaison with the MFA. Cabot redirected to clarify the difference between the old curatorial style to the issues that Moffett faced. The museum's annual acquisition fund was capped at $1.5 million including restricted funds. As a new department and one with no endowment, Moffett faced competition for funding and programs.)

I sat in on all of the acquisition meetings. Mostly the trustees doled out $2,500 here and $3,500 there. They didn't tend to go for the big (expensive) object. The time has come to an end (as an encyclopedic museum) of getting one of everything. In that theory, they would buy 400 objects in the hope of coming out lucky on one of those purchases. It has become important to narrow our choices and pick one instead of another.

CG Under the new rules, what do you go after? What about major acquisitions like the Met's Rembrandt, *Aristotle with the Bust of Homer*, which generates media coverage and excitement? (In 1961 the New York museum spent $2.1 million, which was a record for the purchase of a work of art at the time.)

LC That's why we wanted to buy the Jackson Pollock *Lavender Mist* (1950). You have to understand that we were working with limited resources. Ken believed that one of the great painters of our time is Jules Olitski. There are a number of good Olitski's in Boston collections that will come to the museum. We do not want to duplicate the effort to buy what we will receive.

If we bought the Pollock, other great works would have come to us. It would have brought us a great cubist picture for sure. The idea was that this great picture was to be the gem of our collection and would attract attention to the collection.

(Through Moffett, overtures were made to the artist/collector Alfonso Ossorio. He was a neighbor and friend of Pollock in Springs, Long Island. The painting was offered for $900,000, and Cabot was involved in raising the money. He persuaded the Cabot family to sell a Gilbert Stuart portrait of George Washington for $150,000. It was one of three identical versions of the portrait. Merrill Rueppel, then MFA director, opposed the deaccession and questioned the work, which was then at the museum. A conservation study raised potential restoration issues that alarmed Rueppel. The price quoted by a lawyer representing the owner was off by some $35,000 from the original quote. "In a rage and on the spot" Rueppel demanded that the painting be crated and returned to Ossorio. The painting was sold soon after to the National Gallery at allegedly twice the price offered to the MFA. A few weeks later, in 1973, a major Pollock, *Blue Poles* (1952), was sold to the National Gallery of Australia for $1.3 million in Australian currency. Cabot told me that he was "up in arms" about Rueppel's behavior, but was convinced by trustee Bill Coolidge to drop the issue. Cabot discussed boardroom issues with me because "Rueppel violated a trust by running to the press after he was given a generous settlement by the MFA when he was fired.")

CG The museum is doing well in acquiring post war abstract art, but what about other movements of contemporary art? You are missing the boat on many directions. The top Pop artists are just as important to collect as formalism. There are new artists whose prices have not yet peaked. John Arthur was guest curator for a successful exhibition by the realist Alfred Leslie (then teaching at Boston University). Why not follow up with an acquisition? (Arthur also curated an exhibition of the realist Richard Estes whose works are included in major museum collections other than the MFA.)

LC We have to have faith in Ken. The idea is to have a strong curator and it is then up to him to come forward with recommendations of what we should buy. He only has $45,000 to work with although we can raise funds for a special purchase. There are only so many choices he can make. To some extent he is buying younger artists with lower prices.

(During the MFA exhibition, the Leslie paintings were insured from $25,000 to $45,000 each.)

In the area of Pop Art, we don't want to duplicate the holdings of Brandeis University (The Rose Art Museum, under founding director Sam Hunter, acquired 25 works for $45,000. When Brandeis president, Jehuda Reinharz, attempted to sell the Rose collection in 2014, it was appraised at some $300 million.)

CG Regarding your position with the MFA, concerns have been raised about conflict of interest as collector and dealer.

LC In the city of Boston the extent of annual purchases of contemporary art is in the order of some $2 million. This is nothing compared to what New York and Los Angeles corporations spend on major works of art. The purpose of my business is to see that we can divert some of that money into better art, which will benefit the community.

There are very few businesses in the city which will allow some do-gooder like Cabot to do something with them about art. But they will let you come in as an art advisor, which is rather like an investment counselor. They provide a buck and get a service, like the Friedel Dzubas mural that was commissioned for the Shawmut Bank. That was an ambitious project with a big company. I am very proud of that commission.

(The mural was the artist's largest work. He was, at the time, on the faculty of the Museum School.)

CG Can you answer the question regarding conflict of interest?

LC That may be a legitimate issue or not. I'm not so sure. The MFA is an august institution and it is a matter of pride for each trustee to serve. Every trustee derives some benefit, both social and commercial. I can't deny that. The question is, do I walk around town trading on that in the course of my business? Or, am I keeping two lives quite separate? My interests stem from different sources.

Until I started doing what I'm doing, people thought they needed a gallery and a warm body to walk through the door in order to make a sale. I offer a different approach. I work with the client or corporation and plan ahead and explore a grand design, and then move the pieces accordingly. The business is now changing in this direction. When I decided to start this business, I went to the board and told them what I am doing. I said if they have any objections, let's hear them. I don't have to apologize to anyone for what I have done.

When I was on the board pushing for contemporary art at the MFA, I have been criticized before, during, and after our decision.

CG The galleries say that this is unfair competition, in view of the fact that, as an MFA trustee, you have certain clout that they don't enjoy. When you walk into the Emmerich Gallery, for instance, does anything different happen for you that would not happen for another dealer?

LC Even when I'm buying for myself, I don't get any better deal than anyone else. If I am buying for a corporation, I customarily ask for the gallery to take ten percent less in the knowledge that I charge the client ten percent of the cost of the work as my fee. Most galleries are willing to do this with me. In this manner, I do not actually sell the work. It is sold directly from the gallery to the customer. At a later time, the client sends me a check for ten percent of the sale. As they keep saying in Watergate: "Follow the money." I am so clean on this; however, I would even welcome your looking at my books. There is nothing underhanded. The money goes from the client to the gallery. At a later date, Cabot bills the client ten percent of the sale for the consultation fee.

CG For the sale of a $50,000 Frankenthaler, for instance, you would earn some $5,000?

LC That's correct, but sales don't tend to be for that great an amount. People tend to ask for purchases in the range of $2,500 to $5,000. I don't think you appreciate the amount of time that goes into looking at pictures and the endless talk about these deals.

CG How extensive is this business?

LC The Art Council has lost money every year that I have had it. The deficit this year was some $4,000. Last year we negotiated sales of $250,000 for which our fee was some $25,000. I started the business on capital of $5.00 and a $1,000 loan.

CG It is alleged that several MFA trustees have CIA connections. The Cabot family has an interest in United Fruit, which is known for its relationship with the CIA.

("The CIA made Guatemala safe, not for democracy, but for the Rockefeller-owned United Fruit Company. CIA director, Allen Dulles (president of the CFR), owned UFC stock... The CIA was using companies like Zapata to stage and supply secret missions attacking Fidel Castro's Cuban government in advance of the Bay of Pigs invasion. The CIA's codename for that invasion was 'Operation Zapata.' In 1981, all Securities and Exchange Commission filings for Zapata Off-Shore between 1960 and 1966 were destroyed. In other words, the year Bush became vice president, important records detailing his years at his drilling company disappeared. In 1969, Zapata bought the United Fruit Company of Boston, another company with strong CIA connections." *Constantine Report*, September 1, 2009)

LC That's not true. My uncle (Tom Cabot) was president of United Fruit for two days, then he was fired. My father worked for The State Department. He was ambassador to some 25 countries: Brazil, Poland, Colombia, Finland, Sweden, Pakistan. Obviously, the embassies had CIA connected people. My uncle worked for President Truman on the National Security Council. Naturally, he came into contact with the CIA there, but this was part of their work with the government. Both my father and uncle had to deal with the CIA to some extent.

Perhaps you were not aware of my father's career. He was the chief architect of Yugoslavia's split with the Soviet Union under Tito. He was also the last American to leave the China mainland when Mao took over.

The reason the CIA came about was because there was a goddam war going on and it was necessary to identify the enemy. One didn't know the nature or face of the enemy. We had to establish an apparatus to know who the enemy was and what they were trying to accomplish. There was some unlawfulness about their actions but there was greater need for it then than now. I dare say, it is needed even today. People who supported it (the CIA) like my father and Sidney Rabb (the MFA's first Jewish trustee) considered that they were doing something patriotic to help their country. (laughing) I would like to try to caution you in establishing links between me and the CIA. There are a lot of people who felt that we got a bum deal when (Francis Gary) Power's plane got shot down in the Soviet Union.

(On 1 May 1960, a United States U-2 spy plane was shot down by the Soviet Air Defense Forces while performing photographic aerial reconnaissance deep into Soviet territory.)

The feeling was that he knew what he was doing and the dangerous nature of the work. He should have crashed the plane and destroyed as much evidence as he could. People went to the Hellmuth's and Rabb's because they knew they wouldn't do a lot of talking.

(MFA trustee, Paul F. Hellmuth, was a law partner in Boston's Hale & Dorr with President Richard Nixon's impeachment attorney James St. Clair. Hellmuth "retired" from Hale & Dorr the same year, 1967, that the *Harvard Crimson* published an article stating that Hellmuth served as the conduit for funneling CIA "subsidies" to the CIA of as much as $80,000 per year. At the time Hellmuth was the Secretary of the Harvard Law School Alumni Association.)

CG Can you discuss the significance of MFA trustees and their CIA connections?

LC Let me clean up the questions about conflict of interest. I gave them (MFA) their best Morris Louis painting. Overall, my contribution has been some $100,000. The contemporary department and my committee have raised more than $1 million in acquisitions and operating capital if you consider the value of the Louis gift.

CG Aren't you in a position to derive direct benefit through your relationship with the department? That occurs by loaning works whose value is enhanced thereby. That "equity" is recouped when the work is later sold or donated with an increased value and subsequent tax break. (That loophole was later closed which resulted in diminished contributions to museums.)

LC I am aware of that, which is why we proceed with great caution. First of all, Ken Moffett is his own man. I have never told him what to show or collect. On the other hand, the collection is very small and new. If he asks for the loan of a certain work, then it is a sincere request and I have to say yes. If the work is then seen and associated with the MFA, of course its material value increases. Ultimately, however, the works that I collect will have to stand on their own feet in years to come. Just because they are associated with the collection, they won't necessarily stand up to the test of time. If things are here, it is because Moffett asked for them. I have never asked them (MFA) to store a painting for me, as I have my own storage facilities. There is one exception, a Larry Poons that was too big for me to store.

CG But you still benefit as a dealer.

LC I am not a dealer, but rather a consultant. When I got divorced two years ago, I had to sell some pictures to raise money. I wouldn't have sold the work except for that. Nothing that I sold was sold directly by me. It was sold through dealers and nothing was done at the expense of the museum. I have a good reputation in this country as a collector. Until I had to sell some things, I had one of the outstanding contemporary sculpture collections. I don't believe in dumping things into the museum to take a tax deduction. When I deal with clients, they do not see any of my own things. They are not offered for sale.

CG How extensive is your collection, and who are some of the artists?

LC I have some 200 pictures including Jules Olitski, Kenneth Noland, Jack Bush, and others.

CG Did your family collect?

LC No, my family were not ambitious collectors. They collected some personal things, but nothing on the scale that I have. I have a national reputation as a collector. If you were to call Richard Oldenburg (director) at MoMA, for instance, he would be able to tell you who I am.

In all frankness, when I came here, there was a breath of fresh air. The role of collectors and the museum has to be better defined. We are entering into an era of accountability. For the first time, significant federal funding is taking place. The NEA grant of $2 million for climate control wouldn't have been possible two years ago. With this new Federal involvement, they are not going to give to institutions when underhanded things are going on.

They will force establishing guidelines so it is up to us to jump the gun and take on this job ourselves. You have talked about how trustees are in a position to take advantage of their position with the museum.

CG What about the curatorial staff? They are in the position to pick up fees for work on behalf of corporations and collectors. When they go to see an object, for instance, for whom are they looking at it? Is it for the museum or for a client? This has to be defined.

LC Some of this can be quite innocent. A corporation, for instance, approaches a curator with an invitation to spend a weekend on their yacht. Over a gin and tonic, they ask for advice on art. This is quite different from a corporation signing a contract with a curator to buy for a company. These are gray areas and there are no absolutes, especially in the matter of collectors and dealers loaning works of art to the museum.

(While researching high-profile acquisitions of 19th century French paintings for the *Patriot Ledger*, I examined the 501c3 tax returns for the foundation of William I. Koch. John Walsh, the curator of paintings for the MFA, was identified as a paid consultant to the collector. When I asked about this, the director of the museum, Dr. Jan Fontein, stated that he knew of and approved the arrangement. By then Walsh had left the MFA to become director of the J. Paul Getty Museum.)

CG What is your overall prognosis for the museum?

LC We don't have money anymore, so we have to use our brains. The money just isn't there, and we have to take a different approach. This is when it becomes dangerous, because it is tempting to make an end run and do something underhanded. That's how the Raphael acquisition got us into trouble. Also, we have to flow with the times. Like we have how many Monet's? Maybe we could swap one for something else. Instead the trustees bought another one from Brandeis for $200,000 to bail them out of difficulty. It was a direct sale, not through a dealer. They had endowed a chair and there was no money for it because of a market problem.

At the time, I voted against the Monet sale. We were dribbling away our funds for an area in which we were well represented. We could have used $200,000 toward acquisition of a dramatic picture that would bring people into the museum by creating some excitement. We have to shift our focus and realize that right now a good Pollock is more important than another Monet.

Lewis Cabot was a board member and collector who backed the appointment of Kenworth Moffett. Giuliano photo.

Kenworth Moffett was Founding Curator of the Department of Contemporary Art

Kenworth Moffett, 1934–2016, earned a PhD, in art history from Harvard University. His doctoral dissertation, *Meier-Graefe as Art Critic*, was published in 1973. He was an adherent of formalism and colleague of the influential critic and theorist Clement Greenberg. He was a tenured professor at Wellesley College when invited, in 1972, by MFA director Perry Rathbone, to found the department of 20th century art.

This was the first of many interviews and dialogues over a number of years. We remained friends and colleagues. From 1989 to 1992 he was director of the Fort Lauderdale Museum of Art. During holiday seasons in Palm Beach, for several years, I visited the museum and enjoyed lunch with him. These entailed cordial scholarly debates.

With limited funding and resources, Moffett accomplished a lot for the museum. While the museum was largely closed for renovation, he curated an annex at Quincy Market. The program was diverse, as he invited guest curators. His acquisitions, including some sixteen works by Morris Louis, were viewed as too narrow in their focus on formalism. Consequently, he was undermined by the media and art community.

At the MFA August 9, 1976

Charles Giuliano When did you start as the first curator of the MFA's department of 20th century art?

Ken Moffett It was just over four years ago, in the spring of 1972.

CG What priorities were entailed in initiating the department?

KM We had to build a collection from scratch, build a staff, and find exhibition and storage space. We were out to put the museum on the map in this area. Before that time, there was no contemporary art at the museum. We needed to raise money to start all this. In general, that was a time of great difficulty for museums and contemporary collections in particular. MoMA laid off a number of staff, and there was trouble in Pasadena and other places. The ICA was having difficulties. Traditionally, modern art receives very short-term funding, and when trouble occurs those sources rapidly dry up. We did, however, not have the slightest difficulty in raising money.

CG What were your funding sources?

KM We tried to avoid getting funding from any one individual or source. Instead, we intentionally asked a number of people, some 20–25 individuals or sources. We asked them to give the same amount. We hoped to elicit broad interest in this area, and we didn't want anybody to back off because somebody was taking over the spotlight.

CG Who were the individuals and how much did they contribute?

KM I don't know if the amount should be made public, but a number of people were good to us including Graham Gund and Max Wasserman.

CG What are the department's current resources?

KM We now have a staff and office space. We will be moving soon because of construction of an auditorium. We have the Foster Gallery and a number of works.

CG I understand that Wasserman recently sold works because of debts in real estate development. (The Garage in Harvard Square.)

KM That was a terrible loss for him and for us. He had promised a number of pieces, and this is a loss for the entire community. It must be said that Max was very good to me.

(In 1975, the Development Corp. went bankrupt and approximately 160 art objects were dispersed, chiefly at auctions.)

Our idea for funding was to get a number of small contributions and later on we got larger gifts, like the donation of funds for the Foster Gallery. The collection of works by Morris Louis came to us. Some people, however, were not receptive to us as they were totally committed to the ICA.

CG In the 1950s there was a plan under director Thomas Messer to have the ICA merge as the contemporary department of the MFA. Nothing came of that as Perry Rathbone, then new to the MFA, opted to function as curator of painting including modern and contemporary art.

KM I understand that the ICA made unreasonable demands including the number of ICA officers who would become MFA trustees.

CG The MFA has been opposed to modern art since 1900. Of course, there were great collectors of French impressionism prior to that. What kind of support does the department have from the trustees?

KM The MFA was apathetic to modern art. There are some people who are not enthusiastic but, in general, I have had very good support from the trustees, particularly John Coolidge, who I have known for a long time. He taught me at Harvard. Also, from George Seybolt, Lewis Cabot, Henry Foster, Graham Gund, and Stephen Paine. Except for Seybolt and Coolidge, the others I mentioned are recent trustees. Since they have come on board, we have been doing better than most other comparable museums. Without support, how could we have built two major galleries in four years?

CG The trustees did not support your attempt to acquire a major painting by Jackson Pollock. Was it *Blue Poles*?

KM It was a better painting than *Blue Poles*. Pollock himself said that he didn't care that much for it. The painting we wanted was *Lavender Mist*. It's one of the great Pollocks.

CG Why do you have a half-time appointment as curator?

KM The collection is not that large right now, so there isn't the need for a full-time curator. Let's face it, the place (MFA) right now is a zoo. There have been four directors in four years. (Rathbone, Vermeule, Rueppel, and Fontein) It's a very unstable situation. Also, I like to teach, and if we had a large collection of contemporary things, it would be different, but that's not the case. We are geared toward exhibitions. One of our feelings in creating the department was that there are a number of colleges here and many students who would benefit from those exhibitions. We have done sixteen exhibitions in four years. That's quite a lot of work.

CG How were those shows funded?

KM They came from a variety of sources including special exhibition funds as well as private funding sources for particular exhibitions. All shows are not equally successful in drawing a large attendance. The *Elements* show was a big draw (guest curated by Virginia Gunter). When people have a limited idea of modernism, they like a lot of nuts and bolts and moving parts, which was the case with *Elements*. Abstract art shows, in general, do not have great attendance.

(On February 3, 1971, in the *New York Times*, Hilton Kramer wrote about the *Elements* exhibition of 25 artists. "The Museum of Fine Arts, which has long been under attack in Boston art circles for its traditional policy of paying little or no attention to contemporary art, has suddenly upstaged its critics by mounting an extremely audacious exhibition of new art—an exhibition that includes the use of real fire, some wild life, lots of water and sundry other natural and technological phenomena. Entitled *Earth, Air, Fire, Water: Elements of Art* and consisting for the most part of very large and highly unorthodox constructions, tableaus and happenings, the exhibition is the final event of the museum's centennial program.")

CG Was the (Anthony) Caro show successful in terms of attendance? (Shared with MoMA)

KM No, not really, but that doesn't mean we shouldn't do it. We are not alone in this. The (Jackson) Pollock and (Barnett) Newman shows at MoMA were box office disasters. The MFA's (Andrew) Wyeth show drew 216,000, where attendance for

(Jules) Olitski was 10,000. Does that make Wyeth a more important artist than Olitski?

CG Your preference is for abstract art.

KM Not really. We have shown artists like Horacio Torres and even more than MoMA in this area.

CG Are you planning a Kenneth Noland show?

KM No, the Guggenheim is.

CG Is there someone you haven't shown but intend to?

KM Perhaps Helen Frankenthaler. (In 1981, Carl Belz curated *Frankenthaler: The 1950s* for the Rose Art Museum.)

CG The time frame defined for your department is post 1945. What about the era from 1900 to 1945, which is poorly represented?

KM There should be a department of modern art rather than a contemporary department.

CG Why wasn't it set up that way?

KM It was Perry Rathbone who set up the department. (A mandate for a contemporary program was defined in the museum's 1970 ad hoc report.)

CG What has happened to modern art since then?

KM In four years we have established a small but significant collection of contemporary art. It is small, but very choice, and the collection draws visitors from all over the world. We have some 20–25 first class objects.

CG Including examples of sculpture (David Smith).

KM Yes, the ones (two) you see in the courtyard. We have no space to store sculpture.

CG How did the major Morris Louis (1912–1962) acquisition come about?

KM It came from the widow of Louis, but she prefers not to be identified. I was able to bring them (nine paintings) to the MFA by promising that they would be displayed and studied here. They would be better off than in some other institution which has so much work that they wouldn't all be displayed. I also have two Louis paintings given to us by Graham Gund and three from Stephen Paine. Graham has a very unusual, black veil painting. (Lewis Cabot also donated a Louis.) Our feeling is that all of his archives should be here, including his letters, orders for paintings, and other papers.

(A 2018 Christie's sale resulted in a record for Louis's *Devolving*, which sold for $5,712,500.)

CG How do you rate Louis?

KM He was one of our greatest artists in terms of level of imagination and invention that he possessed.

CG What are some of the twenty plus works in the contemporary department?

KM We own an important (Jackson) Pollock (*Number 10*, 1949) and have works by (Barnett) Newman, (Clifford) Still, (Franz) Kline (*Probst 1*, 1960, from Susan Morse Hilles), (Willem) de Kooning and others on display. The first generation of Post War abstract artists are well represented.

CG What about Pre-War paintings?

KM The collection includes artists like (Ben) Shahn, (Jack) Levine, (Georgia) O'Keeffe, Stuart Davis, and others, but this was not my mandate in coming to the MFA. I think that we have made some wise choices. We bought our Pollock at a reasonable price, and it is now worth three times what we paid for it.

(This was after director Merrill Rueppel botched the acquisition of Pollock's masterpiece *Lavender Mist*, which was offered to the museum of $900,000.)

We have tried to cover what is happening. My own taste is for abstract art, but the first year I was here, we mounted a major exhibition of conceptual art in the work of Douglas Huebler, who was teaching at Harvard at the time. (Guest curated by Chris Cook who was then on leave from The Addison Gallery while director of the ICA with a conceptual one-year contract.)

We have also tried to explore artists working in New England, like Alfred Leslie, who has been living and working in Andover for some time now. (Taught at Boston University, the exhibition was guest curated by John Arthur an authority on realism. He also curated an exhibition by the realist Richard Estes.)

We also mounted *Boston Collects* and a watercolor show with (MFA curator) Cliff Ackley, which drew on Boston artists.

CG How do you regard Boston as an arts center?

KM We are overshadowed by the magnetic character of New York, which is nearby. We can't compare with their thousands of galleries, whereas there are just a handful here. Overall, Boston is a better city for modern art than most places in the country. We have a number of places where contemporary art can be seen, including The Brockton Art Museum, The ICA, The Rose Art Museum, Wellesley College, The City Hall Gallery, and other places, as well as some significant galleries. In a lot of ways, Boston is one of the better art centers.

(Before Moffett came to the MFA, I curated two shows for the ICA. One, work by the protest artist Arnold Trachtman, in the Soldier's Field space in Brighton. The show had been censored and removed from a Harvard house. The second, *Images*, with ICA director, Andrew C. Hyde, at City Hall Gallery. It was an overview of figuration. It was an important space later taken over for City Council offices. For a time, the Boston Visual Artists Union had a spacious gallery in a curved building opposite Government Center and City Hall.)

What we don't have in Boston is a lot of collecting. This town stopped collecting modern art in 1890. There are no significant post-impressionist works in private collections here, to say nothing of surrealism and cubism. That's because a lot of the money in Boston is old money. During the 20th century, there was new money in Chicago and New York, and people were buying art. A city like Chicago is larger than Boston, and population counts. Other than New York, the other major art scenes are in Chicago and Los Angeles.

We have a conservative community that tends to create in its own image. It remains to be explained why Boston was a very progressive center for collecting art, and then just stopped in the 1890s, and only started again in the 1960s.

CG The museum took no initiative in modern art, which had an impact in not inspiring Boston collectors. In what manner do trustees who collect benefit from their association with the contemporary department? Doesn't that enhance the value of their collections when works are loaned or included in special exhibitions?

KM That was (trustee Walter Muir) Whitehill's point in stating that we should not present contemporary art—that we are enhancing the careers of artists and influencing their market value. On my part, I have never been pressured by any trustee to show any particular work or to favor any particular artist.

(Ananda Kentish Muthu Coomaraswamy (1877–1947), the influential curator of Asiatic Art, established the policy that the MFA should only include work by deceased artists.)

CG Isn't the primary motive of donations of works of art to museums the prospect of tax write-offs?

KM There are many advantages, not the least of which is to have adequate security for works which have become too valuable to be secure in private hands. I have shown works loaned by dealers, and yes, this enhances the value of the work, but you have to have a basic sense of trust in your judgement and taste. Many trustees are genuinely involved and really care about art, while others are involved in power games, and don't really take an interest in what we exhibit and collect.

Compare the growth of American to European museums in modern times and you will see a difference. American museums have grown because of tax loopholes. Otherwise, we would have never gotten what we received. There had been no vigorous support of the arts on the part of government. This has been a hidden way in which, through no expenditure, government has supported the arts.

CG While a collector donates to a museum, the tax compensation is based on the market value for the work. When an artist donates work, they are only allowed to claim the cost of the materials. I know a dealer who bought the estate of an artist through a bank at bargain prices. He then arranged to sell the works to individuals who donated paintings to museums for inflated evaluations. In some instances the clients never viewed or took possession of the works, which went to museums.

(The Internal Revenue Code was amended in 1969 to restrict the tax deduction available to artists who donate their work to charity. Since that amendment, the number of charitable contributions by artists to museums and libraries has declined precipitously.)

KM We are all against the tax law, which is unfair to artists, and support the Javits amendment. This, in particular, hurts small collections and museums, which depend on donations as they have no real accession funds. Artists don't have lobbying leverage compared to corporations. In government, they don't care if art has a weak lobby. When politicians close art loopholes, they look as though they have done something useful. Most artists don't make a lot of money, and the revenue that the government derives by closing that loophole doesn't amount to a hill of beans.

CG How would you respond if young Boston artists were willing to donate their work to the museum?

KM I don't think we should put artists in that position. That's like arm-twisting. We should support young artists, and we have made some purchases. In particular, we have been active collecting prints and watercolors.

(When Philip Guston was teaching at Boston University, he offered Moffett the pick of the studio for the MFA. The curator was not interested in the current work and asked for an earlier abstract expressionist painting. The artist declined the request.)

CG One of the issues regarding ousted MFA director, Merrill Rueppel, was a conflict with curators when he restricted their teaching other than within the museum. That impacted you as a professor at Wellesley College while holding a half-time position as an MFA curator.

KM That was blown out of proportion. There are some courses that are appropriate to teach at the museum using the collection and resources. Other courses are better taught at the university with slide collections and lecture halls. The latter facilities don't exist here. I am all for teaching, but this is entirely on an individual basis. For contemporary art, we don't have an appropriate collection to teach that kind of course.

(The MFA maintained an extensive slide library, which was loaned to area teachers. It was later discontinued when art history departments ceased using slide projectors.)

CG It has been suggested that the museum's curators were sources for the *Boston Globe*'s series of articles targeting Merrill Rueppel and George Seybolt.

KM Personally, I had a good working relationship with Rueppel. He supported me, and my program. I have never called a newspaper to complain about conditions here. I consider that to be unprofessional.

CG It has been suggested that the trustees had too active a role in museum policy and were making aesthetic decisions beyond their expertise.

(After George Seybolt, John Coolidge, former Fogg Art Museum director, and then former MIT president, Howard Johnson, served as MFA board presidents. After that, boards were primarily chaired by business and financial individuals. There were legacy and ex officio members, but MFA boards were underrepresented by community and arts leaders. The first woman, Frances (Weeks) Hallowell Lawrence, was elected to the MFA board of trustees in 1954. The first Jewish trustee, Sidney Rabb, was also appointed in the 1960s. Phyllis A. Wallace (1921–1993), an economist and activist, was the first African American trustee appointed in 1976. Regarding diversity, Ted Landsmark has served on the ICA (as president) and MFA boards. Patti Hartigan reported in 1995 for *Boston Magazine*, "Landsmark just laughs. 'The number of racially diverse individuals remains extremely small,' he says, and leaves it at that. In fact, just two out of 33 elected trustees represent communities of color.")

KM It is characteristic for curators not to have direct contact with trustees. I don't know what they think, and their views come to us as hearsay. Curators are not consulted on committee actions.

CG It has been stated that Rueppel came to the MFA to initiate the findings and template of the 1970 ad hoc report.

KM I'll pass on that, as it has been a long time since I read the document and its details are fuzzy to me now.

CG We have heard of plans to deaccession key works in the collection to fund modern and contemporary acquisitions.

KM There is nothing wrong with this. Let us say, for example, the museum has 25 works by Jean-François Millet and none by Claude Monet. Wouldn't it be logical to trade or sell Millet to acquire Monet? This is a very sensitive subject. It gets a lot of people scared and nervous, in particular collectors and donors. Some people make unrestricted donations. These works can be traded or sold to upgrade the collection. Other donors make stipulations against this. MoMA has regularly deaccessioned to upgrade the collection. You never hear about it because they do not operate in a controversial manner. MoMA will trade three inferior works by van Gogh in order to get a first-rate picture.

The Metropolitan Museum acted with arrogance when they deaccessioned work through Marlborough Gallery. It was scandalous when they deaccessioned a major painting by Henri Rousseau without having anyone there to advise them.

(In 2009 the *New York Times* reported: "Thomas Hoving, then the director of the Metropolitan Museum of Art, began aggressively pruning its collection in the early 1970s, selling high-profile paintings like van Gogh's *Olive Pickers* and Rousseau's *Tropics*. The Metropolitan owned only one other painting by Rousseau, and the backlash was fierce.")

They should have called on all of the experts who would appraise the work and make a recommendation. The work would then go on the block at a public auction. This is not how the Met went about it. We could have done the same thing, but gone about it in the correct manner, and there wouldn't have been a word of criticism. Deaccessioning goes on all the time toward the end of refining and improving collections.

CG How do you go about acquiring works when there are such large gaps in the collection?

KM We try to buy top quality works at a reasonable price. We would like to acquire a (Roy) Lichtenstein painting, for instance, but his prices are now more than $100,000 and too expensive for us. We have to pass on pop art, which is too expensive for us. Besides, we have collected prints in this area and pop is primarily a multiples art form.

A museum should be collecting and documenting all phases of art, but we have to make choices and buy shrewdly. We would like to have a major piece of pop art, but we missed the boat and the market is now too high. Also, there isn't that much in Boston collections that might come to us. We should be buying younger artists at better prices.

If you have to spend $100,000 for a Lichtenstein, we have to ask ourselves, is it better to use the money to buy Miro, Picasso, and other artists we don't have? Pop art is a special case and no museum can build a great collection on their own. Until recently, there hasn't been serious collecting here. Take the new realists, for example, Richard Estes has already soared in value. His works bring about $80,000. His work is already out of our range, even though we would like to have one. On the other hand, Stephen Paine has three works by Estes and eventually we would probably get them. This is how you have to work on it.

Kenworth Moffett. Giuliano photo. Moffett at the Ft. Lauderdale Museum during our then annual meetings. Giuliano photo.

John Arthur guest curated exhibitions of Richard Estes and Alfred Leslie. Giuliano photo. Artist Helen Frankenthaler (center) with Rose Art Museum/ MFA patrons Lois and Dr. Henry Foster. Giuliano photo.

Barry Gaither,
Curator of Afro-American Art

Edmund Barry Gaither, born 1944, earned a B.A. from Morehouse College and an M.A. in art history from Brown University in 1968. The following year he moved to Boston to work with the arts activist and entrepreneur, Elma Lewis. She had founded the Elma Lewis School of the Arts in 1950. Gaither took over her National Center for Afro-American Artists.

Elma Ina Lewis (September 15, 1921–January 1, 2004) was one of the first recipients of a MacArthur Fellows Grant, in 1981, and received a Presidential Medal for the Arts from President Ronald Reagan in 1983. At its peak, her school had 700 students and 100 faculty. The site she acquired for the school, which overlooked Franklin Park, was previously Temple Mishkan Tefila. It and an adjoining school were turned over by Jewish philanthropists. Before acquiring this site, the school had passed through multiple locations, which caused financial problems. By the 1980s, the debt reached $720,000. The annual production of Langston Hughes' *Black Nativity* became a staple of the organization and was directed every year by Lewis herself. There were fires of suspicious origin in the 1970s and 1980s. The school closed after a fire in 1985.

Elma Lewis was a consultant to the MFA's ad hoc committee. The decision of the museum, in 1970, to support the National Center with the appointment of Gaither as an adjunct curator was a result of her input. The MFA director, Perry

T. Rathbone, supported her efforts prior to his resignation in 1972.

The ad hoc report stated, in part: "The attitude of the museum both within the walls and in the community should be that of openness, helping individuals and ethnic groups in their search for meaning and identity."

Gaither curated eight major exhibitions for the MFA, as well as directing the National Center. The NCAAA has a collection of some 3,000 objects. Gaither has now retired and the museum's board is reorganizing. As MFA director Matthew Teitelbaum told me, the museum continues to support the organization.

Gaither's pioneering programing had a sustained impact on the MFA. In 2015, Lowery Stokes Sims, the former director of The Studio Museum in Harlem, published the MFA's *Common Wealth: Art by African Americans in the Museum of Fine Arts, Boston*. It catalogues a hundred acquisitions with essays by Dennis Carr, Janet L. Comey, Eliot Bostwick Davis, Aiden Faust, Nonie Gadsen, Edmund Barry Gaither, Karen Haas, Erica E. Hirshler, Kelly Hays L'Ecuyer, Taylor L. Poulin, and Karen Quinn.

Gaither, an art historian, curator, and educator, is the recipient of numerous grants and awards. These include honorary doctorates from Northeastern University, Framingham State College, and Rhode Island College.

In a 1976 interview, we discussed development of a home for NCAAA in a former Roxbury mansion. I later visited the museum, when renovation had been completed. Other dialogues and interviews followed, including one in 2015.

I also spoke with Ted Landsmark, a community leader and former president of the board of the Institute of Contemporary Art, and a trustee of the MFA. The former president of Boston Architectural College is now allied with Northeastern University.

September 1, 1976 interview.

Barry Gaither is working to fund renovation at 300 Walnut Avenue in Roxbury. The National Center for Afro-American Artists was originally planned for the large temple building adjacent to the Elma Lewis School for the Arts. The cost of renovation of that structure was estimated at $2.5 million. The second building is more structurally sound and can be renovated for some $250,000.

Together, we drove to the site. The area primarily has private homes with a minimum of apartment buildings. The structure to be renovated was formerly a mansion that was used by the adjacent Ellis Elementary School. The building was among a number ordered closed by Judge Wendell Arthur Garrity, Jr. who presided over the desegregation of Boston Schools in 1974.

We stood before a Gothic Revival structure. It was one of the largest and most elaborate estates in Roxbury during the prosperous mid-19th century. Initially, Roxbury was a rural neighborhood of Boston that included farms.

Barry Gaither We plan to keep the exterior as is. In terms of the galleries, a number of windows will be removed. Those on the ground floor will be replaced with bronze-toned plexiglass which will admit light but prevent people from viewing what is going on inside. The building has been vandalized. All of the copper on the roof has been stolen and much of the slate is broken. The estimate to repair the roof is some $14,000.

The building was erected by a Mr. Smith, who made his money in trading. It was built in 1859. The second owners were the Samsons, who were merchants. The family occupied the house through the 1920s.

All of this area (pointing to a grassy knoll) and the surrounding open space was part of the estate, which included outhouses and a barn. There was a carriage house and a guesthouse. There is a watercolor of the appearance of the house from 1860, I believe it was a rendering for the architect, which gives a good sense of the original appearance. The rendering is owned by the Roxbury Historical Society.

Charles Giuliano What school are we next to?

BG That's the David A. Ellis School. Mrs. Edith Simon is the headmaster and she was very helpful in securing the building for us. She very much wanted us to come here. We plan to develop a program directly with the school. We also had considerable support from Kathy Kane. (Deputy Mayor under Mayor Kevin White. Kathy and her husband Louis Kane were supporters of the ICA, and Kathy helped them to lease the former police station at 955 Boylston Street.)

We have been given a letter of award, but have not yet been given a title transfer, as there were some complications. We could not go forward with plans until we had clear title. Some weeks ago, we were assured that the transfer of property had been ironed out. If we had known this some time ago, we could have prevented considerable vandalism to the building. Without title we couldn't afford to hire security, which is costly.

(Moving inside, the interior of the building is in disrepair with rotted floors and holes in the plaster walls. The building is constructed with granite and concrete and is structurally sound.)

We intend to restore the downstairs to the condition and appearance of the original home as much as possible. We obtained a number of photographs from the Samson family, which give us a good idea of the appearance of the house in its prime.

The downstairs will be turned into our special exhibition spaces. There are very high ceilings and good-sized rooms that will be perfect for galleries. We will keep the high ceilings and plaster walls, block up some windows, and install track lights. We plan to do about four special exhibitions a year and leave them up for a long time. Our idea is to have a small number of high-quality exhibitions.

We have checked the heating unit and plumbing, and they appear to be in good order. When this was a school, giant bathrooms were installed which are far beyond our needs. Recently, the gas company checked the furnace, and it appears to be sound. The electrical system was recently rewired when it was a school.

The second floor will contain a semi-permanent exhibition of African and Caribbean art.

We have put together a collection of some 800 objects of traditional African crafts and a number of Caribbean paintings. The African objects came from four donors: Dr. Eli and Carolyn Newberger, Dr. Albert Hinn, and the artist Richard Yarde. He acquired a number of interesting pieces during his travel in Africa. Ken Covington, an Ethiopian trader, gave us some choice pieces.

CG Does the Museum of Fine Arts provide funding for acquisitions?

BG Not really. Primarily, they fund our administration and the museum program of The Center. In several rare cases, they helped us to purchase four or five important pieces. We had the Africanist Richard Long take a look at the collection. He located some areas in which we need to fill gaps. The collection is worth roughly $100,000.

We intend to install the traditional materials in a reconstruction of a Yoruba village. There will be corrugated steel huts and a courtyard in which objects will be placed. We are developing a performance program, which will be held in the reconstructed setting. That will give meaning and significance to the pieces. The program will include storytelling, dance, and musical performances.

There will be programs to bring schoolchildren here for instruction and special events. We are trying to fund this through the school department. To do this installation, will take $6,000 in cash and another $12,000 in curatorial time and administrative overhead.

I was on the search committee for the new MFA education director. One of the things that I discussed with Linda Sweet was about exchange programs between our museum and the MFA. The idea is to develop a program that takes kids here and also send them there. We can each offer what we do best and then follow it up in the schools.

(Our tour continued to the third floor with more exhibition space and the print room. The Center has a collection of some 250 prints.)

CG How are you funding this?

BG We are starting a membership drive. The costs will be students $5, single memberships $10, and $15 for a family membership. There will also be corporate and business memberships. The idea is to keep the cost low and create a large membership to draw on a broad base of support.

We have submitted proposals to the Mellon and Kresge Foundations. We started with $25,000 to develop our plans. $10,000 of this was a grant from the Mass Bicentennial Commission. The other $15,000 was earned by doing a considerable amount of consulting work. For instance, we developed a black calendar for Miller Beer, which they distribute to their black customers.

We have done similar work with ITT and other corporations. This works two ways. It provides us with some income and it also gives us visibility. These are frequently the same people who sit on foundation boards, which dispense funds. If you are known and visible, the chances of being funded are all the better.

There is stiff competition for funding. There are some sixty Afro American museums in the country. Of these, ninety-seven percent are historical in orientation. They are mostly historical houses and national landmarks. Of these, only three percent involve art museums, of which the best-known program like ours is The Studio Museum in Harlem. Ours, however, is the only full-service museum program. We are not just a storefront operation, but rather are trying to put together a high-quality program. I am now trying to put together a five-year projection report in terms of our budgetary needs.

(What follows is a summary since the beginning of the program when Gaither arrived in October 1969.)

1971–1972 $50,000 MFA $35,000 National Center $15,000
1971–1973 $58,000 MFA $35,000 National Center $18,000
1973–1974 $68,700 MFA $35,000 National Center $33,700
1974–1975 $81,000 MFA $45,000 National Center $36,000
(Harriet Kennedy added to staff at $10,000 per annum)
1975–1986 $101,600 MFA $45,000 National Center remaining income from grants, consulting fees and Center support

Budget for new building and yearly operating expenses.

Core expense $177,000

    Costs Breakdown:

        $35,000 Occupancy costs, maintenance, and utilities

        $24,000 Administrative expense and telephone

        $33,500 Programming

        $84,000 Personnel

Annual cost of running the Elma Lewis School $800,000.

For the past year and a half the Center has been making cutbacks because of cost increases after a period of rapid growth.

1977–1978 Cost projection: $52,000 plus $125,000 renovation of the new building.

New revenue to be generated by support systems:

1. Membership drive
2. Admission fees, especially from the School Department
3. External grants (Applications filed with the Kresge and Mellon Foundations, as well as at the invitation of Newell Flather of Boston Company, a trusts management firm.)
4. Personal contributions
5. Annual fundraising drive and events

Costs invested in The Elma Lewis School and nature of the fact that the temple is undeveloped.

1970–1973 Cost of investment for improving the school was $750,000. Recently, The Center has received an NEA grant of $25,000 to develop plans for the temple.

CG Is there a significant black middle class in Boston?

BG There are not a lot of blacks who have money in Boston. In many cities, there are pockets of a younger generation with upward mobility. In Roxbury, all classes are mixed into the same neighborhoods. There are a number of more successful black people who are scattered in the suburbs. Therefore, they do not constitute an identifiable group.

(I addressed these issues with Ted Landsmark in 2000.)

Ted Landsmark (Former MFA board member) Boston's black community (20% of its population) has had historical difficulty with self-sufficiency of its cultural institutions.

Charles Giuliano Is that unique to Boston?

TL That's partly because, unlike cities of comparable size, Boston's black community is spread over a number of widely dispersed political jurisdictions. Often people in Cambridge don't connect with people in Dorchester. People in Framingham don't connect with people in Marlboro.

The result has been a failure to put together a critical mass of black leadership. You need that to sustain for the long haul the kinds of institutions we have been able to create but not support in perpetuity. Chicago has neighborhoods, but is basically one Chicago. Boston has neighborhoods fragmented into smaller city jurisdictions that tend to separate people rather than bring them together.

Historically, Boston has been one of the most racially divided cities in America. One sees far more racial cohesion in Charleston or Savannah than one does in Boston. Savannah has a black mayor. In many cities of comparable size in the south, where one doesn't expect black political leadership, it's there. Boston continues as the capital of the only major industrial state that has not sent a person of color to Congress.

(That changed with the election of Ayanna Pressley to the current (2020) Congress. Massachusetts has had a black senator, Ed Brooke, as well as governor, Deval Patrick.)

There has been an effort on the part of white society in Massachusetts to exclude African Americans from leadership roles. Chicago is not a dominantly black city, but it elected a black mayor, as did Minneapolis.

(In 2018 there were 32 black mayors of cities with populations of more than 40,000.)

This occurred in cities where black leadership came forward, because the community was organized. The white community recognized that strength, and was prepared to support it. That has not been the case in Boston. There has been racism in the schools, police and fire departments, the housing authority, and other places. A group of whites have conspired to deny positions of black leadership. That exists because the black community continues to be divided within itself. Boston has suffered because of that.

Return to Gaither Interview

CG Can we talk about your exhibitions for the Museum of Fine Arts?

BG The first was *Afro-American Artists: New York and Boston*.

(May 19 to June 23, 1970. The Boston artists included: Ronald Boutte, Calvin Burnett, Dana C. Chandler, Jr., Henry DeLeon, Milt Johnson, Lois Mailou Jones, Harriet Kennedy, Edward McCluney, Jr., Jerry Pinkey, Stanley Pinckney (Babaluaiye S. Dele), Gary Rickson, Al Smith, Richard Stroud, Lovett Thompson, Richard Waters, John Wilson. Ellen Banks, Richard Yarde. New York Artists: Emma Amos, Benny Andrews, Ellsworth Ausby, Malcolm Bailey, Romare Bearden, Robert Blackburn, Betty Blayton, Lynn Bowers, Frank Bowling, Marvin Brown, John Chandler, Edward Clark, Cliff Joseph, Eldzier Cortor, Ernest Crichlow, Emilio Cruz, Avel DeKnight, James Denmark, Reginald Gammon, Felrath Hines, Alvin Hollingsworth, Bill Howell, Zell Ingram, Gerald Jackson, Daniel L. Jackson, Benjamin Jones, Toiie Jones, Jacob Lawrence, Hughie Lee-Smith, Norman Lewis, Tom Lloyd, Alvin D. Loving, Jr., Richard Mayhew, Algernon Miller, Joseph Overstreet, Louise Parks, John W. Rhoden, Barbara Chase Riboud, Bill Rivers, Mahler Ryder, Raymond Saunders, Thomas Sills, Vincent Smith, Alma Thomas, Bob Thompson, Russ Thompson, Lloyd Toone, Luther Van, Paul Waters, Jack White, Yvonne Williams, Hale Woodruff.)

CG Can you discuss the controversy about your MFA exhibition *Jubilee* and the issues about not having a catalogue for the show?

BG When I did the show *African Art of the Dogon* (July 1973), I had lunch with George Seybolt (president of the board of trustees) and he asked what exhibition I would like to do. I discussed doing an exhibition that would survey several centuries of the art of Ethiopia (15th through 18th centuries). It was scheduled for November–December 1975.

I worked on it through the spring of 1975, including trips to Ethiopia and Europe to prepare the exhibition. Plans went into limbo because of a political coup at that time with the overthrow of Haile Selassie.

Also at this time, there were administrative changes at the MFA. (The incident with the ouster of director Merrill Rueppel resulting from a *Boston Globe* investigative series of articles.) I had a slot, but no show. I decided to propose a different show. We developed a proposal thinking that we had the same budget as that allotted to the Ethiopian exhibition. We planned an exhibition that would be national in scope. We spent time picking and choosing, then Merrill went out. Through July and August, it was impossible to get a commitment.

When the decision to go ahead was made at the end of August, the budget had shrunk from $175,000 to just $20,000 for the *Jubilee* exhibition. For the Ethiopian show we had planned to spend $35,000 on a publication. Out of the $20,000, when in-house costs were deducted, there was no cash for travel. We wanted very much to show the flavor and the spirit of the material.

There was no time left for a thorough art historical show. Instead, we wanted the visitor to have a flavorful experience, so we planned to have performances and we booked them through the National Center. The sense of the show needed this kind of activity. We made the decision that we would rather spend our money on performances than on a catalogue. The exhibition was successful, in the sense that it drew between 30,000 and 40,000 people. (Attendance for the museum's contemporary exhibitions averaged 10,000.)

CG If you agreed to spend money on performances rather than a publication, what caused all the controversy in the press?

BG Naturally, to an artist, the catalogue is very important. It represents documentation of the work and is part of the artist's promotion. They were very upset about not having a catalogue. Dana Chandler, Jr. decided to see what he could do about it and was pressing for a public airing of the issue. (In response to pressure, the museum did publish a slim catalogue.)

CG Did you support his dissent?

BG Look, if you are doing something black in a white context, then controversy is inevitable. Anybody working in this context had to expect it, and any disappointment can easily be generated into an issue.

You are aware, for instance, of the negative review in the *Boston Globe* by Henri Ghent. There has been a feud between us going back some time, to when I was working in Atlanta. He is one of those individuals who received a grant to solicit papers like the *Globe* and ask for assignments to review exhibitions and activities like our *Jubilee* show.

The idea is to have a black critic review major black activity. He reviewed our entire five-year relationship with the MFA, and said that we hadn't done anything of quality except for the Dogon show. In fact, he hadn't been here for 24 hours when he wrote the *Jubilee* review.

(From 1970 through 1975, Gaither curated numerous exhibitions for the National Center, several each year, outside curatorial projects, as well as five for the MFA: *Afro-American Artists: New York and Boston, Bannister and Duncanson, 19th Century Afro-American Artists, Reflective Moments: Lois Mailou Jones, African Art of the Dogon, Jubilee, Afro-American Artists on Afro America*.)

CG What progress is being made on the museum appointing an African American trustee? Is it true that Elma Lewis turned down an offer to join the board?

BG Howard Johnson (board president) has a number of scouts searching for a black trustee. It was never offered to Miss Lewis, and I doubt that she would take it because of her commitment to the school. I think that she would feel that it would be a luxury that she couldn't indulge.

The post was offered to Adelaide Hill of Boston University. She serves as chairperson of the Center's board. She turned it down because she is already over extended with civic commitments.

(The first African American joined Howard Johnson's board in 1976. Phyllis A. Wallace (1921–1993) an economist and activist was the first woman to receive a doctorate of economics at Yale University. Her work focused on racial and gender discrimination in the workplace.)

What follows are highlights of a 2015 interview with Gaither

Barry Gaither Elma Lewis, going back several years before I came, was saying from time to time to Perry (T. Rathbone, director of the MFA) that she wanted his help to start a museum of fine arts, which she saw as a part of the National Center which did not formally incorporate until 1968.

There was a conference in Chicago convened by Columbia College of creative black intellectuals. Miss Lewis was an attendee there. They spent a lot of time bellyaching that they had no place to be somebody. The National Negro Theatre was being born. There were dance things. There was no place that was for all of the arts and teaching. Miss Lewis came back to Boston with that at the front of her mind…

Miss Lewis had been running the school for some time, since 1950. We are talking now of the period 1967 to 1968. The school never had a home. It kept moving from time to time. She had most recently been at the Lewis School, but the Boston School Committee was very unhappy, and basically, they were ousting her from there…

The Jewish population in Roxbury was plummeting. There was the property where Mishkan Tefila had been. It's a synagogue, now in Brookline. The property we got was the property they had been in.

A group of ten Jewish men put together a piece of money, which they gave to Combined Jewish Philanthropies. They used this money to buy the property, which had been the temple. This allowed the dwindling congregation to have money to move to Brookline.

Then, in what they thought was a gesture of goodwill, they gave the property to Miss Lewis. When she got the property, it coincided with the idea for a National Center as a professional entity with teaching, performing, and visual arts. She saw the opportunity to give that concreteness as the National Center.

She came up with the idea of how to do this while not having a lot of money. She created relationships with cultural organizations that had long histories of doing excellent work. She used those to foster getting her pieces to work out.

From time-to-time, she was saying to Perry that she was going to need his help. In early 1969, she went back to him and said now he needs to follow through on promises. Perry initially balked. He said that there weren't any African American artists. That sort of got pushed back because John Wilson was a graduate of the

Museum School and even at that point was well respected.

What came out of it was him saying, we will help if you find someone who we accept. That's how I got into the picture. In the summer of 1969, I was asked to come and interview by the MFA. I didn't meet Miss Lewis until I had come. Previously, I had not known of the Center, which was very new…

I had a real conversation with Perry and was very excited with Miss Lewis's idea. I was untempered enough to think that you could actually pull it off, just by working at it. So I said yes.

In September of 1969, I came to an appointment that was without a model. On the National Center side, when I actually got here, I discovered that I actually had two jobs in one. I was going to be developing the museum, and I was also going to be teaching in the art portion of the Elma Lewis School.

On the MFA side of it, they were already feeling pressed by the controversy that was hitting large museums in their class. You will recall that just the year before, the Metropolitan Museum had done *Harlem on My Mind*, which had just gotten it into more hot water. When I came, the MFA also wanted me to do exhibitions there. I wanted to do them and tie them to the National Center, so we began a process that ultimately produced eleven exhibitions. They were joint exhibitions, but technically paid for by the MFA. For which I bore curatorial responsibility.

The MFA was not quite sure what to expect, because I was a very new and unknown quantity. The relationship, which got structured between the MFA and the National Center, was never written. There is no document, and nothing was ever signed. If it went south, it could just be dropped.

I wanted to do a national show that would be contemporary. It would have taken a year, to a year and a half to organize.

The artists were afraid that if it took too long, the MFA would find a way to repress it. The artists were pressing me. Then I had to find a way to figure out what, in fact, could be done. It would have to be limited to only New York and Boston. That's how it got to be only those two places.

I had met and started a friendship with Bill Bagnell (director of the Museum School), and he had introduced me to Barney (Rubenstein). I suggested to Barney that we roll together the effort that he had already begun to do something quite small at the Museum School, and flesh it out.

I formed a relationship, and we did what should have been a year of work in three months. We were going to New York every week. He and I were going together because he had this cluster of friends at the Chelsea (Hotel). We started with some of those people, and I had my own list beyond that, which was a broader list. We talked to those people as we were going along. We put the show together in this very compressed timetable…

Boston was, at the time, getting around a particular problem. When I would go to talk to particular artists, like Norman Lewis (1909–1979), they were all bitter about their experience at large. They were a little bitter that people kept coming and talking to them. (Art history graduate students.) Those people all ended up getting something out of it, but they (artists) got nothing.

People were coming and getting their thesis finished and moving their career along, interviewing and talking to them. They weren't selling for that reason. They weren't yet getting the visibility. They felt they were being used by people who had an agenda that didn't move them forward.

If I could create exhibitions which give the artists something, I could use the experience to collect the kind of information that I thought I would need. It wouldn't be a one-way exchange. I didn't intend to be in Boston for more than a year or two. That was my own plan, it's just that it didn't work out at all that way.

CG You describe graduate work in the late 1960s. What was the state of studies of African American art at that time? When we started to interact in the 1970s, you would mention artists that I knew nothing about. Very little of that history was mainstream.

BG Here's where that difference comes in. There were a couple of books, and quite a number of earlier catalogues. There were a number of essays on African American art that you really wouldn't know about, lest you were involved with others who had the same interest. I had had a lot of help in my early thinking about this field from James Amos Porter. He was the head of the department of art at Howard. He was the author of *Modern Negro Art* published in 1942. He was the foremost art historian of this area, as well as David Driscoll, who's a half-generation older than I. I also knew John Davis Hatch, who had worked with the exhibition *Negro Artists Come of Age*, which had been at the Albright Knox Museum in 1942, had been in Atlanta at the same time I was a student there. I had access to him. Plus, when I came to college at Morehouse, in 1962, I found myself immediately studying under the works of African American artists.

Hale Woodruff (1900–1980) had been commissioned to do his most important cycle of murals for Atlanta University in 1948–49. Finished in 1952, actually. They were in the rotunda of the library where I studied. Woodruff had founded the *Atlanta University Annual* in 1942. It was where artists from all across the country sent works for an annual exhibition. The university policy was to buy the prizewinners from the annual. They comprised the Atlanta University Collection. That's now the Clark Atlanta Collection. Those works were distributed through the entire set of campuses of the two undergraduate colleges that were gender-based, Spelman and Morehouse. I was always under those works.

My first acquaintance with art was with black visual artists. Before I got to graduate school, my thinking was grounded in these key works. There was Dr. Porter, who did the primary work for the discussion in the 20th century, and to a lesser degree, James Lewis at Morgan. You're well on the road to getting a framework for how these issues were shaping out. What I was bringing to this experience was a perspective grounded in an entirely different body of work. None of that work was a part of my graduate study. Graduate study had to do with methodology. And broader ideas around art and art criticism, but not very specific to African American…

CG Can you talk about Perry and the MFA?

BG I had a good personal relationship with Perry. The way things shook out at the MFA had to do with the following elements. I'm not sure I can rank these.

There was no real curator of paintings. Perry had that portfolio. It was pretty much Perry's decision that I would get this first opportunity to do that show in 1970.

CG Where does George Seybolt come into this?

BG He was chairman of the board of trustees. Frankly, George Seybolt was, to me, kind of like a Dutch uncle. He was a mentor. He liked me. George was a largely self-made man. His early life had been routed through a military academy. He didn't belong to the social strata that you might have most quickly thought of for a man who was chair of the board of the MFA—because he had made himself and the great success that Underwood Deviled products was, and because he did have a genuine interest in museums. He had a great respect for going against the odds.

He and Miss Lewis held enormous respect for each other. But frankly, they couldn't stay in the same room for very long. They both were enormously willful personalities. Disrespect from some for her was because she made the school, the center, and pushed a place for herself in the arts environment through her will. That kind of willful self-making was something he admired…

I served on two working groups for the American Association of Museums on equity and diversity in the 1980s. Then I served on *Museums for a New Century*. It was a blueprint for 2000. At that time, Seybolt was chair of the subgroup of trustees of the American Association of Museums. He had been instrumental in getting the National Museum Bill passed. I testified in Congress for that to happen. From my view, George had been a very progressive guy.

Perry lined up for this to be able to happen because, from the top, he wanted that to happen. I think that George was joined on the trustees by a couple of other people. Esther Anderson was a strong supporter of the relationship. She was a great admirer of Miss Lewis as well…

No museum in the class of the MFA had done such a show before ours. The closest to that had been the Met's *Harlem on My Mind*. Which, as you know, was not a fine art show. It had come in for a lot of criticism.

The big public issues that were playing out at the time were that these very large public institutions had ignored, and continued to ignore, the presence and contribution of African American artists. So that summarizes the institutional racism argument.

The other discussion was that these institutions refused to give critical voice to thinking from within the tradition itself. The curators were not black. That issue had risen to a very high level in the case of Allon Schoener and *Harlem on My Mind*. When I did the show here in Boston, it was a kind of hearty response to that, as you recall from some of the stuff that transpired in The *New York Times* with my response (to) *Harlem on My Mind* and the Benny Andrews response to the issue of curatorial voice. In New York the Harlem Emergency Cultural Coalition was formalized to continue that argument forward.

In the moment, Boston was actually faring a little better, because we were actually doing a whole series of shows, for which I was the curatorial voice.

CG Can we describe that programming?

BG It happened on two levels. On the strictly art historical side of it in the 1970s show, it was all contemporary, with around 100 to 180 pieces and 70 artists. The next year, I did a 19th century show. It included the artists Bannister (Edward Mitchell Bannister, 1828–1901) and Duncanson (Robert Scott Duncanson, 1821–1872). It was the occasion of acquiring *Dog's Head of Scotland*, 1870, by Duncanson. It brought forward new attention to Bannister, who had been a New Englander. He was active in Providence. He had won a bronze medal at the Centennial Exhibition in Philadelphia in 1876. He was a part of the circle of people who ultimately created the Rhode Island School of Design. So I did the show on him.

Then I did the show on Lois Jones (Lois Mailou Jones, 1905–1998). There had not been a one-woman show of an African American artist in a major museum, so that was new ground.

CG Wasn't there a recent show of her work at the MFA?

BG Yes, a year and a half ago. The family gave work to the MFA. The anchor work in that show was *Ubi Girl of the Tai Region*, which the MFA purchased from the show I did at the MFA in the 1970s. That's a region in Liberia. As I recall, the work was executed in 1972. She was a graduate of the Museum School.

CG So there were people at the Museum School. Obviously, Alan Crite (1910–2007) and John Wilson (1922-2015).

BG The early black figures who went to the Museum School include Edwin Augustus Halston, who went there around 1905. He was a portrait painter from Charleston with a wonderfully romantic touch. He died in 1931. He took back to Charleston the portrait style, which was well established at the Museum School. Sargent Johnson (1888–1967), a sculptor who worked mainly on the West Coast, went briefly to the Museum School. They both went there before Lois, who enters in 1923 or 1924. Allan (Crite) enters in the very beginning of the 1930s, and John Wilson goes there in 1940. Others who studied, but didn't complete the program, include James Reuben Reed and Calvin Burnett (1921–2007). Calvin is more associated with the Mass College of Art, just as Richard Yarde is more associated with BU. We are already now well after WWII…

I see the period from 1969 through the end of the 1990s as a time when I did a lot of work there. It included exhibitions but also a lot of performance events which were related to exhibitions. It brought to the MFA a lot of audience, particularly a black audience, which otherwise would not have been so involved.

Through that period, the kind of changes that my work represented were not really institutionalized. Other than my putting forward suggestions on a fairly regular basis, which got acted on, they didn't tend to come from elsewhere.

I think the changes that came about have three conditions, which made them possible. One condition is that large museums respond powerfully to donors who are holding what are perceived as important collections. So to some degree, the emphasis I was trying to push was never going to get traction until a collector came forward to anchor it. That's what Axelrod did. (In 2011 the museum acquired sixty-seven major works of African American art from the collector John Axelrod.)

The second thing that has to happen, is there has to be a greater amount of ownership of the topic. When I did the John Wilson/Joseph Norman exhibition at the MFA in the early 1990s, I did that with one of the young curators from Cliff Ackley's department (Prints, Drawings, and Photography). It was a show fundamentally about prints and drawings. That was all very good. That was the closest things came to having another department at the MFA embrace this topic. The curatorial emphasis, beyond the one I was making, took a long time to get any traction.

The third condition, is that there has to be some commitment of money to actually sustain the change. In this case the money was closely tied to the coming of the Axelrod collection.

In 1970, when we were pressing, by we I mean the African American community with its various pieces, the audience, we at the Center, that was very much a hot discussion. They were being asked to do two things: to make African American art and artists an essential part of what they put forward in an encyclopedic museum; they were also being asked to do the same thing with African subject matter. Neither of those had curatorial favor at that point in time.

Elma Lewis cruising Boston Harbor with Dizzy Gillespie. Giuliano photo.

Edmund Barry Gaither headed The National Center for Afro-American Artists and was an adjunct curator for the MFA. Giuliano photo.

In 1950 she founded of the Elma Lewis School of Fine Arts. Giuliano photo.

Ted Landsmark chaired the Institute of Contemporary Art board and served on the MFA's.

Ted Stebbins Chaired American and European Painting and Contemporary Departments

Theodore E. Stebbins, Jr. was the MFA's John Moors Cabot Curator of American Art. For three years, he was also head of the departments of American and European painting, as well as, the department of 20th century art. He acquired 400 works for the museum, including 100 from the Lane Collection of American modernism. In terms of acquisitions and exhibitions, few curators compare to his impact on the museum.

When Malcolm Rogers fired prominent curators and consolidated departments, he offered Stebbins the opportunity to head Art of the Americas. Stebbins left to found the Department of American Art for the Harvard Art Museums.

Charles Giuliano Were you appointed by Jan Fontein?

Ted Stebbins First he appointed John Walsh as the Baker Curator of European Paintings, in the early months of 1977. Walsh urged Jan to appoint a curator of American paintings. Jan appointed me in the summer of 1977. I began that September or October.

CG As Jan told me, he was an Orientalist with no expertise in painting. There had been no curator of paintings since before Rathbone. This was the domain of directors. But Fontein felt that it was important to have painting curators.

TS Rathbone was pretty knowledgeable, and he was his own paintings curator. He loved going into the market and buying European paintings, and he had the help of Hanns Swarzenski.

CG I would like to explore the process of building collections, particularly the Karolik and Lane collections. Maxim Karolik (1893–1963) preceded you, but you were involved in the Lane acquisition. What would the American collection be without those two great acquisitions?

TS Karolik married Martha Codman (1858–1948) from one of the great Boston families. She was descended from Elias Hasket Derby (1739–1799) from Salem. Derby had a great house, as well as furniture and silver. He helped her to build on an already existing collection. In 1938 they gave it to the museum. They insisted on a scholarly catalogue of the collection. That included furniture and some Copleys.

By then, his wife was fairly old, and he was looking around for something to collect. He visited an exhibition at the Metropolitan Museum called *Life in America*. It was 1939 and his eyes were opened to American landscapes and genre painting.

He started to collect Thomas Birch (1779–1851), a Philadelphia painter. Then, through Charlie Childs, Fitz Hugh Lane, now Fitz Henry Lane (1804–1865), the Gloucester seascape painter. Then Martin Johnson Heade (1819–1904), Sanford Robinson Gifford (1823–1880), John Frederick Kensett (1816–1872), George Caleb Bingham (1811–1879), and William Sidney Mount (1807–1868). He started during the war years and the collection was finished by 1945.

(Maxim Karolik, an opera singer of Jewish heritage, was born in the Ukraine. A linguist, he taught himself English before immigrating to America. He met Martha Catherine Codman during a performance in Washington DC. They married on the Riviera on February 2, 1928. They were largely snubbed by Boston society. They lived in Newport.)

Nobody else was collecting that material. There were a few, but just enough to keep the dealers having lunch: Childs in Boston, Victor Spark in New York, and several others. They looked to him like Russian paintings.

CG That's a major point of the Robert Rosenblum, H. W. Janson textbook, *19th*

Century Art (1984). It widened the focus from a fixation on French art to include German, Russian, British, and Scandinavian art. In particular, it changed the thinking about the uniqueness of American luminism (the focus of the Karolik collection). That text changed how 19th century art was taught. Luminism, as uniquely American, was the thesis of Barbara Novak.

TS Exactly. John Wilmerding did a big show of luminism at the National Gallery. (*American Light: The Luminist Movement, 1850–1875*, 1980)

My essay in that catalogue discusses German, Danish, and Russian paintings. I was saying, hold on a minute, American art was part of an international phenomenon.

CG There was also the shift from the term luminism to the glare aesthetic.

TS You've got that wrong. Wilmerding was a champion of luminism. Except for my essay, the whole catalogue is based on luminism. Pretty soon after that William H. Gerdts, who died recently, wrote an essay called "The Glare Aesthetic." It was about a group of painters just after the luminists. Wilmerding was strictly a luminism guy.

CG Regarding the Karolik collection, you mention Mount and Bingham, who were not part of the luminist tradition. What was the Bingham in the MFA? Was it *Shooting for the Beef* (1850)? No, wait, it's owned by Brooklyn.

TS I wish they did, that's a great picture. It's owned by the Brooklyn Museum. When I was at Yale, I wanted that painting. A great Yale collector, Francis Garven, had sold it.

CG What was the Karolik Bingham?

TS He had *Wood-Boatmen on the Missouri*. We also had *The Squatters* (provenance Henry L. Shattuck, 1937). I sold one in not very good condition to buy the Stuart Davis (1892–1964) *Hot Still Scape*, the single most important painting in my career.

CG What was the Mount?

TS He owned several, including one called *The Bone Player*. (Also *Rustic Dance After a Sleigh Ride*, *The Barn by the Pool*, *The Fence on a Hill*, and *Julia Parish*

Raymond, provenance Roswell Parish)

CG *The Bone Player* (1856) is one of the most important Mount's; particularly, because of the sympathetic manner in which African Americans are depicted in his paintings.

TS There was so much caricature, as you know, and Mount portrayed the black man as an intelligent equal.

CG As did (James Goodwyn) Clonney (1812–1867), who you sold. (One of six paintings, all from the Karolik Collection.)

TS Somewhere in there I sold a Clonney, but there were several others in the museum. I think that Clonney is more caricatured than Mount, but we can argue that.

CG I first saw a number of Binghams in St. Louis.

TS That's the place to see them.

CG We saw Mount's *Eel Fishing on the Setauket* in Cooperstown at the Fenimore Museum. It conveys the wonderful relationship with the black woman standing to spear fish and the boy steering the boat.
    What was Karolik's problem with (Frederic Edwin) Church (1826–1900)?

TS He thought he had a great one. It turned out to be *The Finding of Moses* by a minor painter. It was one of his few mistakes. He should have bought one or two others, but for some reason, Church was harder to grasp. When Barbara Novak wrote her book, *Nature and Culture: American Landscape and Painting, 1825–1875*, she skipped Church altogether.

CG How did so many paintings by Church end up in the Wadsworth Athenaeum?

TS They came from a number of Hartford families. Church was a native son and much admired in Hartford during his lifetime and after.

CG Where does Albert Bierstadt (1830–1902) come into the Karolik Collection?

(There are 26 MFA works by Bierstadt, of which, 24 are in the Karolik Collection.)

TS The Bierstadts in the Karolik collection are good. He liked Bierstadt a lot. He was the first to buy Bierstadt's oil sketches. There are ten or fifteen sketches on paper like the one on the wall behind me. Nobody was collecting them. They were studies for paintings. They didn't seem collectable to people. Karolik was a pioneer in many ways.

CG Looking through the list of your acquisitions, you also bought Colonial paintings, including (John) Smibert (1688–1751).

TS There was a lady in Brookline who gave us a beautiful pair of Smiberts. I bought Benjamin West's (1738–1820) *King Lear* from the Boston Athenaeum. One of my first purchases was a charming Gilbert Stuart (1755–1828) of a young woman, *Miss Anna Powell Mason*. It was at Vose's, and I thought it was the most beautiful Stuart I had ever seen. I went back to the museum, which had forty Stuarts, and there was nothing as beautiful.

So, I built on strength. I bought a full length (John Singleton) Copley (1738–1815).

CG That was the *Nathaniel Sparhawk*.

TS Yes. The museum had fifty Copleys, but no full-length portrait. When you are a curator of that kind of collection, you want to cement it as the absolute best. To see Copley, people absolutely have to come to Boston.

CG Copley and portrait painters charge by how much of the body is in the picture, as well as, how many individuals. So, as a full-length portrait, the *Sparhawk* would have been an expensive portrait.

TS Copley also charged by size. You could buy a miniature and that was much less. You could buy a pastel the size of a book. He charged for the more he had to paint. If you paint a couple, it's much more because you have to blend them together.

CG I wonder if he charged more for all the fruit in *Mrs. Ezekiel Goldthwaite*. He was a shrewd businessman, starting as a teenager. Yale owns Smibert's *The Bermuda Group*, which is a complex composition. He holds up well.

TS That's one of the landmarks of American art.

CG He was trained in England, so do you think of him as American or British school?

TS He was American enough. We were short of artists and needed everybody. Whistler, Sargent, all those people were equally American in our eyes.

CG (James Abbott McNeill) Whistler (1834–1903) claimed that he was born in St. Petersburg, where his father worked as a military engineer. When reminded that he was born in Lowell, Whistler responded, "I will be born when and where I choose."

How does the MFA compare to other American museums in the area of American art?

TS In 1980, the best collection of American Art was the Metropolitan Museum. Boston was second, and The National Gallery third. By 2000, twenty years later, with the Lane Collection and all these other additions, I acquired 400 paintings, about a fifth of the whole collection. By then you could argue that the MFA had the best American collection.

In those 20 years the Met did very little. The National Gallery, with John Wilmerding and Nicolai Cikovsky, were very active. By 2000, the MFA and National Gallery had the major collections of American art, with the Met as a solid second place.

CG In my 1984 interview with Jan Fontein, I quote you at that time saying that, within the next ten years, the MFA would have the nation's best collection of American art.

TS I don't remember saying that. Even for me that would be a bit of hubris, because collecting takes a lot of luck. But it's right that I was ambitious.

CG How did the Lane collection come about?

TS I kept noticing when I went to shows like Marsden Hartley I was seeing great pictures that said, "Lent by the William H. Lane Foundation." Who was this? I discovered that he lived near Worcester. I wrote to him and said, "I would like to come and see you." John Walsh and I drove out. We had a noon appointment. I knocked on the door, barely touched it, and it flew open. This big guy, shaped like you, said, "Where have you guys been?"

We staggered back and thought, oh my God, are we late, "I thought our appointment was for twelve." He said, "No, where have you been for the past twenty years?"

I think you have this in one of your interviews, Perry Rathbone had discovered who he was and put him on a committee. Then Lane gave one of those colored Franz Kline's (1910–1962) to the MFA.

At some point, Perry told Moffett to go see Lane. He went and saw the collection and Bill (Lane) said, "What do you think? What can we do together?" According to Bill, Ken said, "I don't think there's much here for the MFA." I hate saying that, because it's so sad.

CG As much as we liked Ken, he was very narrow.

TS He was narrow, but is it possible to be that narrow? How would you turn down Klines, (Hans) Hofmanns (1880–1966), (Arthur) Doves (1880–1946), and (Charles) Sheeler's (1880–1965)?

That's the sadness and mystery of Moffett, who was a very nice man, as you know. When I got to the MFA, he was the first curator to invite me to lunch. He was a serious and good scholar. He should never have become a curator. We're inclined to blame Ken, but that was exactly the point of view that the MFA wanted when they hired him.

CG What you really mean is, that's what the trustee Lewis Cabot (1937–2020) wanted.

TS Yes, Lewis Cabot. Ever since Michael Fried's 1965 exhibition at the Fogg, *Three American Painters: Kenneth Noland, Jules Olitski, and Frank Stella*. The Fogg immediately bought a big Morris Louis (1912–1962). By the time that Ken got to the MFA, that was Boston's taste and where they wanted to go, Color Field paintings.

I have spent a lot of time sorting out the differences of taste between New York and Boston. It's interesting to see what a curator can do, like Sam Hunter (1923–2014) at Brandeis a decade earlier than Ken. That's still the best collection of modern art in the area.

CG With a gift of $50,000 from the New York collector Leon Mnuchin and his wife, Harriet Gervitz-Mnuchin, he made numerous studio visits and bought some twenty-five works. As Hunter told me, that might have gone to buy a single work, but he wisely spent it on emerging artists. When Brandeis president, Jehuda Reinharz, tried to sell the collection in 2009, it was estimated to be worth some $300 million.

TS There should be a statue of Sam Hunter next to the Rose. He's never gotten enough credit.

CG I knew and liked Ken. We had different taste, but a very cordial relationship. I visited him a number of times at the Fort Lauderdale Museum of Art when he was its director. At the MFA, he was open to working with guest curators.

TS What curators did he work with in Boston?

CG John Arthur, the realism expert, curated very successful Richard Estes (B. 1932) and Alfred Leslie (B. 1927) shows. Chris Cook did a conceptual Douglas Huebler (1924–1997) show.

When the Evans Wing was closed for renovation, Ken was assigned to curate the MFA's temporary galleries at Quincy Market. One of his most amazing projects was the Anthony Caro (1924–2013) York Series of metal sculptures. They were displayed on Mass Avenue, on the grassy area in front of the Christian Science Church. There were two Jules Olitski (1922–2007) shows, one of paintings, and one for sculpture.

TS The Caros were wonderful and stand up well.

CG His strategy was to make formalism the focus of the contemporary collection. The crown jewel was to be the Jackson Pollock (1912–1956) masterpiece *Lavender Mist* (1950). It was Merrill Rueppel who rejected that acquisition.

TS Who actually ended it was Betty Jones, who was the head of paintings conservation. She loved to give negative opinions about pictures. She did the same thing to me when I proposed the great John Trumbull (1756–1843), *The Sortie from Gibraltar*. The Met bought it immediately after the MFA turned it down. She did that with *Lavender Mist* and the trustees, in that situation, were looking for an excuse not to go ahead. She was a much beloved and trusted person at the museum. That was the end of it.

If the curator and director really believe in something, they can get it done. As you point out, the director didn't support the acquisition, but the curator has to be willing to fall on his sword. That's your legacy. That's what you live for: to get that work into the museum.

CG Imagine the contemporary collection if its centerpiece was *Lavender Mist*. Also, he had a very good David Smith (1906–1965), *Cubi XVIII* and *Zig VII*.

TS That was given by the Paines. Ken didn't spend a cent for it.

CG I understood that Wayne Andersen of MIT had proposed *Cubi XVIII* for City Hall Plaza. That didn't happen, in fact, there are no works of art on that vast open space.

TS I don't know about that.

CG Lane may be described as eccentric. Everything he bought had to fit into his station wagon. He brought works to New England libraries, small museums, and schools. His intent was to use the collection to educate people about modern art. Most of the work was purchased from the Downtown Gallery.

(Edith Gregor Halpert (née Edith Gregoryevna Fivoosiovitch [1900–1970]. Her Downtown Gallery was founded in 1926.)

TS That's correct, but he went to other galleries as well. When the weather was nice, on weekends, he would drive to New York in a big old Chevy station wagon. And yes, the works had to fit. He would take a dozen or so pictures and look at them during the week. He would select one or two, and take the rest back the following weekend. So, it was constant looking and learning.

CG He visited the studio of Franz Kline.

TS He knew Kline well.

CG The colored paintings were in the studio during a time when the artist was evolving to black and white paintings. Lane preserved a transitional period.

TS Exactly. Lane was an instinctive scholar. He never graduated from college, but he wanted to know the roots of the art. When he bought an artist, he wanted to know what the early work looked like. He did the same with Hofmann and Dove. Sheeler became a good friend.

He asked Kline for advice. He said, "I've got you and Hofmann, who else should I be collecting?" Kline said, "You should go see Jackson Pollock." So Lane went to the Broome Street Bar. Pollock already had too much to drink and was rude to Lane. He went home, and never bought a Pollock. That could have been a turning point (for the collection).

CG There were major collectors who were bargain hunters. They would visit studios and try to strike deals to buy a number of works at cut-rate prices. That often resulted in acquiring a phase or moment in the artist's development. That happened notably with Walter Chrysler, Joseph Hirshhorn, J. Patrick Lannan, Sr., and Roy Neuberger.

Did Lane do that? Was he a bargain hunter?

TS Not at all. He never bargained and always paid the price that was asked. The strange thing is that, the most he ever paid was the same amount that was the most that Karolik ever paid, which was $2,500. Edith Halpert showed him the Georgia O'Keeffe (1887–1986) of the deer's head. It was a classic O'Keeffe. Lane said, "Oh my god, I can't believe it is still available." He thought he was very lucky because everyone else with education and taste was buying School of Paris.

My theory is that great collectors are often outsiders like Karolik and Lane.

CG You sent me some of your essays, as well as a video disc of the MFA interview with Matthew Teitelbaum. Reading histories of the early years of the museum, its directors, trustees, and collectors, there is the perception of a commitment to collecting the artists of Boston from colonial times through the 1930s.

The museum has presented major exhibitions celebrating that legacy, including *New England Begins; The Seventeenth Century; Paul Revere's Boston; Back Bay Boston: The City as a Work of Art; The Bostonians: Painters of an Elegant Age, 1870–1930; The Boston Tradition: American Paintings from the Museum of Fine Arts, Boston; Paintings by New England Provincial Artists, 1775–1800; A Studio of Her Own: Women Artists in Boston 1870–1940.*

These survey exhibitions end between 1930 and 1940. That's precisely when there was a paradigm shift and the leading Boston artists were Jewish immigrants. There was a recent show, *Hyman Bloom: Matters of Life and Death* (2019) but the MFA has no interest to create a survey of Boston artists in the post war era.

During your MFA lecture, you discussed anti-Semitism that Karolik experienced. And yet, why didn't you exhibit and collect these Jewish artists? You collected Frank Weston Benson (1862–1951), and Edmund C. Tarbell (1862–

1938), in depth, but not the Boston expressionists: Hyman Bloom (1913–2009), Jack Levine (1915–2010), and Karl Zerbe (1903–1972).

TS I particularly liked Zerbe's work. Lane and I had a long negotiation about what he was going to include in our acquisition. I got the Hyman Bloom of the female corpse, which I always liked. And I got two Zerbes including *Job*, a wonderful painting. You and I disagree on this, but I thought this represented them well. I was never enthusiastic enough about their work to form a large collection of it.

CG This is the first time that I'm hearing this. To be honest, I'm astonished. Those are such important acquisitions. The Bloom female corpse is a major picture, and one of the great pieces in the Lane collection. What was your role in that? The *Job* is also a great Zerbe. How did that fall in place?

TS There they were in the Lane collection. Very few pictures were on the walls (of his home). He had a storage area in his house, like in a museum, where everything was on racks. I should pull out for you from my archive a couple of earlier proposals. I would write to him and say we would like these sixty or seventy pictures. He would write back and say, "You're an idiot." (laughing) So I would start again. I can't exactly remember the sequence.

I don't think he used that word, but he would say you're on the wrong track. I was asking for too much of this, and not enough of that. I wasn't doing well enough by Sheeler, say, or Dove. Honestly, I forget the details of that.

I'm looking for my catalogue of the Lane Collection. He bought the Bloom from Durlacher Brothers in 1958. That was a pretty late acquisition. By then he had mostly stopped.

CG He never bought a work by Jack Levine.

TS No. He didn't like figurative painting. He was interested in abstract painting.

CG Aren't Bloom and Zerbe figurative?

TS Well, ah, yes. That's interesting. So, I don't know. Basically, Lane was very much an abstraction guy, but he must have seen the abstract strengths of Bloom and Zerbe. Levine was an excellent painter, but didn't have that same sense of underlying abstraction. It's possible that's how Lane viewed it.

CG Did you see the MFA's Bloom show?

TS My protégée Erica E. Hirshler did it.

CG Did it change your thinking about Bloom?

TS She did a fantastic job, and I also saw the Bloom show at the Alexander Gallery in New York. I read Erica's book very carefully. She made the best possible case for Bloom. I took a lot of different people through that show trying to get people to look at it.

CG The question is, did it change your opinion of the artist?

TS It enriched my view. There were a lot of paintings I had never seen before. It didn't change the way I would rank him.

CG Okay, how do you rank him?

TS I rank him as a very interesting, not quite great, painter, because of his local background, absolutely worth showing at the MFA, and worth acquiring.

CG When you were a curator at the Fogg Art Museum, did you ever visit the prints and drawings room and view the juvenilia of Bloom and Levine? As teenagers they were students at Harvard of Denman Ross.

TS I did. They were both terrific draftsmen.

CG When you were a Fogg curator, why was it never discussed to show that work?

TS I thought there were better things to show.
   (Hirshler included some of the Fogg drawings in her Bloom exhibition.)

CG You were interested in the group of Northampton realists.

TS I'm glad you noticed that. They were worth noting and recording. The realism that Gregory Gillespie (1936–2000) and others practiced shouldn't be forgotten. I have great respect for abstract art, but I don't think it's fair or right to neglect talented people like that. They were very honest and dedicated artists.

CG Greg was a genius of his generation. No less so, his first wife, Frances Cohen Gillespie (1939–1998). Also in Northampton were Jane Lund (B. 1939), Randall Deihl (B. 1946), and Scott Prior (B. 1949).

TS I got a great Scott Prior of his wife, *Nanny and Rose* (1983) on their porch.

CG You acquired a group portrait by Randall Deihl.

TS That painting, *Lust for Life*, is a great visual summary of those artists. I got to know them. They are connected to Boston. In a way, they were local artists and homogeneous enough a group to make sense of. I didn't see anything like that in Boston.

CG I was embedded with the Boston art world and greatly disagree. Did you look at Henry Schwartz (1917–2009), Gerry Bergstein (B. 1947), Bob Ferrandini, and Domingo Barreres?

TS I didn't think much of Schwartz's work, but I liked Bergstein's. He's absolutely one of the best Boston painters. I had one in the exhibition of Boston collectors.

CG You're holding up the catalogue.

TS In this catalogue (*Boston Collects*, 1986) you see Graham Gund owning some fabulous works. Some of the best artists in America, including Frank Stella (B. 1936) at his absolute best. He owns a great Jasper Johns (B. 1930) a couple of (Mark) Rothkos (1903–1970). He was after big game.
(For the MFA's 150th, Gund gave a Rothko to the museum.)

CG Gund, and wealthy collectors like Eli Broad (whose collection was shown at the MFA), did nothing to establish the career and reputation of the artists they acquired. When they bought work, it went to the highest bidder. Compare that to say, Robert Scull, who bought from studios and established the market for Pop artists. There was great resentment when he cashed in on that body of work. Like Charles Saatchi he used the money to refinance collecting the next generation.

Dorothy and Herbert Vogel were people of modest means who filled an apartment with works of minimalism. The artists became their friends. What they acquired for a pittance became priceless. They were true collectors. Their collection went to the National Gallery.

Karolik and Lane were risk takers. They were ahead of the curve. They were taste makers who made the MFA what it is today.

TS You're absolutely right. What Karolik and Lane did is hard to imagine. Don't forget that Lane did it again when he discovered photography in the late 1960s. He formed the greatest private collection of photography in the world.

CG What about the Wagstaff collection?

(Samuel J. Wagstaff, Jr. [1921–1987] was a curator, patron, and collector. In 1973, with the assistance of his lover Robert Mapplethorpe, he believed that art photography was significantly undervalued. Over the next decade, he assembled one of the most important private collections of photographs in the world. He sold his collection to the J. Paul Getty Museum in 1984.)

TS Sam was a very good collector and adventurous in later decades. Lane was there in the late 1960s. So, they are very different. I love the Wagstaff collection. In collecting, how a few people get into things before anyone else does, is one of the great mysteries.

CG Do you believe that the museum has an obligation to collect the artists of Boston? This has been the case in other cities: Chicago, New York, or LA. That in turn enhances the national reputations of artists and communities.

TS I know that's your favorite subject. I admire what you've done with that. The Boston artists need a champion, and you, Sinclair Hitchings (1933–2018, Boston Public Library), and some others filled that role admirably. (Marjorie) Jerry Cohn was the long-time print curator at Harvard. She spent a lot of time going to see local artists and buying prints. That was a fantastic, wonderful thing. The local printmakers were connected and recognized. Their works are now in Harvard's distinguished collection.

For me, I had limited responsibility in contemporary art for a short time. During that period, I wanted to acquire the best available modern artists. I had a brief opening to do that. Buying Boston School painters wasn't on my agenda. Sorry to say.

CG I liked your comment that you were a big game hunter. There's nothing wrong with that.

TS Boston had so far to catch up. Still has.

CG That game wasn't big because you made it big. It was already big. You just had a big rifle.

TS I had a nice-sized rifle. The 1980s was a great moment in time. Works by great artists could still be bought for a few hundred thousand dollars or less. Like

Warhol, Lichtenstein, Richter; those works cost millions now.

CG Does that describe the (Anselm) Kiefer (B. 1945, *Untitled*, 1984)?

TS We got that (from Marian Goodman Gallery) for about $70,000. At the time, that was a ton of money. I don't think the (Georg) Baselitz (B. 1938) was much more.

CG In my 1984 interview with Jan Fontein, I quoted from a then recent Boston *Globe* article with MFA curator Amy Lighthill. She stated, "You can buy twenty Doug Andersons (B. 1954) for the price of one work by Chuck Close (B. 1940)." Who hired Amy?

TS I did.

CG If you describe me as a champion of Boston artists, she certainly had that role. She was close to artists and the community.

TS Amy is a very wonderful person. As you say, she was very dedicated to artists. But in retrospect, hiring her was a mistake of mine. I could have hired anybody. When I met Amy, I was so excited. She seemed good. I should have looked for a better-trained, more intellectual, young modernist. It wasn't Amy's fault at all. She did well, and was nice to work with. I feel badly about this, but I put her in a position she wasn't quite equipped for. Looking back, what it meant for history, I didn't do her a great service, or the museum.

On the other hand, she did a wonderful show of Sean Scully (B. 1945). He is a very tough painter whose reputation continues to rise. She also did a very good Leon Golub (1922–2004) exhibition. Those are two excellent shows that Ken (Moffett) would never have done. Ones I wouldn't have thought of doing myself.

CG Wasn't she close to the Northampton group? Wasn't it through Amy that the museum acquired Gillespie's *Imaginary Pregnancy*?

TS I don't think so, though it's possible. I went several times to see Greg and his wife Peggy. I don't remember Amy being part of that. But I could be wrong.

CG I had negotiated with Nielsen gallery to curate an exhibition of Gillespie's psychedelic paintings. They didn't sell, but it was very interesting work, and I was excited about showing it. Just before the show, he died (suicide), and the project was cancelled.

TS That was such a shock, and I still remember when I heard about it. Did you see the show we did with Greg and Fran's work?

([*Life as Art, Paintings by Gregory Gillespie and Frances Cohen Gillespie, 2003–2004.*] From a press release, "In November 2002, the Harvard University Art Museums established the department of American Art at the Fogg Art Museum and appointed Theodore E. Stebbins, Jr., as its first curator of American art. The exhibition is organized by Stebbins, along with his wife, Susan Ricci Stebbins, an independent scholar; both shared personal and professional relationships with the Gillespies.")

CG I was close to Fran and included her in a 1988 traveling exhibition *Here's Looking at You: Contemporary New England Portraits* (James Aponovich, Gerry Bergstein, Mira Cantor, Randall Deihl, Elsa Dorfman, Frances Cohen Gillespie, Jane Lund, Scott Prior, Suzanne Vincent, Kelly Wise, and David Zaig.)

The painting by Frances was *Leah-Rome*, which she sold to Ellen Poss. She had started it in 1985 and kept working on it until the last minute. Just before her untimely death, she formed a relationship with a scientist. She seemed to have reached real happiness. I'm so pleased that you acquired a painting (*Purple Gloxinia*) for the MFA.

TS When my wife and I were in Rome, she was spending a year there at The American Academy and we got to know her well.

CG You talk about that two-year window of collecting for the MFA. How did that come about? You expanded your portfolio from Heade to Kiefer.

TS My introduction to art started in 1960–1965 with Robert Neuman (1926–2015), Albert Alcalay (1917–2008), and Pace Gallery, which Arne Glimcher started (on Newbury Street) in Boston in the 1960s. That's when I was attending Harvard Law School. I immediately met these painters. I still like the work of Bob Neuman who is a very underrated Boston painter. The sculptor Mirko was also at Harvard.

I had background and enthusiasm in the contemporary field. I had worked with Bill Lane, which was all modern art. There was a lot of pressure on Fontein that the contemporary program wasn't going anywhere. At some point, he asked me to take it over. I'm glad I did it, but I regret that Ken Moffett (1934–2016) was treated badly by the MFA.

So, there I was, and John Walsh had left (to head the Getty Museum). What you should ask me is, "Where did you get the money to buy Warhol and Kiefer?" When Walsh left, I became head of the paintings department. European and American painting were in one department. Then I also became head of contemporary art. So, it was at my discretion how to spend the acquisitions money for paintings.

I spent it to get the best for the museum. I spent it on Kiefer, Gerhard Richter (B. 1932), Francesco Clemente (B. 1952), Ellsworth Kelly (1923–2015). I bought a great Joseph Stella (1877–1946) of the Brooklyn Bridge, Warhol, Alice Neel (1900–1984) *Linda Nochlin and Her Daughter Daisy*. I acquired works by California artists like Joan Brown (1938–1990) and Robert Hudson (B. 1938).

CG Can we talk about the museum's politics at that time? There was a lot of pressure on Fontein and dissatisfaction with his overall performance and administrative skills. There was talk of a tearful breakdown during a trustee's meeting. When I did an interview with him in 1984, he was then 59 years of age. He was surprised when I asked his plans after retirement. He wanted to know where I heard that?

In fact, he was gone three years later. I heard that the plan was for Jan to be forced out and that Walsh would become director. It came as a surprise when Walsh departed for the Getty. So, arguably, Jan survived a bit longer.

Fontein left earlier than he could or should have. When Walsh went to the Getty, Clementine Brown (MFA PR) said to me, "He'll be back in a couple of years." If he could be MFA director, why would he want to go to the Getty? Walsh was the presumptive heir at the MFA, and that was a lot of pressure on Fontein.

TS That's quite accurate. John was a very attractive, well-spoken guy. He was well liked and respected. He did good shows, Chardin, and others at the MFA. He was talked about as the future director. There was no question about that. That must have made Jan nervous, though he was a pretty secure guy. Everyone assumed that Jan would leave in a year or so and that John would become director. Then he suddenly left for the Getty.

CG Around that time great pictures by Manet and Cézanne were showing up in the galleries as loans from a private collection. I investigated and found that they were acquired by a Boston billionaire, William I. Koch. They were acquired through his foundation. I pulled the tax records at the charity desk of the attorney general. The documents revealed that Walsh, while an MFA curator, was paid some $25,000 annually as a consultant. We reported it in the *Patriot Ledger*. I called for comment and asked Fontein if he knew of this arrangement? He said that he did, which greatly surprised me. By then, Walsh had just been appointed to head the Getty.

TS Fontein did know. That arrangement had to be cleared by the director and Howard Johnson, the chairman of the board. I remember the discussion. They Okay'd it. So, you were wrong on that one.

CG Was that arrangement ethical?

TS I'm too close to John to have an opinion about that.

CG You say that everyone knew about it.

TS Howard and Jan knew about it. Beyond that, I don't know who knew.

CG You came up in my interview with (art dealer) Mario Diacono. He didn't speak well of the Boston art world, to which he made few, if any, sales, but praised your interest and support. (Purchase of a painting by Ross Bleckner.)

TS It's so sad. One of the great tragedies of Boston is that they missed the boat, not only on Mario, but countless other aspects of modern art; anything made after the Armory Show of 1913. I told Jan, "It's not too late," this was the early 1980s. "It's not too late to rectify our position in the modern art world. In that field we are about the 60th or 70th ranked museum in America. It's embarrassing. For the next decade all of the museum's acquisition funds should be spent on modern art. Fontein said 'Oh my god. The curators would kill me. The trustees would kill me. I could never do that.'"

CG You actually had that conversation?

TS Yes, basically, for the two years when I was in charge, that's what I did. Then Kathy Halbreich (from MIT's List Visual Arts Center) was appointed curator of contemporary art, soon followed by Trevor Fairbrother. They didn't have the funds I had, and Jan didn't make the effort to get it for them.

CG You said that Jan was helpful to you in terms of acquisitions.

TS He loved objects. He liked people. He loved collecting. The director is all powerful. If he doesn't like your proposal, it's dead in the water. It doesn't go to the trustees unless the director approves. Jan approved everything I proposed. He understood it and wasn't just rubber stamping. With Lane I said, "I've got this great collector who I've visited a couple of times. He's been badly hurt by the museum and needs to know we're serious." A month later I drove Jan and Howard Johnson out to Bill Lane's house. We came hat-in- hand to say that we were sorry about that happened before. We're here to say we love you, and we love your collection. Jan was an active guy.

CG Of the 400 works you acquired, how many were from Lane?

TS The Lane collection included a hundred works.

There are only two reasons to acquire something. You're adding to strength or filling in gaps. You always use one of those two arguments when trying to persuade the trustees. I tried to do both.

You criticized acquiring Benson, Tarbell, and those people. They were Brahmins without a doubt, but they could produce. Three quarters of their paintings are pretty bad paintings. I was after the top five percent, and the MFA didn't have their very best work. I felt it was my duty to acquire them. Some we got through gifts. Some we purchased.

CG If they were the best Boston artists of their generation, why would you not extend collecting to the next generation?

TS We already had that discussion. I don't know. We already talked about that.

CG You're not going to budge.

TS No. I would like to please you, but I would do the same again. Someone like Hyman Bloom doesn't have the national or international legs. He doesn't have the grandeur of a great artist. He literally lays out everything in front of your eyes. What the art world is looking for is subtlety and abstraction, complexity. With Bloom it's very interesting, beautiful, and powerful. But he doesn't leave anything to the imagination. He seems to me to be a follower of Soutine, and not a modernist in any way. He didn't grow over the years. You and I just see that differently. I admire the paintings, but don't see them as deserving of a national or international reputation.

If you go to Chicago, you will see a whole gallery of Ivan Le Lorraine Albright (1897 –1983). He's sort of Chicago's Hyman Bloom. He's a better painter and deserves to have paintings on view at the Museum of Modern Art. Bloom doesn't quite reach that level in my view. That's how I see it.

CG Boston dropped the ball on supporting its (post war) artists. Bloom's reputation today would be different if the MFA and ICA did more to support its artists. There were Bloom and Boston expressionist shows from the ICA of Stephen Prokopoff, to deCordova, Danforth Museum, and Fuller Museum of Art.

If the MFA provides limited support for Boston's artists, how can we expect museums beyond the city limits to take an interest?

TS MoMA gave Bloom every chance in the world. They showed him in 1942. He was shown at the Venice Biennale. The art world goes to Venice and they all saw the work. There were traveling retrospectives in the 1950s and not enough people saluted. In Boston, or out of Boston, Bloom had every chance. He wasn't neglected, but not enough people reacted.

CG Let's turn our attention to the relationship between the MFA and ICA. In the 1950s, when Thomas Messer was director of the ICA, there was a plan to merge with the MFA as a department of modern/contemporary art. Messer would become an MFA curator. He advised on some acquisitions, which have held up well. This is discussed in an *Archives of American Art* interview between Messer and Bob Brown. Rathbone killed that.

TS This comes up every decade or two. I'm sure that Rathbone killed it for a whole variety of reasons we could talk about. Boston is a richer place with both institutions. You can't attach a small adventurous institution onto a larger cumbersome one. It doesn't work. It's better that they didn't combine. Look at what Jill Medvedow has accomplished.

CG Had the merger gone through, the MFA would have had a strong modernist program a generation before launching one in 1971. The few acquisitions that Messer was involved with give a glimpse of what might have been.

Rathbone insisted on being his own curator, which was hit and miss for modern art and mostly miss for contemporary art. Because he knew Max Beckmann (1884–1950), he had a taste for German expressionism.

In general, particularly the Busch-Reisinger Museum, and what (James Sachs) Plaut and Messer showed at the ICA, Boston's taste was for Northern European art.

Moffett was appointed in 1971. I quote you as telling me in the 1970s, "The MFA recognizes 20th century art now that it's almost over." Do you recall saying that?

TS No, but it sounds so good, you can keep quoting me.

CG You worked with David Ross on The Binational. It was a rare instance when the MFA and ICA collaborated.

(In 1988 the MFA and ICA jointly presented *The Binational: German Art of the Late 1980s/American Art of the Late 1980s* in cooperation with the Stadtische Kunsthalle and the Kunstsammlung Nordrhein-Westfalen of Dusseldorf and with support from the Mass. Council on the Arts and Humanities, AT&T Foundation, and the National Endowment for the Arts. The multi-venue exhibitions presented emerging American and German artists. The MFA team included Stebbins and Trevor Fairbrother, David Ross, Elizabeth Sussman, and David Joselit comprised the ICA's.)

TS I don't remember it in detail, but it was an extraordinary experience. David Ross was a totally fun, charismatic person to work with. He connected us with an excellent German team headed by Jurgen Harten. Later, he had a Pollock/Siqueiros show and I persuaded him to add (photographer) Edward Weston (1886–1958). I sent a selection (from the Lane collection) and they fit in beautifully with the abstract painters.

CG Let's talk about Pollock's *Troubled Queen* (1945, acquired 1984).

TS I saw it in a gallery I had never been to before (Stephen Hahn). I thought, that's an ugly, powerful, important painting.

CG When *Lavender Mist* was turned down, Ken later bought a smaller drip painting (*Number 10*, 1949), which he maintained was a very good Pollock.

TS Yes, but it was not great enough by itself to show a major American artist. Here was a 1945 painting with a bit of drip in it and two anguished figures. I had to have it. That really enriched the collection and linked Pollock to earlier expressionist painters.

CG I recall being shocked when it just showed up hanging in the museum. I wondered where it came from. The wall label read, "Charles H. Bayley Picture and Painting Fund [and Gift of Mrs. Albert J. Beveridge and Juliana Cheney Edwards Collection, by exchange." In exchange for what I wondered?

(By exchange, 28 November 1984, with Stephen Hahn Gallery: Two works by Pierre Auguste Renoir; *Young Girl Reading*, 16 x13 and *A Woman with Black Hair*, pastel on paper, 23 x 18 , and Claude Monet's painting from 1884, *Autumn Scene*, 24 x 29 ,)

TS The *Globe* wrote an editorial criticizing the purchase. It was the only time I got bad press, but the art world applauded.

CG I was at the *Patriot Ledger* where my editor, Jon Lehman, and I were about to post the Pollock story. We got a call from Clementine Brown (PR director for the MFA). In a friendly manner she said, "Charlie, I heard that you have been poking around. What are you up to?" Jon nodded that we should ask her for confirmation of the deaccessions we had uncovered. She said she would get back to us so we waited to hear from her. The *Ledger* is an afternoon paper and we missed the deadline waiting for her call.

The next morning the story ran in the *Globe*. She had betrayed years of trust working together. We ran a second-day story. That Sunday, the *Globe* posted the editorial you were mentioned in. They acknowledged that it had been a *Patriot Ledger* story.

TS Damn. You should have called me. We had sixteen Renoirs and that picture was never shown. To me, the one I sold was the least of them. Actually, it was a great trade.

CG At the time, the question that I asked was about trading apples for oranges. In this case, French impressionism, for American abstract expressionism. Is that kosher?

TS Of course. Why not? They are all paintings. I would have traded a Chinese painting, if I could have laid my hands on one. (At the time, Stebbins was the museum's combined curator of painting. Had there been a curator of European painting, it is unlikely the three French impressionist works would be sold for one American painting.)

CG Did you have a relationship with Barry Gaither?

TS Some. I always respected him. I went there, National Center of Afro-American Artists on Elm Hill Avenue in Roxbury.

CG In addition to important exhibitions, Barry also made acquisitions, including important Boston, African American artists. Did you ever visit Alan Rohan Crite (1910–2007)?

TS No. I knew about his work, Boston street scenes. I thought it was interesting, but not MFA quality, top-ranked art.

CG Of course a lot of work has now come with the John Axelrod collection of 67 works by African American artists.

You were involved in negotiations to retain a half stewardship of the Gilbert Stuart portraits of George and Martha Washington.

TS I'm glad you asked about that. I had just arrived at the MFA and learned that a couple of years before, the Athenaeum asked if the MFA would mind if they sold George and Martha? (They had been a long-term loan to the MFA.) John Coolidge, who was then president of the museum, said, "No, we don't mind." I got there and they were about to sell them to the National Portrait Gallery. I said, "This is outrageous. They're Boston treasures." They had been purchased for Boston by something called The George Washington Trust. It was illegal, outrageous, immoral, and unwise. I created a huge ruckus. Half of the Athenaeum trustees were also MFA trustees. It was a very hard battle to fight. What resulted is joint custody of the paintings.

CG You have earned your art combat medals and wear them well.

Maxim and Margaret Karolik donated American art to the MFA. Courtesy of the Museum of Fine Arts, Boston.

MFA curator Theodore E. Stebbins, Jr. Giuliano photo.

William H. and Saundra Lane donated American art and photography to the MFA. Courtesy of the Museum of Fine Arts, Boston.

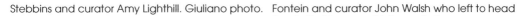

Stebbins and curator Amy Lighthill. Giuliano photo.   Fontein and curator John Walsh who left to head the Getty Museum. Giuliano photo.

Stebbins and MFA director, Jan Fontein. Giuliano photo.

Contemporary Curator
Amy Lighthill's Brave New Works

As the second curator of Contemporary Art for the MFA, Amy Lighthill had a brief, but impactful tenure. She followed Kenworth Moffett, who launched the department with limited resources. He was a tenured professor at Wellesley College and was hired by Perry T. Rathbone to a half-time position. He was eased out, based on his narrow focus on formalism and abstract art. Reporting to Ted Stebbins, Lighthill brought a focus on social justice, feminism, and support for Boston artists.

Charles Giuliano You were with the Museum of Fine Arts for two and a half years. Prior to that you were associated with Pat Hills and the Boston University Art Gallery.

Amy Lighthill Prior to the Art History Department taking over the BU Art Gallery, it was run by BU's fine arts program. For reasons that I don't know, the fine arts faculty didn't want to run it anymore. Or the administration decided. I worked with Pat Hills running the gallery program. She was the logical person, as she came to BU from a curatorship at the Whitney Museum. She selected me as the first grad student to manage the gallery.

That was in 1979 or 1980. I'm not sure. I had finished my master's degree and was starting on a PhD. I was feeling more likely to go into museum work rather than become an academic and scholar. I was excited by the opportunity to work with and learn from her. I did that for two years.

CG What was your thesis topic?

AL Rockwell Kent's prints and political leaning. His WPA murals were of interest in that regard. He was eccentric and contrarian, also a compatriot, if not a member of, the Communist Party. By the time I started at the gallery I was doing the doctoral course work, but it became clear that I loved being in the gallery and working with artists. I stayed on the second year to continue with the gallery, which was my job.

I was offered a job organizing traveling exhibitions by the Ohio Arts Council in Columbus. Not long after I went there, it was clear that the person who offered me the job had misrepresented the financial stability of the Council. They wanted me to do three jobs instead of one.

Casting about, I took a job at Kent State running their art gallery. I spent one year there and began to look around, as the gallery was very underfunded. I did what I could and got a grant.

CG When did you start at the MFA?

AL I started in June of 1983, and I left at the beginning of January in 1986. I was there only two and a half years.

CG Can you describe to me what were your position and duties?

AL First, I would like to describe how I got the job. I had taken a course with Ted Stebbins while in graduate school. It was a seminar that met at the MFA.

I did some research for him on a picture that turned out to be useful. He was impressed and stayed in touch with me. He came to the BU Art Gallery to see what I was doing.

When I was at Kent State, I wrote to him saying that I was looking for another job. He called me and said, "I think we are going to have an opening in contemporary art here at the MFA."

He brought me in to interview with Jan Fontein in the spring of 1983. The job was assistant curator of contemporary art. I was only talking to Ted and yet Ken Moffett (curator of contemporary art) was still at the museum. He was relegated to the basement with his assistant, Debbie.

Ken was not involved in this at all. Ted said, "Well, the situation is in flux." The museum was in a position to deal more actively in contemporary art, which he defined as anything after 1945…Ken would be doing what Ken did. I understood that it was an awkward situation.

CG When did Ken leave?

AL From when I came, six months to a year later. I was introduced to him, but I worked upstairs in the paintings department. That was the time when, as you know, Ted was running all things painting. It was an interesting and usual time to be at the MFA. It was a unique situation with Ted running such a vast empire. (Three departments: European painting, American painting, and 20th century art.) That was unprecedented.

CG Did you go through storage and take measure of the depth of the contemporary collection?

AL I went through storage periodically. I went with my assistant, sometimes with Ted, and sometimes with Trevor (Fairbrother). It depended on why we were going.

CG Can you give me an idea of the collection at that time? Was there anything other than Color Field painting?

AL Not really. I don't remember much else post-1945.

CG Did you see all the Morris Louis Color Field paintings?

AL I'm not sure that I saw all of them. We did look at them and I know that there was concern about their condition. There were some twenty or so, and some of them may have been out on loan.

CG What was defined as your domain? Did it entail outreach to Boston and New England artists? In particular, I am interested in where the Northampton group comes in.

AL It was never clear. Ted had a lot of freedom and Jan's backing. He was enjoying that sense of openness and possibilities. He was moving into an area which was quite away from 19th century and the luminists.

He was interested in modern art, and I say that advisedly, because I don't think he had been following contemporary art. He was relying on his eye, and I don't think, at that point, he had a clear sense of the parameters. As time went on, it became clear that he wanted to "fill in the gaps" to use his terminology. His focus was on acquiring "masterworks."

CG On his watch the museum acquired an Anselm Kiefer.

AL Yes. I recall that Ted got Senator John Heinz to buy that painting for us with funds from a foundation he had set up with his wife, Teresa (who later married John Kerry after Heinz's death). We also bought Pollock's *Troubled Queen*. I had ambivalent feelings about that.

(*Troubled Queen*, 1945, was acquired in 1984. There is also a print, *Untitled*, 1951, two *Psychoanalytic Drawings*, which were created during therapy sessions and sold by Boston's Nielsen Gallery, and a 1939 painted ceramic bowl, *Flight of Man*.)

CG What do you mean by that?

AL I thought it was a very fine Pollock, but came at such a huge cost. (Deaccession of two Renoirs and a Monet.) Then, basically, we had the one Pollock. We used a combination of cash and deaccessions.

CG Ted defends the acquisition. When I spoke to (former director) Alan Shestack, he said that on his watch he would never have made that swap.

AL I agree with Ted on that point. We had a lot of Monet and Renoir. But my point is that it was also a half million in cash. That much money was a big commitment at that time. I felt, was it worth all this to get this one Pollock? It was not going to make us a destination for Pollock. It felt like chasing, and getting, too little too late.

CG Think how different the Moffett legacy would have been with *Lavender Mist*. It would have attracted donations from major collectors. Ken passed on Pop art and minimalism. Trevor Fairbrother later acquired a Warhol.

(*Red Disaster* a 1963/1985 diptych acquired in 1985. The museum, in 1986, acquired a number of works on paper, and since then, other works, including album covers, silk screen portraits, an *Oxidation* painting, and Polaroid photographs.)

AL Trevor pushed for that.

CG What was his role at that time?

AL He was in the paintings department and Sargent was his thing. He was trained in American art, but not contemporary. He was working for Ted in 19th and early 20th century American art.

He was fun to work with, and I liked him. I was also a colleague of Carol Troyen. She worked in 19th century American paintings. We were all working for Ted in the paintings department.

There was a certain amount of blurriness of responsibility. Trevor would be drawn in when Ted needed him or where Trevor's particular interest was, like Warhol. Occasionally Trevor and I went to New York together and looked at things. Sometimes Ted had things for Trevor to do. That happened increasingly during my second year, as things shifted for the worse between me and Ted.

CG Shestack lured Kathy Halbreich from MIT as contemporary curator. Trevor was assigned to work under her. After a relatively brief time, she left to become director of the Walker Art Center. Trevor took her position, and worked well with Shestack, who supported his exhibitions program, including a major exhibition of props created by Robert Wilson for theatre productions. Shestack told me that he prioritized exhibitions over acquisitions.

When Malcolm Rogers became director, he attempted to micro manage the contemporary program. When Trevor opted to leave, Cheryl Brutvan was appointed to do Roger's bidding.

You worked with the ICA.

AL A little bit. Not a lot, just the *Boston Now: Emerging Mass Painters and Sculptors* that we did together. Occasionally, I did things with them, like jurying a show with David Ross. Elizabeth (Sussman) and I had planned a trip to Montreal to look at contemporary art with Ted, but he bagged on us at the last minute, and we didn't go. Now and then I would run into them. Sometimes we had meetings together, but *Boston Now* was the only thing we planned together.

As you know, I was very interested in showing local artists. We all thought it was a great way to broaden exposure and deepen the show by including both painting and sculpture at the two venues.

CG Give me an idea of Boston galleries and artists you were interested in.

AL I tried to stay current and went to open studios, when possible. Of course, artists wanted me to come to their studios, and I tried to do as many as I possibly could. Some of the artists became friends. I was interested in a lot of work being made in Boston. Ruth Bauer, the landscape painter. I liked Mela Lyman's work. Adam Cvijanovic was young, already very talented. I loved Tim Harney from Beverly. Clara and Bill Wainwright became dear friends. I think Clara's work is beautiful, but I also greatly admire how much she accomplished working collaboratively with different communities around Boston. I was close with the painter, sculptor, and author, Leslie Sills, as well. I thought both Todd and Judy McKie made wonderful work. Marcy Hermansader of southern Vermont, I'll count as local, and she became a friend. She continues to make delicate, mystical, excellent work, which deserves much more recognition.

CG Did you acquire any of those artists?

AL This was a frustration for me. There were some people, local artists, whose collectors offered us gifts. Dealers also said they were able to make it happen. One offered-work was by Ruth Bauer, another was by Roger Kizik. We were offered a really good James Aponovich.

CG The museum acquired an Aponovich, the nude portrait of his daughter Ana. She was then a child going through chemotherapy and later recovered.

AL Yes, that's the one I was thinking of. I'm not sure whether that happened on my watch or after. (*Portrait of Ana*, 1984, was acquired in 1985. Amy left in early January 1986.) I loved that painting and wanted it to happen.

CG Was the Gregory Gillespie, *Peggy Seated: Imaginary Pregnancy* (1982–1983) your acquisition (in 1984)?

AL Yes. It was a struggle. That was a hard sell. There was worry on the part of some because of Greg's unorthodox painting method. The concern was with possible conservation issues down the line. There was an internal struggle. We took it to the conservation department. I talked with his dealer, Bella Fishko of Forum Gallery. The painting cost $80,000, as I recall, which was a lot.

At first, I wasn't going to be allowed to talk about the picture with the 20th century visiting committee. Jan was talking with them, then at the last minute, I was told that I could come and talk about it—to say why we wanted it. I recall Jan giving me a cue that I could mention the conservation issues, and that we thought we could handle anything that arose.

(The museum acquired *Purple Gloxinia* (1982–1983) by Frances Cohen Gillespie, the artist's first wife, in 1984.)

CG Did you have a hand in the 1983 acquisition of Alice Neel's *Linda Nochlin and Daisy*? Was that you?

AL Yes, that was me. I knew Alice from the Boston University Art Gallery and a show organized by Pat Hills. I think it's one of her best works, a comment on the changing face of art history, as well as a great portrait. When Alice, who looked so grandmotherly then, came to give a talk at the MFA, she told the audience I reminded her of Annie Sprinkle, a stripper she knew!

CG Ted takes credit for the Gillespie acquisitions.

AL I checked that out with Peggy Gillespie, who confirmed that I introduced Ted to Greg.

CG Were you involved with the Doug Anderson acquisition?

(*Lovers Will Contrast Their Emotion in Times of Crisis* from the *Perfect Mom* series, 1981, acquired in 1983. Represented by Stux Gallery, the Boston artist was included in the Whitney Biennial.)

AL I don't recall how we got it. That was around the *Emerging Mass Painters* show so I must have been involved. My recollection is that we bought it.

CG There is a quote from you in the media that you can buy twenty-five Doug Andersons for the price of one Baselitz.

AL (laughing) Yeah, that sounds like something I would have said. (still laughing)

It's a brash, unvarnished comment, an un-nuanced way of describing an issue. But it's true, and you have to decide what you are going to do when collecting contemporary art. I thought it was better to take a chance by buying younger artists whose work was inexpensive if we believed in them. Let history sort it out.

You have to be brave and accept the fact that you're going to be criticized. Later you find that some acquisitions haven't held up. There are tons of works like that in the basement of the MFA. Things go in and out of fashion and a museum is, to a point, a repository of culture. If a museum is willing to collect the art of its time, it has to be willing to take a chance.

CG You were reporting to Ted, and contemporary art was a relatively unknown area for him. It was a stretch that his domain was expanded from Heade to Baselitz. The same might be said of Trevor, whose training was Sargent and American Impressionism. These are examples of over-extended scholars. Ultimately, was that best for the museum which lacked strength in modern and contemporary art? The Met, by comparison, had Henry Geldzahler, who was in the thick of it.

AL Clearly the MFA was not ready to make a full-fledged commitment to contemporary art, but was prepared to dip its toe in. Before we got started, I'm not sure that Ted was much involved. He was buying things.

CG For himself or the museum?

AL Both. Occasionally, he would say, "I like these two works. I will buy one and buy the other for the museum." It was a gray area. Like many curators of his generation who came from wealthy families, he was a collector.

CG What did Ted think of your interests in acquisitions?

AL The first year he was very positive. He liked my show ideas and approved of purchases I wanted to make. He wrote me at the end of that year that I had made "very, very few mistakes." Things shifted after *Emerging Mass Painters*, when I fell out of his favor. The show didn't get great reviews, and I think there was blowback. It was hard for him to withstand that. Our views had become more clearly differentiated, and he started saying to me that he didn't "trust my eye" anymore…

He felt I was out of my depth. However, the whole first year he was extremely pleased and positive. He wanted to move forward together "for many more years," he said.

We were able to do the first show, *Brave New Works*, in museum terms, in no time at all. I arrived in summer, and we had that show up in the later fall. I had never worked at a big museum, and I had no idea how unusual that was. It was very well received. Robert Taylor, the *Globe*'s art reviewer, described *Brave New Works* as "a brilliant curatorial debut."

It also included some local artists, as well as others from New York and California. The Massachusetts artists were Greg Amenoff (who had moved to

New York), Doug Anderson, Liz Awalt, Ruth Bauer, Greg Gillespie, Michael Mazur, William Beckman, and Paul Rahilly. In addition to the Massachusetts artists, it also included the Chicago artist Roger Brown—a great picture about Vietnam, which I hoped someone would buy for us, but it didn't happen. Nationally, it had Joan Brown, Leon Golub, Alice Neel, Lucas Samaras, Miriam Shapiro, Joan Snyder, Sydney Goodman, Robert Longo, Donald Sultan, Cy Twombly, and a few others.

I got the work from mostly from New York dealers, a couple in California, and some from Boston dealers. There were three Samaras' pastels. I liked his work a lot. His manipulated Polaroids were fantastic, and I loved his fabric work as well. Some of those works did end up in the permanent collection—Alice Neel and Joan Brown's paintings, in addition to Greg's.

Ted was very enthusiastic that year. He knew exactly what he was getting when he hired me. He was into it—up to the point where criticism came.

CG Can you describe the criticism of *Emerging Mass Painters*?

AL Generally, it was that we hadn't chosen the best painters out of the 787 who sent in slides. People quarreled with our choices. That it was a mish mash, and that we picked people that the critics didn't appreciate and didn't agree with. Basically, that's what it was. Every survey show of contemporary art faces this complaint.

CG At that time, what interest did you have in artists of diversity?

AL I wish I could say I had that already in my head as a pressing issue that I needed to focus on. I can't say that I did. I know that I was skewed toward things that were outside the mainstream. I was interested in the art of women, and pushed for their inclusion. I made a little bit of headway.

I was very much interested in breaking down barriers between media. I didn't understand the need for boundaries between say fiber art and craft. I was interested in seeing what I could do to ameliorate that. That was another kind of diversity. I think I was out in front on that one.

CG When I asked your interests at the time, you told me of wanting to do an exhibition of Pattern paintings.

AL There was an article by a group of younger artists, critics, and curators recently in the *Times* about the 25 most important art objects of the past century. It mentioned both Miriam Shapiro and Faith Wilding, a Boston painter, who was part of *Boston Now*. As it turned out, Wilding was one of the artists that Ted particularly disliked. Both of them were mentioned in a feminist context with Judy Chicago and Pattern painters.

CG You did a Leon Golub show.

AL Yes, I'm very proud of that. It was a struggle. I had met Leon through Pat Hills and thought his work was, though challenging, very important and powerful. At first Ted agreed when we started planning it. Then Ted and Jan changed their minds, I think because they thought the work was "too tough." It was a traveling show and we pulled out of it. It then opened with rave reviews, at which point the MFA became interested again. We had to scramble to get back into it.

CG Talking with Ted I have him saying that, in effect, he didn't think that there were any important contemporary Boston Artists.

AL (laughs) This is a note from Ted, May 7, 1985. "Amy, who are all these people anyway? Can you fill me in?"

It was about a lecture you gave at the Boston Public Library on Boston artists on May 5, 1985. The letter says "Charles Giuliano" then lists a bunch of Boston painters. You mentioned Jack Levine, Hyman Bloom, Dana Chandler, Trachtman, he didn't know the first name which is Arnie, Alex Gray, Doug Anderson, Paul Laffoley. Anyway about fifteen people. Ted didn't know them.

CG A lot of artists came to that slide lecture. It occurred because I was working closely with David Sutherland, who was doing a film on Jack Levine. Tess Cederholm, the BPL curator, was working with David.

CG It appeared that there was a lot of support for what you were doing at the MFA.

AL When I left the museum, I got a ton of notes from artists and dealers as well

CG Did you have any interest in the Boston Expressionists?

AL Gerry Bergstein and Henry Schwartz.

CG They are part of the lineage, but I'm referring to the first generation of Hyman

Bloom, Jack Levine, and Karl Zerbe.

AL Yes. At one point, Ted, Pam Allara, and I went to New Hampshire to see Hyman Bloom. We had been talking about a show of his work. Ted wasn't super keen. You talked with Ted about Bloom, as I recall. He was not willing to say that we (MFA) had done a poor job of serving Hyman Bloom.

CG He was more interested in the Boston Impressionists, particularly Frank W. Benson, than the Boston Expressionists.

AL Boston Expressionism wasn't Ted's cup of tea.

CG Stebbins offered Bloom a show and then withdrew. Sources have discussed with me having seen the letter to Bloom, which is best described as a carefully worded snub.

AL I'm looking at a draft of Ted's document from December 1984. It's a report on 20th century art at the MFA. I did some initial work, just to gather data for him. Ted was writing this as a way of pitching to the board and those who were interested in 20th century art, particularly in contemporary, what we needed to be buying.

He starts with European modernism, the Nabis, Fauve, Cubism. He is saying, "We have nothing, we have nothing." The Blue Rider, German expressionism. Then he comes to American painting, "We have excellent Ashcan School. We have excellent Stieglitz group." He says Social Realist and Regionalism, "Fair." His list only goes as far as Pop. Then he writes, "We must buy masterworks!"

Regarding boards: the general split was old money supporting the MFA, with new and Jewish money interested in the ICA.

CG You were junior on the curatorial ladder as well as female and Jewish. How did that factor for you? Were there other women curators to derive support from? Was there a women's caucus at the museum? What was the working environment? Who would you have lunch with?

AL There wasn't a lot of congeniality. I was friendly with Carol Troyen, but I didn't have lunch with her. I did feel rather isolated. When I got there, I was naive. I had had just two university gallery positions. This was a huge leap forward onto the Boston and national stage…

CG Was there anti-Semitism at the museum?

AL On a deep level, it seems clear when you look at who held the power and who didn't, in staff, board members, and art that was collected. Personally, I wasn't born Jewish. That entered my life subsequent to the art world... When we had the Leon Golub show, for whatever reason, Ted begged off from the opening dinner with Leon and his wife, Nancy (Spero). When we visited Hyman Bloom, he was really not interested. He often confused those two artists.

CG As I heard it, the idea of a Bloom show had been proposed by Pam Allara.

AL Probably, though I'm not certain of it. She was with us that day when Ted and I visited Hyman and Stella. I remember that the appointment was for two, so we ate our lunch in the car. As soon as we arrived, Hyman proposed that we go to his favorite restaurant. We looked at each other, went to the restaurant and had to eat a whole second meal...

There were people that I tried but failed to acquire for the museum. We were offered a beautiful Mary Frank called *Lovers* for $35,000. It's crime that we didn't get that. Ellen Poss, a psychiatrist, was married to Mitch Kapor. (He founded Lotus Development Corporation.) She was a collector and offered to help us buy a major work by Miriam Shapiro, the one I had in *Brave New Works*. At the time it was $30,000, and she offered to give us a third of the price. That didn't happen. I also desperately wanted to buy a Martin Puryear.

(In addition to a number of works on paper, the museum acquired a major Puryear sculpture, *Confessional*, 1996–2000 in 2012.)

That major Puryear was $13,000. I wanted to buy an Audrey Flack, *WWII (Vanitas)* (1977). I don't love all of her work, but that picture is amazing. We should have bought that picture, which is now in a private collection. But, again, how could there be a more Jewish picture than that? It combines memento-mori still life passages and an element of Holocaust victims depicted behind barbed wire. There was a beautiful Joan Snyder that I wanted called *Tell Me Any Way You Can*. I wish we had a Lucas Samaras.

CG Who was turning down these acquisitions?

AL I would present the offer. For the Miriam Shapiro, I told Ted that Ellen Poss would give us $10,000. We then needed $20,000 to buy the work. But then nothing would happen. It would just disappear. Those were some things that, sadly, we didn't get.

CG Matthew Teitelbaum discussed with me plans to display contemporary art throughout the museum. Cy Twombly sculptures, for example, will be shown in the Classical galleries. He is attempting to activate new ways of looking. We may, at last, be evolving into expanding legitimizing the art of our time in the context of a traditional, encyclopedic museum.

Lighthill at an MFA panel. Giuliano photo.

With Peter Sellers at an ICA event. Giuliano photo.

MFA conference (L. to R.) Lighthill, Jan Fontein, Ted Stebbins, David Ross. Giuliano photo.

Contemporary curator Amy Lighthill. Giuliano photo.

Director Alan Shestack Succumbed to Downturn

On April 14, 2020, Alan Shestack passed away at 81. From 1987 to 1993, he was director of the Museum of Fine Arts. He was notable as a mediator and problem solver. As director, he presided over twenty-six departments with an uneven distribution of resources and power. After the MFA, he was deputy director of The National Gallery. He also served as director of the Yale Art Gallery and Minneapolis Institute of Art.

There were highlights, like the blockbuster 1990 Monet exhibition. Support for contemporary art was a priority. Kathy Halbreich was an early hire to head the contemporary department. She soon left to become director of the Walker Art Museum, where she remained for sixteen years. He supported *The Binational: German Art of the Late 1980s/American Art of the Late 1980s*, a collaboration with the Institute of Contemporary Art. Shestack raised some $600,000 for the programming of Trevor Fairbrother who took over from Halbreich.

As I reported for *Art News*, he turned down the offer of a gift from Cambridge-based photographer Elsa Dorfman. It was a large-format Polaroid, double portrait of poet Allen Ginsberg, nude and clothed. He told me that he wouldn't acquire a work that he could not display. She died in 2020 before the opening of the MFA exhibition *Elsa Dorfman: Me and My Camera*. The museum owns other works by the artist.

By the end of his tenure, Shestack was contending with an economic downturn. He sought creative strategies to monetize the museum. This partly entailed establishing a twenty-year relationship to show a range of works from the MFA in Nagoya, Japan.

Ted Stebbins, who was the MFA's John Moors Cabot curator of American paintings while Shestack was director, said in a museum statement, "Alan was one of the finest people I have ever known. A superb scholar, a lover of all kinds of art, a person of the highest integrity, he also had a terrific sense of humor."

"Detroit, with a dominantly black community, came to realize that it needed a collection of African art," he told the audience during an inaugural address. "The hope was that groups of school children who came to the museum would relate to that work. In order to understand it, they would want to know more about it. They would be more interested in that, than say, a portrait of George III. Last year, in Minneapolis, I urged the acquisition of a very handsome Shoshone elk hide with pictographs, because Minneapolis sits in the largest concentration of Plains Indians in North America. I felt that we needed, not just one object, but many in the museum that Indian children could relate to. You couldn't bring in a group of Indian children from a reservation and just show them Italian baroque paintings. There are legitimate reasons for doing this."

If Shestack came to the museum with hopes of diversity, there were mixed results. He fought for change, but encountered resistance, as the *Globe* reported in his obituary. "I do not choose the board, of course; they choose me," he told the *Globe* in January 1991, "but I have certainly let them know my feeling that the board is a little homogenized…

"Nearly all the museum's department heads were white then as well." In the same interview, for a *Globe* report on the lack of diversity in the museum's staffing and holdings, Shestack noted that change occurs slowly at institutions steeped in tradition.

"We haven't been in the vanguard, I'm sad to say. But finally, museums are getting a little social conscience," he said, adding with a note of frustration, "I am a member of the American Civil Liberties Union. It's hard to be a liberal and lead an institution like this."

Shestack was the museum's first Jewish director. Matthew Teitelbaum, the second, is currently director of the museum. The museum had a legacy of racism and anti-Semitism. Shestack attempted to initiate change. Accusations of racism rocked the museum in 2019. Teitelbaum has been effective in facing them. Prior to coming to the MFA, he was an activist as director of the Art Gallery of Ontario in acquiring and displaying work by Canada's First Nations artists.

This is the first of several interviews with Shestack. It occurred in 1987 when he was new to the position. That is followed by one from 1992.

Charles Giuliano I attended your inaugural address. Can we pick up from there with an overview of coming to the museum at this time?

Alan Shestack The truth is very hard to define. Everyone has a different version of the past and any particular instance that has occurred. I'm not really sure I know the recent history of this museum in specific terms. I know where it stands at this moment. I'm not quite sure I know how it got to where it is; who made certain decisions or why.

There has been a recent spate of articles criticizing the museum. There was one three weeks ago. It seems that my arrival has been accompanied by a series of critical articles. They seem to be digging up problems of the past, including things that Walter Whitehill (1905–1978) said fifteen or twenty years ago, but not stating that he said them fifteen or twenty years ago. As far as the reader is concerned, they may have been uttered recently. It's a bit unfair in that respect.

The media is critical of the traditional, elitist image of the museum. I told my staff that, unlike Ronald Reagan, who was described as a Teflon President, we seem to be The Velcro Museum.

Problems that were legitimate fifteen or twenty years ago, no longer are, but stick because of the museum's reputation. Opinions lag reality for quite a long period, because frankly, I have not, in my very short tenure here, but also in my negotiations with the board when I was deciding if I wanted to come to this job, I have not sensed any elitism in terms of keeping anyone out of the museum or keeping the board pure. I have not sensed that at all.

I find the board here to be very much in line with boards of other major American museums. Its diversity, or lack thereof, is very much in line with how it is in most museums. Typically, trustees are people with money, civic pride, and jobs that allow them a lot of free time. As it is with most museums, I do not find the board in any way unusual.

As it is for every museum director in this country, there is an attempt for a proper balance between traditional values of art museums, and the new initiatives that museums have taken. Maintaining our integrity is going to be a tricky business.

For these initiatives, we have to find money because these museums are so expensive. The admission fee to this museum is, admittedly, a bit on the high side at $5 a ticket. The admissions pay for only a fifth of what it actually costs to run the museum. In other words, each visitor who walks through the door costs us $25. You derive that by taking the number of visitors and dividing into the annual budget.

Compared to other major museums, we get no money from the city, unlike The National Gallery, Met, Philadelphia, and Art Institute of Chicago. They all get substantial subsidies from their cities. This museum does not.

CG I believe the city helps to fund the program to bus school children to the museum.

(Then $60,000 annually,)

AS I wasn't aware of that. To be fully honest the Mass Council for the Arts and Humanities has been very generous of late, and that has been very heartening. When I walked through the door, the first thing I heard was a grant from them ($300,000) for the German show we are doing next year with the ICA, *The Binational: German Art of the Late 1980s/American Art of the Late 1980s.*

Compare that to $13 million a year the Met gets from New York City.

CG What's the annual budget of the MFA?

AS Twenty-six million dollars. We have to find that money. Marketing is part of the American way of life. But if we do it, that has to be done with integrity. We have to look at the quality of what we sell in the shop. I went down to the shop the other day, and didn't see anything objectionable…

No matter which direction we took, there would be room for criticism. This museum finally got on the bandwagon in the past fifteen or twenty years, and began to think about how do we survive into the 21st century? You can't do it the old way anymore. That speaks well for this museum.

CG What was the motivation for showing a corporation like Tiffany?

AS Tiffany has been a very classy company over the years and has employed the best designers. It's been at the forefront of design experimentation. We justify the exhibition based on the quality of the objects in the show. The fact that they were produced to be sold by a store, rather than an individual artist, is not an issue. I have no idea how it was decided to have that show. It was installed when I got here.

CG I understand that the Met turned it down.

AS That would have no impact on me. What they do makes no difference to decisions that we make. The National Gallery and Detroit chose to have it, as did San Francisco, and I think, Dallas. There were plenty of museums that chose to have it. I don't want to second-guess my predecessors.

Let me say this, though, about *Helga* (Andrew Wyeth). It's ironic that the MFA has been criticized for being stodgy and elitist, but the minute that it does a show that is bound to have a large audience, because it presents a beloved artist of the people, then we get accused of pandering to the public.

It can't go both ways. Either we're doing something useful for the public's good, indeed, a show that is bound to be mighty popular and we're not stodgy. Or we're stodgy for not doing that kind of show. We get criticized from both directions at the same time. I have mixed feelings about *Andrew Wyeth: The Helga Pictures* (1987)...

I'm not sure that it's wrong for a museum such as this one, that's desperately trying to shed its old, outdated, elitist image, to put on a show from time-to-time that most people will like...

We have some shows planned, which are not what you call blockbusters. You shouldn't get the impression that all that happens in this museum is a season of blockbusters. We try to have a nice mix. We're having Ellsworth Kelly. We're doing much more with contemporary art.

This winter we're doing a show of 17th century Dutch landscapes that Peter Sutton has been working on from the moment he got here. People will love the show if they give it a chance...

If *Helga* brings people in, it helps us to do the scholarly shows we have an obligation to present. We are not able to find a corporate sponsor for the Dutch show, yet we are able to do it, and have our fingers crossed.

(The influence of Sutton and that exhibition proved to be palpable. In 2017 the museum announced a major acquisition of two collections that include 113 works by 76 artists. The gifts represent the largest donation of European paintings to the MFA, and nearly doubled the museum's holding of Dutch and Flemish paintings. Boston-area collectors Rose-Marie and Eijk van Otterloo and Susan and Matthew Weatherbie began collecting Netherlandish work in the '80s. Rose-Marie van Otterloo said Peter Sutton, a former curator of European art at the MFA, encouraged her and her husband to focus on collecting this genre.)

We're having a show of Charles Sheeler's photography from the Lane Collection. For me, that represents the perfect show. We have staff members with great expertise. The show makes a point with a two-volume catalogue. It's the last word on Sheeler with complete assessment and reappraisal. It's the biggest show of this work ever mounted, and Sheeler is just famous enough that people will want to see it. At the same time, it serves a scholarly function. It's the kind of thing I like to see happen.

We have a Goya show for 1989. Our curator, Eleanor Sayre, is one of the great Goya scholars. It's paintings, prints, and drawings. It's coming from all over, with thirty or forty lenders. It opens in Madrid, then comes to Boston and New York.

We have the Fitz Hugh Lane show (now Fitz Henry Lane) which Ted (Stebbins) wants to do. But Lane is not a household name. That will be coming here in '88. It's a show I'm very excited about, but not sure it will attract crowds.

We are collaborating with David Ross and the ICA and Jurgen Harten for Germany, on a show that we are organizing of avant-garde American and German art. Half will be at the ICA, and half will be here. (*The Binational: German Art of the Late 1980s/American Art of the Late 1980s*) The museum in Dusseldorf will be organizing a show of avant-garde German art. When the shows end, they will then exchange. We'll have the German show, and they'll have the American show. Younger staff members of both institutions are involved in the selection of the art.

I don't know how Boston will react. It's very experimental. Many of the artists will create works for the exhibition. That's why the deadline for the catalogue is held to the very last second. It's expensive, with a lot of complex logistics, but an exciting idea. Of course, I had nothing to do with the planning of the project.

I just signed a letter of commitment to a show of Ancient Greek bronzes from American collections. It will be us, Cleveland, and another museum.

We are doing a lot of scholarly shows. The mix is good. Over the next two years here the museum will provide something for every taste. To be judged solely on accepting *Helga* for 1987 would be a very unfair thing. *Helga* is controversial and that's interesting.

CG It will take some time before you have an impact on the exhibition schedule.

AS It won't be until 1990.

CG As said before, there has been a period of growth and change. What shape do you find the museum in now? There has been enormous renovation. Do decorative arts come next?

AS I'm not sure what comes next. There's renovation pending for classical, Egyptian, European, and American decorative arts.

CG Completing renovation of Evans Wing of Paintings and the Asiatic Wing gives a false impression that the work has been done.

AS That's a tremendous start. The other day, I said to the board, it feels as though I have leaped onto a fast-moving train. My job here will be to access what's going on. It's a little too soon to say. Around Christmas, I will have enough of a handle to make strong recommendations.

CG Will you be a bricks and mortar director?

AS That will be determined by what's needed most. I'll probably be a little of everything. I don't think I categorize myself easily. I enjoy every aspect of museum work. I'm interested in what's going on in the education department. I'm a part of the reassessment, which is in full swing now. I'll look at our space needs. Every curator wants more space.

CG When you were negotiating for the position, you likely had overall impressions of the institution. What did you feel you might achieve, and why were you the right person for the tasks at hand?

AS From a distance, my impression was that it was at the cutting edge of the problems we are talking about. If you were looking for a museum that was struggling with the issues of the day, you couldn't find a better case study than the MFA. The museum has a great professional staff.

Two things made me want to be here. The collection. Most people don't sense to what extent a curator or director feels attached to a collection and enjoys the job, even if it is full of other problems, financial and political. If the collection is great, it makes up for a lot of other problems.

I knew the collections here. Not intimately, there were parts I hadn't looked at in depth. But I had a sense of the greatness of the collections.

That was number one. Then the curatorial staff is one of the best in the world. To be affiliated with this group of people was attractive to me. The combination of collections and staff being of very high quality, to tell you the truth, being in Boston was very attractive to me.

I was very conscious that there are problems here. The curatorial staff is concerned about what they see as the commercialization of the museum. This end of the museum is where all the authority lies and the curatorial offices are in the older, other side of the museum. That's a perception that some curators have. I can change, not just the perception, but the reality. I enjoy curatorial opinion, and I think of myself as a consensus manager. I love to hear what people think about things…

The curators are welcoming my management style, which is to hear people out. To listen to what they think, and mix it all together, before I come up with my own opinion.

CG As a reporter, I investigated the acquisition of the Jackson Pollock painting *Troubled Queen*. I found that, to raise money, it partly entailed selling two Renoirs and a Monet. That was an apple for oranges issue. The museum evaded my fact-checking efforts. Rather than answer, Jan Fontein ordered PR director, Clementine Brown, to leak the story to the *Globe*. Should the museum make public the components of such an acquisition?

AS In New York City, it's mandatory.

CG If you make major deaccessions, should you do that at auction?

AS On the other side of the coin, should we publicly be discussing what we are acquiring?

CG Yes.

AS Before the fact?

CG No. In this case the issue was swapping 19th century French impressionism for American modernism. That's drawing on a strength of the collection to make up for negligence in another area of collecting.

AS I feel very strongly about deaccessions. That's a word I don't like. I prefer to say sell. If you sell from the collection, there are several steps that have to be taken.

One. Find out where you got the work of art in the first place. See if the donor is alive, the children, or grandchildren. You go to them and inform them of your desire to sell. If they have any issues whatsoever, the whole issue is dead. If people have left works of art to a museum, they have the expectation that the work will be there forever. If the donor is no longer alive, you must go to the next living relative for permission, even when the written will doesn't require that. It's a courtesy that must be followed. If you don't get permission, you forget the whole deal.

Two. With permission in hand, you next go to your curatorial staff. I like to confer. I don't like it to be one curator and myself. I want everyone to have input regarding the work that's under consideration.

For example, we have so many Millets. (Jean-François Millet, 1814–1875) Why not sell one? You could argue that we don't need so many. I would argue that we are a resource and scholars come here to study the artist. I'm against selling any Millets. I would take that as a very important consideration in a deaccessioning decision. It would diminish the importance of Boston as a Millet center. If the staff agrees, then it goes to the trustees. They may know more about the family or background of the donor.

If there is one strong dissenting voice among the trustees, for me, that's a veto. Once the object is sold, that's it. That's within the walls, however, I can't have a thousand people writing and telling me what to do about deaccessions.

At that point, you put the work in a public auction. That way there can be no doubt that you got full value for the object, that you did not waste the assets of the institution.

The other option, to sell it, is to approach several dealers. You can approach a dealer in London, Paris, and a couple in New York. They do not know of each other. You ask if they are interested in buying or taking on consignment. You get back four bids. The competition between dealers is so great that they won't confer.

You also ask the auction houses what they would estimate at. Then you make a decision about the best way to go. In terms of getting the greatest yield for the works of art.

There are safeguards against doing it wrong. You must then publish what you did in your annual report, in the same way that you brag about what you acquire. It should be public record, particularly for scholars. Also, you keep a file alive in your institution indicating where and when you sold it. A scholar should always be able to track the object if possible.

When I was at Yale, I established there a very clear policy regarding the process for deaccessioning. It's pretty much what I just described to you. You can be embarrassed when you sell. Particularly if you get too low a price. You can be embarrassed years later if a distant relative of the donor shows up and wants to see the object. It's not there anymore and that can be humiliating. That's why you have to proceed in the most cautious and conservative way.

CG The King Tut exhibition was supposed to come to the MFA, but didn't. In many ways that was a turning point for the museum.

AS In a way, it was.

CG In competing for major traveling exhibitions, what is the current status of the MFA?

AS It depends on what criteria you use for judging, if you base it on the permanent collection of the MFA. We are without peer in this country in Egyptian and classical art. That doesn't mean we have the biggest collection, but I would say that you've got to judge it department by department. For classical, object by object, there is no greater American collection. The National Gallery does not collect classical, and we are far ahead of Chicago and Philadelphia. Because of the UNESCO convention, it is now harder to buy classical art. I would take our collection over that of the Met based on the consistency of quality.

In Ancient Egyptian art, there is no museum in this country that matches us, though Brooklyn comes close. Then in European decorative arts, without doubt, the Met is ahead of us, but we rank second in the nation. American decorative arts are spectacular and needs to be reinstalled someday soon. The collections of silver and furniture here are just fabulous. There we are on a par with the Met. There's Winterthur and museums that specialize in decorative arts, but among encyclopedic museums, we are not beaten by anyone.

Where we fall down, as everyone knows, we failed to collect modernism and the 20th century. We're paying the price now, as we can never catch up to

Philadelphia's (Louise and Walter) Arensberg collection (of Marcel Duchamp and others). Our goal over the next decade can be to add ten to twenty wonderful early modern works. We can try to have a respectable showing. To play catch-up would take hundreds of millions of dollars. You can get on Amtrak and go to Philadelphia to see Duchamp and Dali, Picasso and Braque.

Our prints collection is spectacular. It is a collection that, as a prints and drawings person, I have come back to over the years. It has been a place to recharge my batteries. The collection is so ravishing.

CG It has been described as the area of the museum that has the greatest potential for growth.

(There is a gallery named for collectors Lois B. (1926–2020) and Michael K. Torf, who focused on modern and contemporary prints. Lois Torf was a trustee of the MFA and ICA. Although the MFA neglected to collect 20th century painting and sculpture, the prints and drawings department was active in modernism. The Torf collection has expanded this with depth in contemporary prints and works on paper. In 1984, the Williams College Museum of Art and the Museum of Fine Arts, Boston both exhibited *The Modern Art of the Print: Selections from the Collection of Lois and Michael Torf.*)

AS The print collection has 500,000 sheets of paper. With Cliff Ackley there, he's done a great job.

In American painting, with our Homers and Washington Allstons, we are one of the best. The Met and National Gallery are also very strong in this area. You may argue our Thomas Cole vs. your Albert Bierstadt. Boston has depth in Copley while Philadelphia is notable for Eakins. Chicago may have a tiny edge in French Impressionism.

With all these other strengths, add to that our Asian collection, which is the best in the world. Most Japanese scholars would acknowledge that the MFA's collection is better than anything in Japan.

CG In areas of weakness, how do you gain ground?

AS On average, some twenty to thirty great works come on the market each year. The Getty has the deepest resources for acquisitions, as well as the greatest need. They are having the fun of being in the market with its rough and tumble.

CG What lured you here?

AS After seventeen years in New Haven, I got restless. So, I went to Minneapolis. (As director, in 1985 for two years before the MFA.)

CG There were media reports that you were going to Chicago.

AS That never happened, and I stayed at Yale from 1971–1985. With Chicago, it worked out for the best. They got a wonderful director. I was the wrong person for that job. I went to Minneapolis in 1985. I loved that city and thought I would have a lot of fun there and stay for who knows how long. Then I got a call from the MFA search committee to be a consultant for them.

I met with them in January in that capacity. They asked me all kinds of questions about what I would do were I director. It was a couple of hours. They asked what kind of person they should hire and I answered to the best of my ability. When I got to the airport, I called my wife and said, "I think they offered me the job, but I'm not sure." They called about three weeks later and said we would like to talk seriously with you about offering you the job.

I went back for another dialogue. It was a place I had always loved and I felt that I could be useful. I felt badly about leaving Minneapolis so quickly. Things I wanted to accomplish there were just getting started.

CG You have detailed the status of the museum and its collections. Where does it rank in terms of getting the major international traveling exhibitions?

AS In the top five.

CG There was a time when we weren't getting those shows.

AS But that didn't have to do with the reputation of the institution. What I have been told is that the museum didn't have the appropriate special exhibition facilities with proper climate control. It wasn't a lack of distinction for the institution but a facilities thing.

Boston is the smallest of the three major East Coast destinations. In that game, Philadelphia never seemed to be big. The question is, how much attendance can you generate and handle. That is part of the economics of organizing these very expensive projects. You have to draw enough of an audience to pay for the cost of doing the show. A lot of that has to do with the size of the market.

In that respect, Boston hasn't been able to compete with New York. The percentage of tourists who visit the Met is far greater than tourists who visit the MFA.

CG How does the museum get its share of major traveling exhibitions?

AS I'm not so much interested in blockbusters, but rather good, solid, balanced programming, to present something for every taste, and a mixed diet of quality exhibitions, as well as ones with the potential to bring in good attendance.

CG When John Walsh was head of European Paintings, the museum had major shows of *Chardin 1699–1779* (1979) and *Renoir* (1985). The Renoir show drew some 500,000 and produced a net of some $1 million. The primary source of major exhibitions has been from the departments of paintings and prints and drawings.

(Renoir's 97-painting exhibit drew record crowds in London and Paris. In Paris, Renoir drew crowds averaging 8,668 visitors per day. In London, it surpassed the attendance record of the Hayward Gallery. Boston was the only American venue of the exhibit. The prior MFA attendance record was for *Pompeii, A.D. 79*, with 432,000 visitors in 1978. *Renoir* topped 500,000. Under Shestack there was *Monet in the '90s: The Series Paintings* in 1990, curated by Paul Hayes Tucker, which drew capacity attendance. The exhibition was also seen at the Art Institute of Chicago and London's Royal Academy of Arts. Tucker curated *Monet in the 20th Century* another blockbuster in 1998 that the MFA shared with The Royal Academy of Arts.)

AS We have shows scheduled through the classical and Egyptian departments. In the Gund Gallery in '88 we have *The Funerary Art of Ancient Egypt*. We have a show of the figure in classical art in '89. *Classical Bronzes* is also in '89. So those departments will emerge. Little by little, until the turn of the century, everyone's turn will come. Decorative arts and textiles are in line, but we will soon have to make decisions about where next to turn our attention.

Cornelius Vermeules' term expired before we got to a project with the classical department. We have two classical shows now scheduled. Little by little those things will happen.

As I try to explain to everyone around here, in every museum paintings, prints, and drawings are the major progenitors of exhibitions. That's the way it is.

Two-dimensional objects are easy to work with. The works are relatively easy to install, where an Egyptian show is hell on wheels. The objects are fragile and hard to move. Classical marbles are not to be moved at all if it can be helped. There are good reasons for these priorities. Prints and drawings are easy to transport.

So that's the reason for showing a lot of photography, but not the only reason. The logistics are so much simpler. But we are not ignoring the other departments.

CG There is financial inequality among the twenty-six departments of the museum. Some are rich, while others are relatively poor. That's been reflected in the priorities for renovations, particularly when Jan Fontein, a former Asiatic curator, was director.

AS We've been fundraising for Asiatic renovations and have been very lucky to get Japanese support.

CG When the Asiatic department wants to build a new garden, they can get Japanese funding, but the Egyptian department can't rely on Cairo for support.

(During renovation, the small, internal, traditional raked sand and boulders garden was relocated at grand scale to the exterior of the museum. The Tenshin-En Japanese Garden, designed by Kinsaku Nakane, opened in 1988.)

AS You can ask any museum director or college president, and they will tell you that it is impossible to move forward with each department with equal energy, simultaneously. You just can't do that. You've got to establish priorities. The energies of your staff and resources available dictate that. You just have to do it one at a time…

CG How the twenty-six departments play out is primarily an internal affair. To the outside community there is particular concern about the status of modern and contemporary art.

AS I haven't been here long enough to address that. Generally speaking, I hope a new curator will be on board soon. We haven't started interviewing. Because I knew this was an issue that would come up, I've been talking with friends from around the country in the contemporary art world. We have a dozen candidates.

(Kathy Halbreich was director of MIT's List Visual Arts Center [1976–1986]. She was appointed as curator of contemporary art at the MFA. She left to head the Walker Art Center, where she remained for 16 years. At the MFA, her assistant was Trevor Fairbrother. From a field of eleven candidates, he became curator of a three-person department, which Shestack was active in supporting.)

CG What does the institution have to offer that individual?

AS I can talk about my commitment and the commitment I'm hearing from some of the people in town. But I can't give you specifics. If we hire the right person, everything will fall into place. I'm very optimistic about that. If we get someone in there full time, it looks like the MFA is committed to contemporary art. People in the community will see that as a message to support that program...

CG To what extent will you use your expertise (prints and drawings)?

AS Probably not, as all of my energy will be focused on solving the museum's problems. I see myself as a facilitator, and one who can bring messages back and forth between people who don't agree with each other. I am trying to be a mediator and solve problems here.

(In 1993 he joined the National Gallery of Art as deputy director and chief curator until his retirement fifteen years later.)

CG There has been a change in how museums are run. A Perry Rathbone, for example, had complete authority. Later there was a shift to the director, as presiding over aesthetic decisions, acquisitions, and exhibitions. Now there is the more usual approach of major museums to divide that with a director and business manager.

AS When Rathbone stepped down, it took two people to replace him. When I step down, I recommend that the museum have a coequal president. I prefer the situation I inherited, where I'm CEO and there is a deputy director who deals with administrative problems. I don't worry about purchasing paper clips. A museum director shouldn't have to focus on that. The former directors didn't have all the problems of the new museums with expanded marketing, retail, and food services.

If there is a situation where the division of responsibilities overlap, I would have the final decision. We have to do what balances the books at the end of the year. But we are a long way from having sold our souls to make that happen.

A 1992 interview follows.

CG When we first talked, you described jumping onto a fast-moving express train. Through a time of economic downturn there has been a slower pace. The negotiations with Nagoya, Japan have been a part of creative ways to generate more revenue for the museum.

AS What we are doing with Nagoya is very different from the satellite museums of the Guggenheim.

In those cases, they are administered by the central museum. The city of Nagoya is building a museum. We are a consultant to that project. When the museum exists, we will provide it with exhibitions. It will be a Nagoya Museum and not be our museum. They are appointing a director who will be working with me and the architect.

The Guggenheim Bilbao will be staffed with people sent from New York. That will not be the case with us. Nagoya is a wealthy, prosperous city, which felt the need for more cultural opportunity. We are helping them to do what they want to do for themselves. We are not going to run that museum.

CG How did the project come about?

AS We were approached by an emissary from the Nagoya Chamber of Commerce. That was about a year ago, in early 1991. They asked if we had interest in helping them. In Japan, we are considered as the *ne plus ultra* of museums, mostly because of our Japanese holdings. They asked if we were interested in assisting them in forming a museum. That led to me going there for two days of meetings. I wanted to know more of the scale they were talking about. What kind of participation were they looking for on our part? I wanted to know what they wanted from us. What was in it for us?

This marriage occurred for two good reasons. Nagoya is perhaps the only large industrial city that does not already have an abundance of museums. As you know our museum has basements full of stuff that we don't show. The combination proved to be unbeatable. That couldn't happen with an American museum that didn't have great reserve collections. Nor could it happen in many other Japanese cities. It is a city of four million in its metropolitan region. It has headquarters of Toyota and Yamaha. The city is fully employed. The major corporations got behind the Chamber of Commerce. The prefecture in which Nagoya is located and the region were all eager to help. The city decided that they would build the museum. Everyone came together.

CG They made you an offer you could not refuse.

AS Not at first. It took a while to negotiate what it would take to make it happen. The first thing I said was that there could be nothing out of pocket for us. We were not in a position to subsidize a museum in Japan. We needed to be reimbursed for the effort we would make. It would take additional staffing to make it happen. The already stretched staff of the museum couldn't be expected to do it. They agreed to cover between five to seven salaries. We are still negotiating that. That would entail a registrar as well as exhibition planners and so forth.

We discussed a signing bonus for the project, which we are still negotiating, so I can't give you those numbers. Though we're not out of the woods, this project will go a long way toward a balanced budget. It's going to be substantial help. But this is not going to solve all of our problems.

CG What are those problems?

AS We have a structural deficit of $3 million a year. We have been working hard to cut costs and enhance revenue. Those are the two things you do when there is a financial crunch. Against general trends in New England, our attendance is up eighteen percent over last year.

To be crass, I've been pressing our retail people. They have increased our mailing list, also bucking trends. We are looking at restructuring staff, which could result in annual savings. We cut back forty-six and let go twenty-six positions. We have a staff of about 500. That's about ten percent, which, compared to Detroit and Brooklyn, we have been riding high. We have yet to close galleries, as has the Metropolitan Museum. We have not cut programming.

CG In the past there have been times when galleries were not staffed.

AS That's something we might have to look at. That has not occurred in light of the current financial troubles we have been facing.

CG Had Nagoya not come along at an opportune time, what were you facing? What is the role of state and federal funding?

AS As you know, the museum has never had substantial state funding. We'd gone from $60,000 to $8,000 a year. It's virtually pennies.

CG What can you do with $8,000?

AS That pays for one children's program.

We have been very aggressive in seeking to make up for that reduced state money, and have been very successful. Not one of our education programs has been terminated. But it's through private donations from several sources.

There have been a large number of expenses. For example, just covering health benefits for the staff, that cost has quadrupled in the past five years. Those bills go up by hundreds of thousands of dollars annually. That's one factor.

We have had some extraordinary expenses in our school. The HVAC system was not functioning properly. It had to be completely redone at a cost of several million dollars. We had to make life tolerable and get all the toxic fumes out. It required an enormous retrofit job.

You have a staff of 500 with a budget of $15 million. That's an average of $30,000 a year. And when you give a five percent pay increase, that adds $600,000 to your operating budget, in a year when you don't necessarily have additional attendance. That compounds, and how are you going to cover that? Museums and all cultural institutions are constantly in that position of having their costs compound while income increases arithmetically.

I'm happy to say that giving to the museum has not fallen off. It is as it was before, and membership is actually up over what it was last year. We have taken on additional debt service. We built our garage on borrowed money. It was not part of our prior budget and now we have debt service. That has suddenly been added onto our operating budget. We have debt service on the bond issued for the West Wing. Debts are coming due and we are having to pay for them.

The positive of this is that the board recognizes that we have debts and sees the need to build a capital base. There will be a capital campaign starting probably some time this year.

CG What is the endowment?

AS One hundred forty-three million dollars. That's about half of what it should be.

(Malcolm Rogers who followed Shestack started with an endowment of $180 million and raised it to $602 million. Matthew Teitelbaum estimated the endowment at $650 million. Since then, there has been a market correction as well as losses to balance in 2020 and 2021. There is also debt service for the construction projects of Rogers.)

CG How does that compare to other major museums?

AS The National Gallery has no endowment, but gets $45 million a year from Uncle Sam. That's the equivalent of having $1 billion endowment, which you're paying for through taxes. The Met endowment is something like $300 million but I'm not sure. The Cleveland Museum has $300 million for a museum a third the size of this one. The difference between us, the Art Institute of Chicago, and the Philadelphia Museum, is that they are handsomely supported by their cities. A third of their operating budgets come from their cities. We get nothing. We are at a tremendous disadvantage. We are one of the very few, major, urban art museums in the country that get no support from their city.

We are a private museum. That's a detriment to us. There's no question about it, that's just an historical fact. The reasons for it are complicated and not worth going into...

I think we're finding some creative ways out of our hole. Nagoya is not the only money we're raising in Japan. We are packaging and sending to Japan other exhibitions. We have one on right now of screens from the Weld-Fenollosa collection. It's in Tokyo, and will be in Hiroshima in a week or two. We are sending a French impressionism show next year that does not yet have a title. It's about 70 works.

CG The MFA has the greatest Asian collection in the world. Is that what Japan wants to see? Will you send a national treasure like *Burning of the Sanjo Palace*?

AS We will not let what we send to Nagoya reduce the strength of what we display here in any way. What we send will mostly be from the storage collection.

The Nagoya committee that will be working with us is yet to be appointed. We will be dealing with museum professionals in Japan. They will work with us on the specifications for the building and begin to work on the programming.

From the initial talks with powers that be, they want a mixed diet with Egyptian and classical, Greek and Roman, European painting, prints, and drawings. I asked how about photography shows? They responded, if they're good enough. I thought of sending the Ansel Adams photographs from the Lane Collection. There seems to be no restriction. They don't want contemporary. They are less interested in Japanese art, as there is already a Japanese art museum in Nagoya. The Tokugawa Art Museum is a quite good museum.

CG Jan Fontein sent *Burning of the Sanjo Palace*, but told me that he had overcome an estate restriction against loans.

AS That was an exceptional circumstance for a temporary exhibition that required board approval. That was at most a few weeks. We are talking about a general exhibition program with a great variety of works. They are not interested in contemporary art, but when the program is up and running, five or so years from now, we might say "how about this?"

It's also possible, but not likely, that shows that we organize for ourselves might also travel there. But that's not what they're looking for. They want representative sampling and exhibitions that come out of our collections. We have promised that they can be there as long as six months. Actually, five months with a one-month turnover. We would send two exhibitions a year.

We will fill two spaces, each approximately 5,000 square feet. One would be more or less permanent. It could be *Art of the Ancient World*. That would include Egyptian, Greek, and Roman. We could put together a hundred objects that would remain on view for up to five years. That would be plugged into the curriculum of their schools. That's enough lead time to really use those collections.

That would be very important to them because there are no Japanese museums that own Western antiquities. This is an opportunity for them to draw on the rich reserves in our collection. They would have exhibitions that do not exist anywhere else in Japan. There are some small museums that have three Egyptian objects. They were collected in the last decade. Of course, it's too late. You don't start in 1992 to collect that material…

In the past couple of years, I've been to Japan five times. It has taken a year to negotiate a contract, because it takes time to develop rapport. We have now reached that point.

CG Given the depth of the collection, what is the possibility for the museum to develop satellite operations. When the Evans Wing of Painting was closed for renovation, for example, Ken Moffett was curator of an MFA gallery in Quincy Market. What about MFA related retail operations?

AS The Quincy Market venture lost money. It was limited because the elevators were small. The venture was a loser because of money. As to retail, virtually every museum in the country is doing this. The Met maintains eleven shops. There's a museum shop in Columbus, Ohio, in a shopping mall. We're looking into that.

CG What about satellite exhibitions with corporations?

AS We have not looked into that. The climate is not right now to find a corporate sponsor. Not when they are laying off because of the recession.

(There was a Guggenheim satellite in Las Vegas, which has since closed. Steve Wynn had a small museum in his hotel that included a Vermeer and other choice works from his collection. Despite wealth and tourism, Las Vegas does not have a major museum.)

CG All museums, great and small, are exploring ways to monetize their collections. That includes deaccessioning. The Fuller Art Museum (Brockton) sold a dozen works at auction. The Rose Art Museum has sold works not within their core mandate. How do you feel about museums in dire financial straits selling works from their collections?

AS I am opposed to deaccessioning for any reason other than to upgrade the collection. To sell works from the bottom of the collection that we would never show, to upgrade to better works, is done all the time. Since I have been here, we have sold at least a thousand works. A lot of what we sold was just junk.

CG What about Pollock's *Troubled Queen*? The museum deaccessioned two Renoirs and a Monet.

AS That was before my time. I had nothing to do with it, so I do not wish to comment. I'm telling you what we do now. I'm telling you what my policy is. You start down a slippery slope when you do what Brockton and the Rose did.

CG I understand the concept for major museums to deaccession to upgrade collections, but there are now museums like the Rose, Danforth, and Brockton facing desperate situations. Their very existence is in jeopardy.

AS What is their purpose for being? Their *raison d'etre*? The purpose is to collect, preserve, and display works of art. If it cannot do so for lack of money, it is better to go out of business and distribute the works to other 501c3 institutions that can take care of them. It is better to go out of business than to deny your birthright…

A museum's primary mission is very clear. It doesn't matter if it's big or small. It's to collect, preserve, exhibit, and interpret works of art. The minute you start raiding the collection and thinking of it as a commodity, that can be utilized at the moment for expedient reasons, for solving your problems, rather than having your board working on more creative solutions, working with Nagoya, Japan, or whatever else you decide to do.

This museum has been in trouble many times. On one occasion the decision about what to do was about going into the retail business—to become a marketer. That's a solution we're still benefiting from. Some museums package and market exhibitions that tour around. That's another thing that you can do.

Some museums go out and find an angel who says, I love your museum enough to underwrite what you do. Cultural institutions in this country have never made it on their own. They have always depended on charitable institutions. If you don't get that charitable support, you don't exist.

That five or six dollars per visitor at the gate adds up to $3 million a year. Half of our visitors are members who don't pay for admission. That $3 million a year at the gate is just ten percent of our budget. You are never going to make it on admissions.

As a colleague described it to me, when a museum sells its works to save itself, it's like a Siberian peasant. He's cold and starts to take his house apart and throwing it on the fire. He may have kept warm for a couple of weeks, but in the end, he doesn't have a house. That's what deaccessioning for cash flow is like.

CG I'm the one you may recall who made a case about deaccessions for the Pollock. The issue was swapping French impressionism for American modernism.

AS I don't agree with that. If I had been director at the time, that would not have happened. I don't believe in that and think it's a mistake. Regarding the original donors, if you buy art using their money, to buy in a field they might not have admired, to put their name to a label, is a betrayal of trust.

CG It was apples and oranges in this case, three French impressionist works for one American modern painting.

AS Once you have depth in particular artists (Renoir and Monet) you become a resource for their work. It's a mistake to reduce the critical mass of those artists in the collection.

It was a terrible mistake. I disagree with that entirely.

I was a director of a university museum at Yale for many years. You set priorities and for me, it was the collections. I would cut back exhibitions, I would reduce staff, I would do a lot of things before I would sell works from the collection to cover costs. Selling works is the last thing, not the first thing you do when facing financial crisis…

CG I was surprised that you opted not to return a stolen Egyptian pectoral that was acquired by the museum.

AS I was following the advice of several well-paid lawyers. I acknowledged to Lafayette College that the pectoral had been stolen from them.

(It is a fascinating story that includes theft, and even the unsolved murder of a 64-year-old librarian. She was stabbed multiple times. The 3,600-year-old pectoral, a breastplate from a royal Egyptian sarcophagus, was stolen from Lafayette College in the late 1970s. In 1858, Roxbury, Massachusetts civil engineer George Alfred Stone acquired the piece in Egypt. The breastplate, as well as papyrus and several other artifacts, were from a royal tomb in Thebes. Fearing a curse, Stone's widow, in 1873, sold the objects to Lafayette for $425. The breastplate was on display at the college from 1873 to 1968, when an art expert advised the college to protect it from deterioration. It was then placed in the library's rare-book vault. It is alleged to have been stolen by reference librarian Robert G. Gennett. Records of the Egyptian objects were destroyed. The pectoral went on the block at Sotheby's on December 11, 1980. It did not draw the minimum $110,000 the seller required, and later that month was transferred to the Museum of Fine Arts in Boston for $165,000, in a sale arranged by Sotheby's. The college didn't discover the pectoral was stolen until late 1987.)

When you have something stolen and you don't report it for ten years, when you're covering up murders and all kind of things by not reporting to the police. The theft was announced ten years later, when a new president came to the university.

When it was first discovered that what we owned, purchased from Sotheby's, which had put it on the cover of their auction catalog, nobody denied that this transaction had taken place. Regarding provenance, there was no mention of it, and we had no idea where it came from. Prior to 1981, there was no notion of where it came from. We did a thorough search prior to the acquisition.

We were led to believe that Lafayette had deaccessioned it. We were not to mention Lafayette, as they would be embarrassed for having deaccessioned it. There were all kinds of funny things involved.

When it was taken from the vault of the rare books collection of the college library, one could argue that it had minimal value. It was suspected to be a forgery, and when it was consigned to Sotheby's, it was bad-mouthed in the trade. When it came up at auction, there was not one buyer willing to bid on the reserve price for the object.

Kelly Simpson (MFA curator of Egyptian Art) had the intelligence and eye to see that under all the grime and grit it might be something. He believed in it, and came back here and persuaded Jan (Fontein) to buy it. We went to Sotheby's, which acted as middleman with the consigner, an antiques dealer in Pennsylvania, and the museum acquired it. At that point, it was said to be worth $150,000 (actually $165,000 with fees). It then came here and was worked on for one year. It was studied intensively and put on view in our collection.

(The pectoral is from Egypt's Second Intermediate Period, Dynasty 13–17, 1783–1550 B.C., and was fit for a king. The pectoral was made as a piece of funerary equipment, rather than as jewelry to be worn in life.)

It was published four times and became a rather famous piece. We greatly enhanced its value by virtue of the fact that we accepted it. We validated its authenticity. We did the scientific studies that proved its authenticity. We restored and published it.

In the law, an institution or new owner of stolen property, who enhances its value, is entitled to that enhanced value if it goes back to the original owner. Some kind of accommodation has to be reached between the original owner and the new owner. If in fact, the object is worth five times as much now because of the very activities of the new owner.

When I learned of the theft, I made an immediate plan to meet with the president of Lafayette College. We sought to reach an out-of-court settlement. We have been negotiating, and are now very close. I offered him cash immediately for title to the piece. It's now been six to eight months.

We came a long way, but couldn't decide on money, so we have just gone to mediation. That report has just arrived and I'm not at liberty to discuss it. The piece will stay here and we'll write a check to Lafayette...

The statute of limitations had run out. Then try to find out why they didn't report the theft. You hire detectives and they find all kinds of funny reasons why it wasn't reported. If you don't report the theft, it is no longer your property by law. It's not a simple case.

Mr. Rotberg and I get along fine until we talk about money. One joke he made was, "Which of us gets the TV rights to this?"

If you were director of a museum and someone came along and claimed one of your objects would you just say, sure, here it is?

(Museums return things. Jan Fontein spoke with me about returning a statue of Shiva. The MFA was sued by Italy for the return of the [alleged] Raphael portrait [of Eleonora Gonzaga]. We see more and more examples of this with museums.)

CG This year there were changes in the tax law for deductions for gifts to museums of works of art. How did that impact the museum?

AS It was a good year for us. There was no avalanche, but it was a good year. In the painting department, for example, we got a Copley, a Heade, and a very important Sargent. The window of opportunity, because of the tax law, encouraged donations. In musical instruments, we got a harpsichord, which may be the most important object in our musical instruments collection. Enormous collections of American silver were given.

CG You have been able to generate exhibitions based on collections. Ultimately that has saved money in terms of expensive loans and insurance.

AS There's nothing wrong with that. You seem to be saying that I should be more sympathetic to smaller institutions with fewer resources to deaccession to cover their costs. I have trustees who would agree with you. There are fewer and fewer who take my position.

Last year we managed to raise $600,000 for Trevor Fairbrother's contemporary art exhibition program. That money came from foundations, private individuals, Uncle Sam, small grants. He put together a pretty damn good year. We had a major Robert Wilson show, Brice Marden, a body show. It was a pretty lively program. We begged and cajoled with people who care about contemporary art. We put the money toward those shows.

We could have taken the money and bought one major work of art. Or could have allowed Trevor to purchase six works for $100,000 each. The program right now is more important to us than adding to the collection. I asked Trevor, because I knew I would be seeing you, how many works of art were acquired by his department? He said that there were 35 acquisitions in the past six months. That's separate from buying prints and photographs.

Considering the financial state of things, our contemporary program is doing very well. I wouldn't want to trade any work of art to solidify that program.

To come back to your question with permanent collection and loan shows, we're mixing them up. We're coming out of a very tough year. We are doing somewhat more out of the basement shows, but have some great shows coming up, including *The Lure of Italy*, which Ted Stebbins is curating, and Peter Sutton is doing *The Age of Rubens*. We're trying to balance things.

Alan Shestack was MFA director during an economic downturn. Giuliano photo.

Shestack supported Trevor Fairbrother's contemporary program. Giuliano photo.

Gallerist Mario Diacono donated his Piero Manzoni conceptual certificate to Fairbrother.

Peter Lacovara of the Egyptian Department

Soon after graduating from Brandeis University, I joined the Egyptian Department of the museum, where I worked in the basement for two and a half years, starting in fall 1963. Some years later, Dr. Peter Lacovara had a similar experience.

We compared notes, as well as his behind-the-scenes insight of palace intrigues.

Charles Giuliano When and how did you join the MFA Egyptian Department?

Peter Lacovara I was an undergraduate at Boston University and enrolled in a course taught at the museum. It was an introduction to Egyptian art taught by Ed Brovarski. While I was there, I volunteered to intern for the department. That was the fall of 1976.

I got to know the members of the department. I decided to go to graduate school, so they suggested the University of Chicago, where I specialized in archaeology. New Kingdom town planning was my dissertation topic. After four years of course work, it took some time to write my dissertation. Part of that entailed fieldwork. I went back to the MFA in 1980 as an intern and stayed there for a while.

CG Who was in the department at that time?

PL It was still Dows Dunham (1890–1984) and Sue Chapman (an artist who did technical rendering for department publications), Ed Brovarski, Edna Russmann, and Timothy Kendall as assistant curators. The chief curator was William Kelly Simpson (1928–2017). The secretary from hell was Mary Cairns.

CG She was indeed. I read the long interview with Perry Rathbone in the *Archives of American Art*. He mentioned with pride appointing both Simpson and Cornelius Vermeule to head the classical department.

After Rathbone resigned in 1972, Merrill Rueppel, who followed him, attempted to professionalize the jobs and commitments of the curators. In addition to their MFA responsibilities, a number of curators were professors and earned fees as consultants to galleries and collectors. They were told to confine their teaching to within the museum. As compensation they were given modest pay increases.

Simpson was also a tenured professor at Yale, as was the part-time contemporary curator, Ken Moffett, who taught at Wellesley. While Rathbone praised Simpson, you have a different assessment.

PL He was hired, in part, because of his social connections. He was very wealthy and married to a Rockefeller. His father had been a senator. He concentrated mostly on Yale, and the MFA was just another feather in his cap.

He didn't fight for the department. Under him, they lost gallery and storage space. When climate control was discussed, his response was that the material was old and didn't need it. Actually, it is the most fragile material in the museum.

He sold objects that he shouldn't have. He was cheap with important purchases, because he was waiting for the price to go down. He told both Brovarski and Russmann that they would be the next chief curator. That created conflict between them.

CG Who succeeded him?

PL Ann Russmann went to the Met, and Brovarski served briefly. He was removed because of an alleged incident. Eventually Rita Freed became curator.

CG Let's sketch an overview of the department. Other than Cairo, it is regarded as the world's finest collection of Old Kingdom objects.

PL And Nubia.

CG That came from the decades of excavations of George Andrew Reisner (1867–1942, who was MFA curator from 1910–1942). While rich in objects, it seemed that, compared to other departments, it was relatively underendowed.

PL It was less a matter of money, than not having support from trustees. There were no trustees who collected Egyptian art. Painting and decorative arts had a cadre of wealthy supporters. It was popular with the public, and the Egyptian Department was far more important, for example, than the department of paintings.

CG What resources did Simpson have?

PL He was wealthy, but rather penurious. He didn't contribute much to the museum. The museum was hoping he would. Katherine Lane Weems sculpted the life-size, bronze rhinoceros in front of The Museum School. She gave $250,000 to refurbish the Egyptian galleries, which were then quite shabby. Jan Fontein (MFA director) took all that money to refurbish the Asiatic galleries. He similarly took funds from the department of European decorative arts.

CG What was the negative impact under Simpson.

PL The department had an archives room in the basement. It's where excavation records and maps were stored. Mr. Dunham worked down there on his publications. Simpson let them take that space, so all that material was shoved into the basement with no rhyme or reason. I tried to reorganize the records but it took a long time to get them together again.

CG How did he let that happen?

PL He didn't care, as long as the museum let him spend time in Katonah, New York City, and New Haven. When he was actually at the MFA, he would spend his time on the phone fundraising for Yale.

CG Then Rueppel was right.

PL Yes, certainly in the case of Simpson. Staff should teach, but in a way that benefits both the museum and themselves. He was exploiting that privilege. They hoped to get something out of him, and they clearly didn't. It only got worse later on.

CG Did he mentor you in any way?

PL No. He was so strange that I stayed as clear from him as possible. He lived on Beacon Hill in The Green House. It was a mansion given to the museum by a Mr. Green. It was intended to be the director's house, but the director didn't want to live there. They let Simpson have it for just paying utilities.

CG What was his expertise?

PL Egyptian language. He wasn't an archaeologist, so he didn't have much understanding or interest in it.

CG Are you a linguist?

PL No, I'm an archaeologist, but I have some ability to read hieroglyphics.

CG Is Egyptian art African or somehow Near Eastern and connected to Eurocentric traditions? If you look at the Old Kingdom reserve heads of the royal family, for instance, you encounter Semites, a Negro princess, and features of hybrid individuals. The latter represented by images of King Mycerinus and his queen. The wall text for the MFA's Nubian Exhibition quoted Reisner with rather racist comments. Can you give me a sense of the context of race in Egyptology?

PL It's changing. There was a lot of racism, and earlier on, there were attempts to divorce Egypt from Africa with an emphasis on Mediterranean connections. Of course, you couldn't do that with Nubia, so it was regarded as a degenerate African reflection of Egyptian culture, rather than as something of value in its own terms.

The MFA's Nubian collection is the greatest in the world. Even in Sudan, there is nothing comparable. When I reorganized the basement, I dealt a lot with that material. Mr. Dunham had done a book on earlier cemeteries in Kerma that Reisner excavated. I helped him to organize that. So that gave me an appreciation of Nubia.

Boston City Councilor, David Scondras, helped us to get some money from AT&T to do a Nubian gallery. We got a fairly substantial grant. The museum took most of the money for other purposes. They did the gallery on the cheap, and put it in an area where the shop used to be. (Near the Huntington Avenue entrance.) They used old cases and old carpet. I complained to Brent Benjamin, an executive who is now in Saint Louis. The mirror image of that space was the Indian sculpture gallery, which is now a shop.

I said, "You're doing this as outreach to Boston's African American community. They can just look across and see that you spent nothing on Nubia compared to the Indian installation." His response was, "Those people will never be able to tell the difference."

You probably remember the great Aspelta sarcophagus. It's a masterpiece, and the largest royal sarcophagus in the New World. (Napatan Period, reign of Aspelta, 593–568 B.C. From Nuri, tomb of Aspelta, hawk figure from tomb of King Amtalqa.)

It was long installed in the lower rotunda. The Ladies Committee decided that they wanted to serve tea there. Simpson agreed to have it moved to storage in the basement. In any other museum, it would be a highlight of the collection. It's so large, they were barely able to jam it in.

Under Kelly, they also lost a gallery which had Old Kingdom reliefs set into the wall. They decided they wanted to use that for chair storage. They simply walled up millions of dollars' worth of beautiful reliefs.

CG During the Lord Norman Foster expansion, the department lost Gallery E1.
(From the grand Fenway staircase, on the right off of the rotunda, under the John Singer Sargent murals.)

PL It's crazy. That was a historic installation. It was under Malcolm Rogers. There was this Greek American, George Behrakis, who said, "Greece is the pinnacle of civilization, so its gallery should be on the top floor." To please him and get more money, they started sticking classical things in that gallery. They moved the Egyptian sculpture out of there. It makes no sense.

(In a 2021 interview, Matthew Teitelbaum discussed new galleries for Greek and Egyptian galleries, as well as plans to create space for Nubian art. It was unclear that this might entail the Aspelta Sacrophagus.)

CG The heroic-scaled, alabaster sculpture of King Mycerinus is now installed in a gallery off the atrium of the American Wing. Those galleries are unimposing considering the significance of the Egyptian collection. The display has declined from featured to an afterthought.

PL It's as though Egyptian art is being punished. Part of this is inherited from

Kelly, in the sense that the department was not seen as politically important. Even after the time of Jan Fontein, nobody messed with the Asiatic department. The curators who followed Simpson have not really fought for the department. They don't have the backing that they really need.

CG You say that Simpson deaccessioned objects. What was his motive? Was he trying to raise money for acquisitions?

PL When objects were acquired through excavations, the agreement with the Egyptian Government was that they could not be sold. This was a violation of that contract. There were lots of things that were not acquired through excavations that could have been sold.

The Memphis Museum got a grant to buy things for a collection, any collection, and notified a number of museums. Kelly was one of the only ones to reply, and he sold them objects from excavations. He sold them a wooden paddle doll, which has wonderful painting on its bottom. Apparently, he never turned it over to observe that. He sold them the head of an Old Kingdom woman. I was doing research and found fragments of a triad sculpture of two men with a woman in the middle. We found the pieces and were able to reconstruct the sculpture, except for the head in the middle, which he had sold to Memphis.

He sold half of an Old Kingdom granite sarcophagus from the basement to Boston's Museum of Science. He didn't realize that the rest of it was also down there. He had to get it back from the Museum of Science. They had it outside…

CG (William Stevenson Smith, 1907–1969, joined the department in 1941. After service, 1942–1946, as a lieutenant commander in the Navy, Smith was director of the Giza excavation from 1946–1947, until the excavation agreement from 1905 expired. He returned to the museum, and was chief curator from 1959 to 1969. He authored the *History of Egyptian Art* from the Pelican History of Art series, among other publications.)

Smith died before you first joined the department. I was fortunate to know him for two and a half years. You told me an interesting story about the department secretary Mary Cairns.

PL When Smith died, she went to his house to help clear it out. She burned his personal papers. She assumed that nobody would be interested. She didn't like to file things, so she threw papers out. It's hard to go back and research things because there is so little.

CG Where did she get the authority to do that?

PL Again it was Kelly because he just let her do that. He was there so seldom that she really ran the department. They spoke every night by phone when she gave him her take on what happened that day. She would express an opinion on whether or not they should acquire things. It was bizarre.

CG Can we talk about *Ancient Nubia Now* the 2019 exhibition. Is the art of Nubia equal in status and quality to that of Ancient Egypt? The wall text for the exhibition displayed racist comments by Reisner.

PL The art of Nubia is different. It's a matter of comparing apples and oranges. It's different in many ways. The artists of Nubia didn't have access to the same raw materials that the Egyptians had. Their sculpture does not compare, but they did superb gold work and pottery, in advance of anything the Egyptians manufactured. You have to take it on its own terms, and the MFA has the cream of the crop. It's a spectacular collection. A lot of the pieces are breathtaking. But it's all in storage. The installation made an issue of Reisner's racism. It is viewed as African art, which is crazy.

CG You were at the MFA from 1980 to 1998, some 18 years. What was the sense of internal and administrative politics?

PL It was the waning days of Jan Fontein. John Walsh (curator of paintings) and the other curators were upset because all the money was being directed to renovation of the Asiatic department. They were meeting to try to undermine him. Ed Brovarski offered to host the meetings in the Egyptian department. He would throw us out of the office while they had their secret meetings. Brovarski was playing both ends against the middle. He would report to Ross Farrar (associate director) and tell him what was going on.

CG Walsh wanted to become director, but the coup failed when he left to become director of the Getty. When he left, PR director Clementine Brown told me, "He'll be back."

PL There was a search, and they appointed Alan Shestack.

CG How would you evaluate Fontein as director?

PL He was successful for the Asiatic department, but less so for the rest of the museum. Overall, he wasn't bad, but not great like Perry Rathbone, or as bad as Merrill Rueppel.

CG I published in the *Patriot Ledger* that John Walsh was paid about $25,000 a year as a consultant to the William I. Koch Foundation. Some works he acquired for Koch, by Manet and Cezanne, were briefly hung at the MFA. It is viewed as the job of curators to work with collectors in the hope that objects will eventually come to the museum.

PL Some of the curators were working with dealers, and in some cases getting kickbacks. There was someone fired from the painting department for doing that. There was a lot of that. There was a junior member of our department running his own publication business. He spent department time working on his books using museum stationery and postage. There was no oversight, so people could get away with doing things…

CG In ousting Rueppel, the curators got what they wanted in elevating one of their own as director.

PL Yes, but that didn't work out, as Fontein was only interested in elevating his own department.

CG He did a great job, as the Asiatic collection looks magnificent.

PL Yes, but they squandered a lot of money. They had finished a large gallery. Fontein decided that he didn't like it and had them rip it out and start over again. He had a special wooden case made for objects in storage, including silk-lined drawers for shards. They were form fitted for each object. It turned out that the cases were made with formaldehyde-soaked plywood, which was giving off gas that was damaging the bronzes. They had to rip them out and throw them away. Fontein and Ross Farrar wasted vast amounts of money.

CG How did things change with Shestack as director?

PL When the new wing opened, there was a revenue increase because people wanted to see it. A big bonus was voted for everybody, but it was scaled to their salary.

Shestack and Farrar got huge bonuses, and everyone else got smaller ones. Then the stock market tanked. There was a meeting to talk with the staff about that.

A curator in the textile department asked if the director was taking a pay cut? Shestack refused to answer, but the curator was let go the next day. Earlier, when the chief textile curator, Larry Salmon, had left, they hired Jean-Michel Tuchscherer, and he was a disaster. Within months, people left who had been with the textile department for twenty years. The new staff he hired were complaining about him in a matter of months.

During the economic downturn, Shestack had meetings of curators and department heads to discuss the financial situation. Tuchscherer got up and said, "Enough of this talk of money. When I was director of the Textile Museum in Lyon, we had none of these talks about money." Shestack ordered him to sit down and shut up.

When he got back to his office, Tuchscherer sent an email to all of the department heads and trustees saying that Shestack didn't know what he was doing. When he found out about this, the director was furious. He called down and ordered Tuchscherer to come to his office. Jean Michel refused and he was told to leave the building for not obeying an order. He refused to leave the building.

Security was sent to escort him out. He saw the guards coming and started to run. They chased him all over the museum. In desperation they called the Boston police. They came and started chasing him. We heard of this from one of our volunteers, who was coming in through the New Wing entrance. It was just before the museum had opened, so there were people gathered in front of the glass doors. They witnessed this guy running back and forth with the police chasing him. They finally managed to take him to the station. Needless to say, he was no longer chief curator after that.

CG Thank you for sharing memories and insights.

Peter Lacovara excavating in the Valley of the Kings. Courtesy of Lacovara.

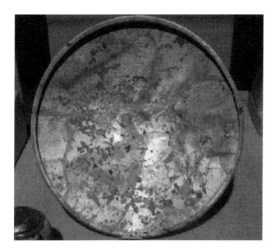

Dynasty Three stone vessel of Ka Ba restored by Charles Giuliano.

MFA curator William Kelly Simpson was also a professor at Yale University. Courtesy of the Museum of Fine Arts, Boston.

George Andrew Reisner excavated for decades on behalf of the MFA. Courtesy of the Museum of Fine Arts, Boston.

MFA curator William Stevenson Smith worked with Reisner in Egypt. Courtesy of the Museum of Fine Arts, Boston.

Malcolm Rogers, Expansion and Controversy

Malcolm A. Rogers, CBE (Commander of the British Empire) (born October 3, 1948) served as the Ann and Graham Gund Director of the Museum of Fine Arts from 1994 through 2015. Rogers was Deputy Director of London's National Portrait Gallery before seeking a position in Boston.

A native of Scarborough, North Yorkshire, England, Rogers was educated at Oakham School and later went on to receive degrees from Magdalen College and Christ Church of the University of Oxford, where he earned a B.A with first class honors and a Ph.D in English His area of scholarship was 17th century British Portraiture.

In the upper level of the arts, the class system prevails in the U.K. He lacked aristocratic rank, so when passed over for director of the National Portrait Gallery, he pursued opportunities for his talents in America.

His management style proved to be déclassé. On a Friday afternoon in 1999, in a corporate manner, security escorted eighteen curators from the building, including Jonathan Leo Fairbanks (28-year tenure) and Anne Poulet (20-year tenure). Other curators resigned, including Theodore E. Stebbins, Jr. (22-year tenure) having declined Rogers' offer to head the new conglomerate, Art of the Americas.

Belinda Rathbone described to me how her father, Perry T. Rathbone, had wooed Fairbanks to become a curator of American decorative arts. In 1982, he curated *New England Begins: The Seventeenth Century*, which came with a three-volume catalogue. A replica of a 17th century home, resembling that of his family, was constructed in the museum's courtyard.

Poulet, though ousted by the MFA, ascended to the position of director of the Frick Museum. As a dowry, she brought a stunning exhibition of sculpture by Jean-Antoine Houdon (1741–1828) that she had worked on for Boston.

While the manner of firing struck many as unseemly, it was not unprecedented. As Michael Conforti, the former director of the Clark Art Institute, told me, "One could say that the trend began at the Metropolitan Museum under Thomas Hoving in the early 1970s, but it was famously advanced internationally at the Victoria and Albert Museum in the 1980s, when director Elizabeth Esteve-Coll fired a number of curatorial department heads causing a world-wide outcry.

"The goal was to take control of the institution away from curators and distribute it to other, more publicly centered departments. That became an ambition of the MFA a bit later, and while it transpired in different ways over time, Malcolm Rogers was more effective in making this change than anyone previously. Whether you believe that the diffusion of curatorial authority is a desirable goal or not, it's been an evolutionary characteristic of art museums with historical collections over these past decades. It played out in Boston in a way that was specific to them, but there are parallels everywhere in art museums, both in the U.S. and Europe."

The opinion of the late critic David Bonetti, in a 2014 piece for *Berkshire Fine Arts*, however, was unequivocal, "To begin with, you have to admit that Malcolm—as everyone calls him, whether he likes it or not—was the MFA's greatest director since the end of World War II. Since I don't know the history before that that well, I can't say whether he was the greatest director in its history, but I suspect that he might well be a contender.

"We have to remember what the museum was like before he came—there were dust balls blowing around in the galleries! Under his predecessor, the hapless Alan Shestack, housekeeping languished. Is that important? YES, it is. Because it shows a contempt for the public that Shestack also exhibited by shutting the Huntington Avenue entrance. Malcolm opened that and the Fenway entrance…

"In addition to all the money he raised, Malcolm built the addition the museum desperately needed (which that money paid for). He kept it open seven days a week, he acquired an enormous amount of art, much of it significant, and he embraced cultures that the museum had previously ignored...

"About the so-called 'Friday Massacre,' the way it was done was unfortunate, the result perhaps of a Brit being given bad advice from American corporate types about how workers are dismissed. But was there a loss to the firing of Anne Poulet and Jonathan Fairbanks (who has since been given emeritus status)?

"If you care about modern art, the answer is NO. Did either of them, as curators of decorative arts and sculpture, ever purchase 20th century art sculpture? Basically, no...

"Was Malcolm a populist? Yes. Was that a bad thing? No...Did I like the idea of a Herb Ritts show? No. (I didn't see it—I was living in San Francisco.) But fashion/celebrity photography is a legitimate genre for collection and exhibition in a museum that pretends to collect the material culture of the entire world, and it was a smart area for the MFA to move into since it was undervalued and under-collected...

"Did I like everything Malcolm did? Of course not. He admitted to the *Boston Globe*'s Sebastian Smee that, if there were a legitimate criticism of his taste, it was that he had a jumble shop aesthetic... He has said that he will retire to a cottage in the English countryside. I'm sure his den will be well supplied with Tobey Jugs. God bless the Queen..."

During an economic downturn, the museum had fallen on hard times under prior director, Alan Shestack, who served from 1987 to 1993. Rogers was given a broad mandate to kick-start what had become a moribund institution.

In June 1991, under Shestack, the board ordered the administration to trim $1.7 million off a projected $4.7 million deficit. Forty-two positions were affected, and 21 people were laid off. The MFA had borrowed an estimated $6 million to $10 million from its endowment, which had decreased to $145 million. As a part of cost cutting, the grand Huntington Avenue entrance was closed. Rogers initially made staff cuts that shaved $3.4 million off the museum's $4.5 million deficit. More cuts and shakeups would follow.

Malcolm Rogers and I met for the interviews that follow. There were others, as well as lunch that resulted in a feature for *Art New England*. For the first meeting, in 1994, he had been on the job for just seven weeks. The second occurred in September 2011, during the opening of the Linde Family Wing of Contemporary Art.

As Rogers was then new to the job, there were signifiers of policy positions that would erupt under the mantra of "One Museum." Through growth of the endowment, brick and mortar expansion, property acquisition, and collections growth, arguably, he left the museum in better shape than he found it.

When Rogers arrived in 1994, the budget was about $77 million; it rose to $101 million. The number of visitors was 864,179 in 1994, and 1,227,163 in 2015. The endowment grew from $180.6 million to $623.7 million. The museum's debt, however, grew from $35 million; to $189 million at its peak, through construction and the 2007 acquisition of the adjacent, former Forsyth Institute. The American Wing cost $345 million; the Rogers campaign was $504 million and included endowment. He left a debt of $140 million, which in 2021 is $105 million.

His greatest accomplishment was a major expansion and creation of The American Wing, designed by the British architect Lord Norman Foster. It cost some $500 million, but has garnered mixed reviews. While generous space was given to the multipurpose atrium, the galleries feel cramped, with no room for expansion of growing collections. It seems incongruous that the essential Graham Gund Special Exhibition space is located in the basement. Lacking an appropriate foyer, it is entered inelegantly through glass doors around the corner from the base of the stairs.

While there were undeniable efforts toward fiscal balance and physical expansion, Rogers accomplished this while diminishing the independence of the museum's world-renowned curators and their departments. When the dust settled, it was said that he micromanaged their domain. His mantra of "One Museum" emphasized who was in charge.

There were 375 special exhibitions on his watch, with an emphasis on populism. These ranged from the commercial portrait photographers, Herb Ritts and Yousuf Karsh, to the vintage cars of Ralph Lauren, *Dangerous Curves: The Art of the Guita*; *An Adventure with Wallace and Gromit*, and the mediocre collection of billionaire William I. Koch. The installation included empty bottles from Koch's wine cellar, Native American souvenirs, and two of his America's Cup yachts parked in front of the Huntington Avenue entrance. The Rogers program also included Goya and the prints of Katsushika Hokusai.

Garish kitsch works by the populist Japanese artist Takashi Murakami were installed in galleries of the world-class Asiatic collection. As a renowned gallerist told me, encountering them in that context, "Made me want to puke."

The glitzy glass sculptures, *Chihuly: Through the Looking Glass*, drew crowds in 2011. Money was raised to purchase an enormous, Christmas tree-like tchotchke. It remains in the enormous atrium of the American Wing.

The Chihuly exhibition seemed to bring Vegas taste to Boston. It is no surprise that the museum's priceless works by Claude Monet were rented to the Bellagio for a million dollars. In addition to a contractual agreement with a museum in Nagoya, Japan, the museum's treasures were often on the road to earn their keep. These loans were for commercial gain rather than the quid quo pro of scholarly museum exhibitions.

Rogers treated the collection of the museum as a liquid asset. As former *Boston Globe* critic Sebastian Smee reported, "Visitors to the Museum of Fine Arts this holiday season can see the celebrity and fashion photographs of Mario Testino. But if they wander off into the permanent collection galleries, they won't find the museum's most famous Renoir, *Dance at Bougival*. Nor will they see any of the MFA's five paintings by Cezanne, five of its six great paintings by Edouard Manet, its most distinctive Monet (*La Japonaise* [*Camille Monet in a Japanese Costume*], or its two greatest Van Goghs (*Postman Joseph Roulin* and *Lullaby: Madame Augustine Roulin Rocking a Cradle* [*La Berceuse*]).

"Some of these works have been lent to serious and scholarly museum shows in the United States, Japan, and Europe. Agreeing to such loans is common practice, and builds goodwill for when the museum asks to borrow for its own exhibitions.

"However, the MFA, eager to raise revenues, is also renting out many of its most prized works of European and American art to for-profit enterprises. A total of 26 paintings, including the marquee *Dance at Bougival* and *Madame Roulin*, have been sent to exhibitions in Italy, organized by a private company called Linea d'Ombra, for a large, undisclosed fee…Other absent masterpieces include Velazquez's *Luis de Gongora*, two of the MFA's three great El Grecos, two of its Courbets, its only major painting by Edvard Munch, and arguably its greatest Degas."

My wife Astrid and I experienced this pay-per-view practice first hand during a 2014 visit to The Frist Center for Visual Art in Nashville. It operates as a kunsthalle or non-collecting institution. We were surprised to encounter the

MFA's Japanese prints and interesting, but minor, paintings. The loan show was enhanced by a couple of show stoppers, including a late Monet painting of the Japanese bridge over his lily pond at Giverny and van Gogh's *The Postman Roulin*.

The director of the Frist, Mark Sala, told me, "We don't have the exhibition budget that the MFA Boston has. We do ten to twelve exhibitions a year. Right now, we have a show from the MFA Boston *Looking East: Western Artists and the Allure of Japan*. That was a big budget item for us."

During Rogers's tenure the museum acquired some 67,000 works of art, including a $20 million-plus painting by Edgar Degas (1834–1917), *Duchessa di Montejasi with Her Daughters, Elena and Camilla*. In modern and contemporary art, the late doctors, Melvin Blank and Frank Purnell, donated 60 works by surrealists and an early nude by pop artist Larry Rivers. The museum also sold eight works and drew on funds to purchase *Man at His Bath* (1884). It is regarded as one of the greatest works by the French impressionist artist Gustave Caillebotte (1848–1894). This important painting represents the first impressionist nude to enter the Museum's collection of paintings.

The museum has a long and ambivalent track record on issues of diversity and inclusion.

John Axelrod, the philanthropist, credits Rogers with initiating an internal diversity report and action plan in 2002. In 2011, Axelrod sold 67 works by African-American artists to the museum for $5 to $10 million. He also helped fund *Common Wealth: Art by African Americans in the Museum of Fine Arts*, with a comprehensive catalogue edited by curator Lowery Stokes Sims. It documents some hundred acquisitions since 1970. The museum is committed to expand on this foundation. Vintage acquisitions included renowned Boston artist Alan Rohan Crite and outsider artist Horace Pippin.

We first spoke in 1994 and a number of times after that.

Charles Giuliano Can we talk about Nagoya (Museum in Japan)?

Malcolm Rogers We are getting close to a contract. I have been here just seven weeks now, and I wasn't involved in the negotiations.

CG Your predecessor, Alan Shestack, expressed that this would help to address deficit issues. It is thought of as a key piece of the puzzle of resolving a deficit.

MR It's an important part of the puzzle, as well as a part of our outreach.

CG It has been projected to bring in at least $1 million annually.

MR I don't have an exact figure, as the process is still in negotiation. We have been running a deficit this past year, approximately $4.5 million with an operating budget of $60 million.

There are certain things you have to know about the deficit. Some five percent of the spending capital of the endowment is set by the trustees, so that you can build up endowment. It is set aside and invested as a reserve, in case there is a special project or an emergency. To be perfectly honest, our structural deficit is about $2 million a year.

CG In recent years there has been a lot spent on construction. What is the debt service on those loans?

MR About $2 million a year.

CG In the 1980s there was extensive museum expansion. There was a decision to climate control special exhibition galleries to accommodate major traveling exhibitions, and to provide amenities, as well as refreshed collection galleries. You have inherited the responsibility of paying for those brick and mortar improvements. The MFA has seemed out of the loop. Boston lost out on the *Rembrandt* show that Peter Sutton initiated for the museum.

MR In hindsight, we realize it would have been better to be building and fund raising at the same time. Looking on the positive side, because of the building that was put up, we have doubled attendance.

CG Jan Fontein is remembered for expanding the museum, while Alan Shestack was increasingly burdened with managing the museum through a declining economy. You come in with that over your head, which is a daunting undertaking. Knowing that, why did you want this job?

MR When I was considering coming here, there were some twenty major museum positions to be filled. There I was in London, thinking America might be an interesting place to work. I looked at those twenty positions and one stood out. It was literally the best job, which I started to chase. I knew the MFA very well as one of the greatest museums in the world, in one of the finest cities in the world.

It was also an impossible job to do. I liked the idea that it was a difficult job in a great, great place.

CG What's the difference between impossible and difficult?

MR (laughing) I don't think there are any impossibilities. The impossibility is thinking it's impossible. In my very first message here, and I tend to say and write what I believe, it all broke down into challenges. There are committed, able people here who love this museum, when you enable and empower them to do their job. I was convinced that we can turn it around with the support of the trustees, with the support of our staff and motivating it. Clearly, we have to think long and hard about how to use our resources.

No doubt you read in this morning's *Globe* about Mr. Rogers. I wouldn't put it the way that Christine (Temin) did. Have we got the balance right between permanent and temporary exhibitions? The permanent collections are important, but are they more important? It's difficult to say what's the right balance? My feeling is that we should be doing a certain number of exhibitions a year, but we should also be improving a certain number of permanent displays each year. That you would have budgets for education plans that fit into the museum's mission. Exhibitions, temporary and permanent, should be planned well ahead, and we should know why we want to do them. We can't just exist. We have to be a priority for visitors.

CG The programming has been a bit dull. Because of the deficit and funding there seems to have been too many in-house exhibitions with things dragged up from the basement.

MR (with emphasis) Can I assure you, Charles, that I do not intend to drag up shows from the basement? Can I also say to you, sometimes we try to use a bit more imagination? When we did our recent Egyptian mask exhibition, many of the objects came out of storage and are international treasures. They have been put into a gallery that is used for education. We hope it will be a major public attraction, and that is not an attempt to palm them off as a temporary exhibition. It's quite different.

(Long pause). How do I put it? What it comes down to is planning well ahead and knowing what we want to do. What will be as effective as possible? I sense what you are thinking about, but a retread can be so much more than that. Ah, what's the word I want? (pause) The opportunity to have an exhibition, which just happens to be around, as a long-term planner, we have to explore the bounds between temporary and long-term exhibitions. I'm not saying to do permanent displays because they are cheap to do. Often, they proved to be more expensive. But our permanent collection is incredible and it's what is so special about this museum.

I'm not in the business of doing things to save money. Whatever we do must be professional to the highest standards.

CG In the past few years we have had a diet of in-house shows.

MR What do you mean by diet? I'm not so sure of that.

CG The generic, thematic impressionism show a couple of summers ago played like the basement's greatest hits with some highlights and a lot of filler. It was formulaic in finding a way to recycle crowd-pleasing impressionism. It did not make a strong scholarly or aesthetic point. Actually, it didn't make much of an impression.

MR Could you check the dates about that? The show that's up presently, I did not choose personally. I would have done it differently, and I am not interested in a diet of retread shows. It seems correct to me, from time-to-time, to do shows that attract some 40,000 people. That's quite different from a retread, which is a way to save money and come up with an exhibition. As far as I know, *Awash in Color: Homer, Sargent, and the Great American Watercolor* (April 1993) was a much-appreciated exhibition. That came from our collection. When we do that it's not limited. I'm not just showing things that are lying around. That would make no sense to anyone.

CG What I'm saying is, for now, have we seen the end of blockbusters? Considering the difficulties, won't it be some time before we again see something like Peter Sutton's (1993) *The Age of Rubens*. As Alan Shestack told me, Sutton started working on that show from the minute he arrived at the MFA (1985).

Consider *Monet in the '90s: The Series Paintings*, which Paul Tucker curated in 1990. It's said that the museum had great attendance, but didn't make any money because the insurance costs were so high. On the other hand, *Renoir* in 1985, had a record attendance of some 500,000, and cleared $1 million for the museum. Between then and now, costs have risen cutting into profit margins.

Museums can only do those shows with corporate sponsorship. Shestack told me that he couldn't find sponsorship for *The Age of Rubens*, but believed in the project and took a chance. That gets risky, and museums look more for a sure thing.

MR It doesn't matter if shows make money or not, as long as you know why you are doing them. I do not want to do exhibitions just to make a profit, but we have to get the books balanced. We will put on some exhibitions that take a loss. That's an attempt to balance the picture.

CG Exhibitions create interest in the institution, as did *Rubens* last year. There is nothing on that level in the schedule this year.

MR Oh really, what about our *Nolde* show? Do you think that's a worthwhile exhibition? It's a great exhibition.

(*Emil Nolde: The Artists Prints*, curated by Clifford Ackley, 1995, proved to be controversial because of the artist's membership in the Nazi party. There was a contentious panel discussion at the Goethe Institute with emotional exchanges between the audience and panelists. The artist was presented as völkisch, an adherent of a German ethnic and nationalist movement espousing "blood and soil," which was active from the late 19th century through the Nazi era. By keeping a low profile during National Socialism, *Nolde* was tolerated or ignored in a manner that other German expressionists were not. From critics, there were no debates about the superb aesthetics of the exhibition. There were protests and headlines, however, that the artist's Nazi background was not covered in the catalogue. The museum opted to add that information in wall text for the exhibition.)

CG Is there corporate support for the *Nolde* exhibition?

MR I'm not sure. Frankly, I'm running a museum with worthwhile exhibitions, not developing projects to lure corporate sponsors. We want to do what we want to do. *Nolde* is a potentially wonderful exhibition. You seem to criticize the museum for doing exhibitions to make money, and then are displeased when we do something superb like *Nolde*. It's a wonderfully worthwhile opportunity.

(The backfire of Nolde's Nazi affiliation was an unforced error of the curator. The question is whether Ackley knew of, but opted to ignore, the artist's questionable politics. It underscores an era when the moral compass and sensitivity to social justice by curators and museums were less well calibrated.)

MR We need to do *Renoir* and *Nolde*. That's very important.

CG Because of all the pressures of fund raising on museums, it is interesting that some top curators, like Peter Sutton, leave for the private sector with more income and latitude. He was arguably frustrated not to get the *Rembrandt* show that he had initiated.

MR You will have to ask Mr. Sutton how he is getting along at Christie's.

(Former MFA director, Perry T. Rathbone, joined the auction house for a number of years. What happens when top museum directors and curators lure great collections to the market rather than to museums? With changes in the tax laws there is less incentive for donations. There is logic to selling work, which is then taxed or perhaps donated to charities. Many wealthy collectors, including museum trustees, acquire as an investment strategy. While the MFA's curator of European Painting, John Walsh, the retired director of the Getty Museum, was a paid consultant to collector William I. Koch. An area of concern is the extent to which curators and art historians are compensated for attributions and finder's fees. While regarded as unethical, it is common for curators to collect in their field and accept gifts from artists.)

Our curators have tremendous opportunities for what they want to do. You are generalizing based on one person. I have set my directorship from the time I've been here on the theme of "One Museum." Not to be a museum of separate departments, but a museum of unity. The personality syndrome is subordinated to the museum and that's an important change. I feel the mandate is as an educational institution. There is a focus on the integrity of the collections and their interpretation. We offer great opportunities in our own way.

CG What do you have in mind?

MR Museums tend to focus on painting, but I would like to do more with three-dimensional objects and non-European cultures. I think, eventually, we may get away entirely from just painting shows. We can definitely do more with contemporary sculpture.

CG Why are we missing shows like *Rembrandt*?

MR That's got a lot to do with funding. We need individuals and corporations to give to us and trust us.

CG Recently I was surprised to see *The Head of Sesostris III*, a masterpiece of Middle Kingdom art, on view in the Egyptian galleries on loan from the Metropolitan Museum of Art.

MR We have a regular policy for such exchanges. It is important to have the collections more widely seen at Nagoya and other museums.

CG That's the argument of Tom Krens in creating satellite museums. He states that eighty-five percent of the collections of major museums like the Guggenheim are not on view. In recent years there have been some great exchanges. When the MFA was renovating, it sent its Copley's to the Philadelphia Museum. Similarly, when they were under construction, a great show of their Thomas Eakins collection came here. Do you see more of those kinds of exchanges?

MR We shall see. I am just getting started, and it will take some time moving forward to create a dynamic exhibition program.

CG Do you come from money?

(With benefits and raises his compensation was some $900,000 annually. When visiting as a job candidate, he was put up at the former Midtown Motor Inn near the museum. There was a dinner with trustees at The Ritz at which he has been described as brilliant.)

MR Myself? I'm afraid not. I was born on 20 acres in a Yorkshire hamlet. My family were farmers and butchers. If you wanted me to, I could break down a hog from hams to sausages. But I don't want to be known as the "butcher of the MFA."

CG What's your personal style regarding leisure time. Do you like to cook and entertain?

MR I don't have time to cook and am not a creature of habit. There is not a regular day when I do the shopping and errands.

CG Boston has long been regarded as an anglophile city.

MR I'm not coming here because it's a city like London. I'm coming because there are wonderful opportunities and challenges. I'm paid to run the museum and a part of that job is to mingle with individuals who support our fundraising.

I have a small house in the Back Bay, which is not suitable for entertaining. I felt that if I come to Boston I want to be a part of the city. There was temptation to live in one of the towns around Boston, but I want to be where I can walk to work and to theatre. Back Bay is near the shops and entertainment.

(The museum later provided housing in Newton suitable for the entertainment of donors and dignitaries expected of a museum director.)

CG Talking to museum directors and curators there seem to be different models of how exhibitions are organized and marketed. Generally, that entails finding corporate sponsors. But that appears to be changing. Given the startup costs and touring, with a catalogue, a show may tour for a year or two. Different approaches are emerging with video and online marketing. Do you see a shift in that direction, particularly for funding major exhibitions? It appears, particularly with international projects, that potential media and marketing is a part of the initial stages of exhibitions.

MR The first thing I would say is that there is much more planning in terms of corporate support. We have to put a lot more thought into this. Corporations seem much more interested in health-related and content-related giving. What we have here is great resources for education. It's at the very heart of new ways of getting corporations involved with exhibitions. We have to plan further ahead and with them. They have to see potential in exhibitions and have their demands met as well. The technological and media applications of exhibitions are very important. We are looking at ways in which information can be electronically published.

CG The Getty has been proposing projects to digitize museum collections. The goal would be to have images of objects online. Eventually, one may make virtual tours of major museums. That would be a great resource for curators organizing exhibitions. There has been a decline in federal and state funding. Given this environment, all of the cultural institutions are seeking the same private and corporate sources. There are many mouths to feed.

MR To succeed in attracting corporate support, we have to give them something that they want. If we can do that, we will be successful.

CG It was before your time, but what is your opinion about why the museum was not successful in securing support for its *Rubens* exhibition?

MR It's a matter of creating opportunities for them. Rubens did have opportunities for the right corporation. The elements are there and we have to find the right match.

CG What is your position on contemporary art?

MR We will be doing an extraordinary number of special exhibitions. It's very important to grow that collection. We have to be showing what we have to showcase contemporary art acquisitions to make the case for attracting more giving.

CG It's well known that the MFA is a museum with world-class collections, but not in 20th century art.

MR I understand that, but think that there are a lot of things that can be done. We have significant support for the contemporary department.

(When a respected curator Trevor Fairbrother left, search for top candidates was unsuccessful. Established curators were wary of reporting to Rogers. The position was filled by Cheryl Brutvan from the Albright Knox Museum. Her programming was regarded as less than remarkable. Eventually, she left for the Norton Gallery. In 2011, Edward Saywell became chair of the Linde Family Wing for Contemporary Art with Jen Mergel as the Beal Senior Curator of Contemporary Art. Reto Thüring was appointed to the Beal Family position by Matthew Teitelbaum in 2018. Saywell is now Chief of Exhibitions Strategy and Gallery Displays.)

Interview September 2011, opening of the Linde Wing of Contemporary Art.

Charles Giuliano Is there anything left to do?

Malcolm Rogers The museum is like one of those huge bridges. You start painting at one end and by the time you reach the other end it's time to start all over again.

CG You've had so many projects.

MR I like new things. What a privilege it is to be here during a time of transformation for the museum.

CG How long have you been here?

MR Sixteen or seventeen years I can't remember. I'm about the fourth longest serving director.

CG In terms of bricks and mortar, also one of the most significant.

MR When you think of it, for a museum of this size to have transformed every single façade in a period of four or five years.

CG Let's talk about contemporary art. This was the major museum, which was famous for not having any.

MR We'll have to see what you think. It's definitely new.

CG What have you acquired in the past few years?

MR There's a lot that we've acquired. But I've also said there's a real culture of collectors in town that's growing up. People are backing purchases. Boston is in a process of exciting change.

CG How did that come about? Boston, historically, has been a city that didn't have an interest in contemporary art.

MR It has gradually been gaining momentum. If you think about all the institutions there are in town. Think of the influence of the new ICA.

CG Are you going to work together?

MR Of course. If you look at the labels on the walls, you will see that many of the benefactors are supporters of the ICA and the MFA.
(In 1988 the MFA and ICA jointly presented *The Binational: German Art of the Late 1980s/American Art of the Late 1980s* in cooperation with the Stadtische Kunsthalle and the Kunstsammlung Nordrhein-Westfalen of Dusseldorf and with support from the Massachusetts Council on the Arts and Humanities, AT&T Foundation, and the National Endowment for the Arts.)

CG In New York there has been an interesting relationship between MoMA and the Met. When works in the MoMA collection morph from contemporary and modernist to historic, some of that material gets transferred to the Met. The ICA is starting to collect, but has little or no space to store more than a token of work.

In a generation or so, it will reach a critical mass and perhaps a crisis point. Can you see some of that work finding its way to the MFA using the model of MoMA and the Met?

MR We don't have that relationship at the moment. We have art going back thousands of years. When things grow older, they become just as attractive to us.

CG What is your own definition of contemporary art?

MR My own, very personal definition, is anything that was produced during the lifetime of the oldest person in the room.

(The MFA's Linde Family Wing for Contemporary Art includes Claude Monet's *La Japonaise (Camille Monet in Japanese costume)*, 1876, as a conceptual aspect of a work by Louise Lawler, and *Rape of the Sabine Women* by Picasso, 1963.)

CG That's an interesting definition. I haven't heard that before.

MR I think there is too much emphasis on cutting edge and bleeding edge and wet paint. But I think it should be the art of a generation.

CG The issue is that contemporary art has evolved beyond the object with installations and the epic scaled works that we see on the global circuit of biennials. Much of that work just simply can't be housed in the galleries of the MFA. We are only viewing the object-oriented slice of contemporary art in museums. Has that informed the mandate of what is contained here?

MR I think we have some pretty ambitious installation pieces here. When we are acquiring something, we have to ask, will it stand the test of time artistically? Is it conservationally sound? Will it last? Does it stand a chance of coming out historically? You've also got to show imagination. You've got to love the subject. That sometimes allows you to make risky choices. Contemporary art is about risky choices to some extent.

CG How do you preserve an Anselm Kiefer? You have one actually.

MR Yes, we do have one with straw built into it. Conservation is very difficult.

CG That was a risky piece when it was acquired.

MR I'm not saying we'll stop taking risks. I think you will see some risks around the walls. There are some things that are very conservative and quite New England.

CG Is this a good day for you, Malcolm?

MR It's an exciting day. I always love to see a project coming to fulfillment. The truth is it's never complete. This leads on to other opportunities. I'm particularly happy because everyone involved in this project, it wasn't a huge budget, and everyone has a real sense of joy and achievement in the project.

CG Particularly having works to put on the wall and not fall flat on your face. Why has this historically been such a problematic aspect of the MFA's collection?

MR We are what people in Boston collect, to a very large extent. Certainly, people from other cities are giving us art. In truth, a city collection like this is a reflection of its donors. The taste in Boston has been fundamentally conservative. Now things are perking up.

CG In the 19th century, during the era of French Impressionism, Bostonians were progressive and made great acquisitions.

MR That's absolutely right.

CG Then it tapered off in the early 20th century when business and banking in Boston lost momentum. The taste of old money was ever more conservative. In recent years there had been a boom and new entrepreneurship.

MR Yes, so we are in a way a reflection of the taste and mood of our city. This is an exciting time.

CG What happened when the focus of the Boston art world turned to immigrants in the 1920s and the Depression years of the 1930s? Boston collectors and the MFA passed on the era of the Boston Expressionists.

(During the Linde opening, Kelly, an abstract artist, discussed studying with Karl Zerbe at the Museum School.)

MR You realize that these are artists whom we have on display in the museum. Just remember that we are one of the world's great encyclopedic museums. We have to have a bit of everything. We can't be a museum of New England. We work as hard as we can for New England artists as well. Just look around.

CG You have depth in Copley. The interest in contemporary Boston art tapered off from the 1920s until only comparatively recently. During the 1920s Boston Impressionists like The Ten were phasing out and the immigrant Boston Expressionists were emerging. It is precisely when the mainstream of Boston lost interest, not just in Boston artists, but also passed on Post War abstract expressionism, pop, minimalism, and other contemporary movements. Are you now picking up and coming back to multiculturalism?

MR As you know, multiculturalism is an important theme in any encyclopedic museum.

We're conscious that work has to be done in the Twentieth Century and in the contemporary period. You'll see in these galleries a statement of good intentions. Some achievement. More still to do.

CG A way to go.

MR There's always a way to go. There's always a way to go.

CG Are you under pressure for that? What is your relationship with the National Center for Afro-American Artists and the MFA's adjunct curator, Barry Gaither?

MR It's good. We see Barry here a lot. He works very actively with the museum. It's a source of great interest to us. Watch this space. You'll hear news of interesting acquisitions. What we are presenting here is a salad bar of things you will love and things you won't. The idea is to provoke discussion.

(Regarding "Watch This Space," the museum soon after announced plans to acquire *Man at His Bath* by Caillebotte. To purchase the nude painting, the museum sold works by Alfred Sisley, Maxime Camille Louis Maufra, Paul Gauguin, Claude Monet, Pierre-Auguste Renoir, and Camille Pissarro.)

CG Is there anything you are particularly pleased with?

MR What I am particularly pleased with, which benefits the whole of Boston, is that Boston is acquiring collectors of contemporary art. They are prepared to work with more than one institution, which I feel is critical. It creates a scene here. Looking historically at what you will see here today, I am particularly pleased by the acquisition of a major work by Ellsworth Kelly. It's something we lacked, and he is one of the greatest alumni of the Museum School.

(Ellsworth Kelly (1923–2015) a graduate of the Museum School, was present during the event in support of an exhibition of his work.)

CG Can you ever fill the gaps?

MR I would like to fill the gaps. There will still be opportunities to fill gaps in the next decades. As work is reassessed and things come on the market when collections break up, we'll be active.

CG This week MoMA is opening a de Kooning exhibition, which, with works valued at more than a billion dollars, is the most expensive project the museum has ever undertaken.

MR We just acquired our first de Kooning painting. It's a comparatively small work, but a beautiful head study. Perhaps one day de Kooning's prices may come down and we'll have an opportunity.

Malcolm in the West Wing. Giuliano photo.

Malcolm musing. Giuliano photo.

Rogers courted billionaire William Koch. Giuliano photo.

"Malcolm and Me" Astrid Hiemer photo.

Koch's America's Cup yachts displayed in front of the MFA. Giuliano photo.

Rogers shares a laugh with artist Ellsworth Kelly.

Fellow Brits David Hockney and Rogers.

Lunch with Malcolm Rogers. Giuliano photo collage.

Malcolm Rogers and architect Lord Norman Foster. Giuliano photo

Lord Norman Foster views his American Wing at the MFA. Giuliano Photo

Malcolm's Union-Busting Blues

Malcolm Rogers fought to prevent the security guards from forming a union. It reveals a lot about his corporate approach to managing "One Museum." Many of the guards were artists and musicians who cared about the museum. The guards, some of whom had worked for twenty years, were making under ten dollars an hour. As the protestors noted in their campaign, the director was then making some $500,000 a year with benefits and perks.

We spoke with Gary Lombard who helped to organize the workers. Today he provides independent IT support, in which capacity, I have worked with him long term.

By contrast, in 2020, under Matthew Teitelbaum, the administration and workers negotiated to broadly unionize the museum.

Charles Giuliano When was the protest?

Gary Lombard It was a series of rallies starting in the winter of 1998, through the summer of 1999, during the negotiation of our third union contract with the Museum.

The first contract ran from April 1992–1995, when we were affiliated with the United Plant Guard Workers of America (UPGWA), a national union. The second contract ran from March 1996–1999, when we voted to disaffiliate from UPGWA and form our own independent union. The third contract ran from September 1999–2002.

You will note the gaps in the dates of those contracts. That's when we were fighting for our existence as a union. We held rallies during all of these contract campaigns to put pressure on the Museum.

CG Who organized it?

GL We did. We organized all our own rallies. We were a completely independent union. We did everything ourselves. We hired our own negotiator, our own lawyer, elected our own officers, treasurer, and shop stewards. We had a newsletter called the *Security Blanket* and *Security Bulletins*. We wrote and designed our own leaflets. We designed signs, banners, stickers, and had everything printed by a union printer.

We had guards demonstrating on their days off, before and after shifts, and punching out during lunch breaks.

We would demonstrate outside the MFA, outside donors like Verizon, Fidelity, and Shreve, Crump & Low; outside MFA trustees' homes. We would picket outside Malcolm Rogers', John Stanley's (Deputy Director), and John Paul Kozicki's (Director of Visitor Services) homes or apartments.

CG Was a union involved with AFL etc.?

GL No. We had no support from organized labor. Volunteers from Jobs with Justice would show up from time to time to help with larger rallies. The management of major unions ignored our independent union.

We were reaching out to the public by handing out leaflets and urging them to call or email the director. We reached out to college students or school groups visiting the Museum, asking them to carry signs and hand out flyers. Our guards talked to the press.

CG What were wages and benefits at the time?

GL Very low! Our message was simple and effective. We had many full-time members who worked for ten, fifteen, twenty, and up to twenty-five years. They were making less than ten dollars an hour. There was a guard making nine dollars and twenty-four cents after twenty-five years. Two guards were making eight dollars and eighty-four cents after twenty years. Everyone else was making considerably less money. Hence the sign, "Working Up to 25 Years. Making Less than $10.00 per hour." Our twenty-five to thirty-foot banners stated "Malcolm Rogers makes $500,000 per year. Why can't he treat his workers fairly?"

The MFA director was making as much or more than the president of the USA. It was a point that we made at every opportunity. With board support, he had just led a corporate coup, firing a number of curators, which the press called the "The Boston Massacre."

The MFA was flush in the 1990s coming off three huge Monet shows and other profitable special exhibits. Malcolm was in the midst of raising $500 million.

CG Did the protest result in an increase? If so, how much?

GL We received a three percent raise every year for the next three years for all union members, additional step raises for members at one, four, seven, and ten years of service, a higher starting rate, doing away with lower probationary rate pay for the first ninety days of service. There was a retroactive pay raise to the date of the last expired union contract. Also, a yearly bonus for any guards already making over the agreed upon wage rate for their years of service. By the end of our three-year contract, every member was earning over ten dollars per hour.

We had already negotiated double-time-and-a-half pay for holidays (2 1/2 pay) on a previous contract for guards that worked any holiday. That included part-timers if they worked the holiday. They could work eight hours and get paid for twenty hours. More, if there was a party after hours. The Museum tried to take that away, but failed. A typical union-busting technique forces unions to squander resources to keep what they had negotiated. We only negotiated forward from our last contract.

This holiday pay turned out to be quite valuable, as the MFA opened on some Monday holidays, then eventually all holidays, except for Thanksgiving and Christmas. They even opened on New Years Day, which ended up being one of their biggest days of the year. It was a gold mine for them. We just wanted to share a few of those nuggets.

CG Do you have any personal memories about Malcolm?

GL He was very good at what he did. He made at ton of money for the Museum. He charmed donors into giving money through fundraisers. He opened new galleries, reopened the Garden Courtyard enclosed in glass for parties, and funded the new Art of the Americas wing. We supported that, as we cared about the museum.

Malcolm was thin skinned and easily annoyed, took everything personally, and held grudges. He told us, through the MFA's lawyer, that we didn't make the Museum any money so don't expect a big raise. Only people who make money for the Museum get raises. His first three lowball offers to us were for a five-, eight-, and twelve-cent raise.

That's why we printed stickers with "8 cents is nonsense" on an illustration of a peanut and put them over every MFA advertisement on every MBTA station on the Green Line.

Malcolm resented that banner about his annual salary. As Malcolm was leaving, he took one look at that banner for the first time, and came right back in the entrance and stormed off in the other direction. We were thrilled and printed a second banner with the same message for outside the other entrance.

His comment about not liking curators who ran their departments like "little fiefdoms" shows you his worldview. He thought they usurped his power. He fired independent curators, replacing them with staff loyal to him. He got board approval, forcing trustees to share blame for the media and public backlash.

He treated low-wage workers like serfs. He fired them in several massive layoffs. They blamed the economy. Unlike other employees, the guards had union protection. They had to negotiate layoffs with us. Our contract stipulated firing those with the least amount of seniority and making the least amount of money. That gave workers in other departments ideas.

In 1995, we voted to form our own independent union. The management team, including the Director of Protective Services, the Security Supervisors, Human Resources Director, the HR staff, and even Malcolm Rogers himself, spent many months trying to convince the membership to vote against our union run. They held mandatory meetings before the start of shifts. They gave handouts from their perspective.

Malcolm showed up before the election to hold a mandatory meeting in the break room right before work. They talked to a part-timers who mainly worked weekends, trying to convince them to vote against the union.

He rolled up his shirtsleeves, pretending that he was just another working man, like he was one of us. He told us that he used to be in a union and understood our concerns. He said, "Trust us, just this one time." He took questions, which he didn't handle very well. He couldn't answer the most important question: Why shouldn't we vote for a union when we are the union? We couldn't trust the MFA to do the right thing.

In the weeks before the election, management was talking individually to the entire guard staff. This included the Director of the Human Resources Department, who nobody knew. She was shaking people's hands and acting like their best friend. They were coached on how to do this by some union-busting consulting firm.

While the guards were voting, management, including Rogers, the Director of Protective Services, some Security Supervisors, and the Director of Human Resources were all there. They watched, especially Malcolm, as votes were counted, recounted, then certified. We won by only seven votes. Rogers stormed out with everyone else. We hugged and celebrated.

When we won, they fired members of their management team. In this case, the Director of Protective Services, who was a former state trooper lieutenant colonel and the HR director were fired. They later fired others for their failures. It was like watching the *Sopranos*. So much for "Trust Us!" Had we failed, union management, including me, would have been fired.

CG This past year, the administrators and MFA workers negotiated a union contract with no fuss.

GL During one of the Monet shows, they hired Pinkerton to provide security for the special exhibition store. A Pinkerton guard was caught stealing Monet T-shirts and sweatshirts. He was caught red handed and fired.

Most of our members were artists, musicians, college students, and retirees, who loved the museum. They thought of it as a nice place to work. We actually cared and wanted the MFA to do well. We just wished that the feeling was mutual, and that the MFA would treat their employees fairly.

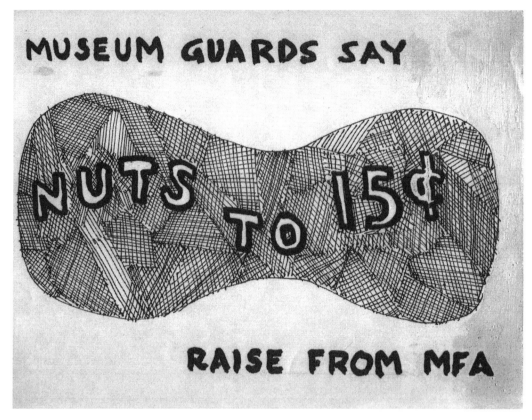

Working for peanuts. Protest images courtesy of Gary Lombard archive.

Protesting for fair wages.

Malcolm's Union-Busting Blues

Car talk.

Jack the Dripper supports the union.

Standing up for fair treatment.

Gary Lombard on the picket line.

Matthew Teitelbaum, from the ICA to MFA

Uniquely, the Canadian-born Matthew Teitelbaum (1956), was briefly the acting director of Boston's Institute of Contemporary Art, which he left in 1993. He then returned to Boston to become director of the MFA in 2015. At the ICA, he was hired by David Ross and worked with the board in the time between when Ross left and Milena Kalinovska became director. He worked with her on complex and provocative exhibitions.

During the interim years, from 1993 to 2015, he was chief curator, then director, of the Art Gallery of Ontario. There he was a brick and mortar director who raised $306 million for a Frank Gehry designed expansion.

More than an administrator, he is a scholar and mediator. As a curator, he made notable contributions to the field of modern and contemporary art with exhibitions and catalogues. He earned a master's degree in European painting and sculpture from London's renowned Courtauld Institute of Art.

In particular, he dealt with issues of diversity and inclusion at the AGO. He was a part of the national museum movement to integrate and contextualize all aspects of First Nations art into strategies for acquisitions and display in exhibitions.

In 2019, there was an MFA instance of racism targeting a school group that drew criticism and media attention. The MFA, which had been widely regarded as elitist, has a 150-year legacy of exclusion, racism, and anti-Semitism. That is now changing under Teitelbaum's leadership.

He had already initiated changes to reverse this when the incident preempted his efforts. Since then, in agreement with the Attorney General, the museum has created funding to bring diversity and inclusion to all aspects of the museum's programming and staff training.

While the mantra of Malcolm Rogers was "One Museum" that of Teitelbaum is making the MFA a museum "For All of Boston."

Rogers was a brick and mortar director who raised $500 million to create the American Wing designed by Lord Norman Foster. Toward that end, Rogers spent more than he raised. He passed on considerable debt.

That could not have happened at a more difficult time. The Covid-19 pandemic shut down museums and theatres and devastated the arts and artists. To balance the books in 2020 entailed cost cutting, layoffs, retirements, and fundraising. The red ink for 2021 is projected at $12 million as the nation struggles.

The MFA is renowned for world-class collections in areas other than modern and contemporary art. It is now impossible to fill gaps, as the market for key works is out of reach. That ship has sailed. But Teitelbaum is charged with making adjustments and engaging in affordable acquisitions geared to the future. Where to display and store these new works is another matter. One strategy is to integrate it throughout the museum creating new ways to look at art of the past through the lens of contemporary art.

Arguably, there has never been a more difficult and daunting time to be the director of a world-class, encyclopedic museum.

I have known Matthew for many years and feel that, for these times, there is nobody more qualified and up to the task than he is.

What follows are two interviews that offer then-and-now engagements. I knew him well when he was at the ICA. I was delighted to meet with him again in his current position. A difference is access. Today, it's tough to schedule an interview and you're on the clock. You have to cover as many bullet points as possible before time runs out. It took from summer to January to negotiate the interview at the beginning of this book. Notably, he looked at his watch and said that we had doubled the allotted time, but he took two more questions. He commented that we have known each other for a long time and there are issues we should bring up "the next time."

This interview occurred in July 1993 as he prepared to leave for a new position at the Art Gallery of Ontario.

Charles Giuliano Will we ever see a fair and objective discussion of the work of Robert Mapplethorpe? Because of the related social and political issues, and attempts at suppression and censorship, the norm of objective critical thinking has been shut down.

Reading recent reviews of the Venice Biennale by Robert Hughes and Michael Kimmelman, they don't give information. There is little discussion of what they saw and evaluated. Their reports deliver polemics. Looking at the current state of arts journalism, we don't see much critical thinking. Shows are endorsed or not, but there is little discussion of the work itself. Critics appear to be voting rather than reviewing.

Matthew Teitelbaum. In part what you are saying is that there is not a lot of independent thinking going on, and I think that's true. You're also saying, and I think it's very true, that truth is equated with the power of speech. The two aren't necessarily connected. I'm thinking of the work of Hans Haacke in the Venice Biennale. It's a piece that works in exactly the terms you are talking about in relationship to "Corporal Politics." When you walk into the piece, there's an image of it in the Robert Hughes article, you have no option but to say, 'this is a great piece.'

There is no ambiguity. There is no internal contradiction, which much great art has. As you say, you cannot be critical of the piece and hold your position on the left. You can't be critical of the Haacke piece and maintain credibility by saying that you support his other work. You can't say that this is a problematic piece, but on the other hand, I really believe in Alan Sekula's work. You're all in or all out. And I think that's a problem. The Haacke piece was strong and powerful, but in spite of itself, because it only allowed a single response.

In this climate, and at this moment, I would like to think of the ICA's *Malcolm X* (*Malcolm X: Man, Ideal, Icon*, 1993) and cross-dressing *Dress Codes* (*Dress Codes:Where Guys Are Dolls*) as having complexities and contradictions. There isn't a single position that you can hold in relationship to these exhibitions. That's part of their strength. It's not, in that sense, didactic. We can provide viewers with a lot to read. We don't make a judgment about whether this art does or does not stand on its own. But we provide a context in which you might more fully understand it

It's not, as you say, that we start with point A and that by the end of the exhibition lead you to point B. I do not believe we did that with the *Dress Codes* show and I don't believe we did that with the *Malcolm X* show. We do not start with when he was a child and then go through when he rejected The Nation of Islam. We do not say, accept Malcolm X as a great orator. We present him with all of his complexities and contradictions. We are trying to find a way for viewers to see different relations to that figure. This, to me, is different from what you are describing regarding the potential tyranny of political correctness. I think it's your responsibility as a critic to keep saying the things you are saying about the quality of works of art.

CG That creates an adversarial relationship with curators.

MT It's your responsibility because I think in those comments people will have a chance to respond, to reflect, and as a curator, my judgment changes. I always remember the context in which those judgments were made. I think that Cathy Opie made an important statement, and in the context of *Dress Codes* it was important and powerful. (Photographs of women as drag kings.) There's very little room to create the context in which it's seen. Most work depends on the context in which you see it. I'm interested in that problematic, and that's why I'm interested in the ICA.

CG The Nan Goldin pieces (in *Dress Codes*) could be seen anywhere. The work has been widely shown. They don't need that show to create context. They don't need the Whitney Biennial. Her work just needs a wall to hang on.

MT I agree.

CG There is a level of work that achieves ubiquitous celebrity and critical acceptance. For example, provocative images by Diane Arbus, Cindy Sherman, Jenny Holzer, or Barbara Kruger. Their work is sufficiently emblematic to stand on its own. They don't require wall text and explanations beyond labels. They don't require elaborate programming to be understood. To confront an Arbus is to be drawn into its wonder. In a recent show, *Alumni Collect*, at Williams College Art Museum, there was the Arbus of an interracial couple in a park with a chimpanzee. You asked how she would find such an image? Her images happened as chance encounters when she went around in public with her camera. We are intrigued by her way of looking at and discovering things. The image is now some twenty-five years old but retains its impact.

MT What I'm driven by is where does art meet its public? My father was a painter. I grew up with wet oil paintings in my house. The act of making art was a part of my everyday life. I'm a part of that desire to make something. But I'm not an artist, and I wasn't then either. I was somebody who received the art. Having been a student, I have dealt with how I have received it. Ultimately, it's been filtered through me. What drives me is not evangelical, but nonetheless, there is a drive to find ways to make art meaningful in the day-to-day lives of people. I walk into the homes of friends and am appalled by what people settle for as enrichment of their everyday lives, in terms of what they hang on their walls, regarding the way in which they are prepared to be involved with visual images that surround them.

CG That's something that bothers me. Through recordings we have access to the full range of music. I can afford to listen to any music that interests me. For art I am limited to galleries and museums. That comments on the elitism of the fine arts regarding the general public as consumers and appreciators. In galleries we have free access to view work, but only the wealthy can own it. Once a work is acquired, it is removed from public view.

That impacts the ICA in terms of audience. It takes an annual budget of $1.5 million to deliver attendance of some 75,000 visitors. For the city of Boston annual ICA attendance is equivalent to one or two Red Sox games.

MT It's a bit more than that. More like two-and-half Red Sox games. But you're right. But this is my point. Is it the failure of the ICA in terms of what it presents? Or is it the failure of the ICA as an institution that engages in some active way? We showed *Performing Objects* with Rebecca Horn, Bruce Nauman, Peter Campus, Gary Hill, all tremendously effective work. Yet attendance was miserable. I don't remember the exact numbers. If you try to figure out overall attendance, it was about half of the audience for *Dress Codes*.

CG What did that show draw?

MT About 17,000, in that range.

CG What was attendance for the Mapplethorpe show?

MT One hundred four thousand, which is mind-boggling. We could have had more visitors, but that was our capacity. My goal, which drives me, is to have the public meet the art, and the art to meet its public. It is an effort to find that meeting place. That doesn't mean that every exhibition I organize has the same goals or the same way of meeting its goals. I certainly believe in all the art we show. It changes its meaning by the context in which it is shown. I wouldn't want a whole program structured on shows like *Dress Codes* and *Malcolm X*. I want those shows in context with other exhibitions.

CG Perhaps it was bad planning to have them run back to back, one provocative theme show right after another.

MT Yeah, maybe.

(Low attendance numbers were a problem for the ICA. The norm for contemporary arts programs was about 25,000 in a good year. Milena Kalinovska presented a survey of feminism, *Inside the Visible*, as well as one-woman shows of artists from Carol Rama to Rachel Whiteread, Marlene Dumas, Charlotte Solomon, Cornelia Parker, and Annie Leibovitz. *The Bleeding Heart* focused on Mexican art. Attendance was generally marginal. There was board pressure to curate more populist shows. *Elvis and Marilyn* failed to attract Boston college-aged population of 250,000. There was a gay audience for *Dress Codes* and blacks came for *Malcolm X*. Perhaps the canine crowd turned out for William Wegman's weimaraners. But those niche audiences did not create a base for ICA programming.)

CG You came here from Canada at an early phase of your career. Now you leave having been like a salmon swimming upstream in Boston. Perhaps the difficulty of navigating the art world here makes you better prepared for challenges awaiting you at the Art Gallery of Ontario in your hometown, Toronto. Can you describe what this transition has meant to you? You came at the end of David Ross as director. There was a transition during a search over two years. That would seem to have given you a lot of curatorial independence. You have had a chance to work with Milena Kalinovska.

MT My time here has intensified thinking about two primary issues. One is that institutions, and not just people, have to take risks in what they do. Institutions have to try to do two things. They have to create themselves as models of thinking that the public will reflect on. That sense of risk-taking has to imbue the whole institution. One of the great things about the ICA is that it doesn't have a permanent collection and it can rethink itself. During the time I have been here, it has done that a number of times. I have been fortunate to be here during a time of change. I have been involved in a lot of this rethinking. I've been able to direct it for a certain period of time and see first-hand how institutions change, if they want to.

The second thing is that it's a public institution and a public space, which for me, means that it has a public dialogue. It is not a place that is constructed from a private or individual point of view. It has to be constructed in a manner that a public dialogue can take place. The ICA has not one public but many publics.

Since I've been here, I've developed sophistication in understanding how different publics can be served. It's the notion of a museum as a space where a variety of things can go on. You can complement an exhibition with ways in which it can be constructed so that it can coexist, not just in a pluralistic way, but in an interesting one.

I'm incredibly grateful for the various kinds of lives that the ICA has had since I have been here. I wanted David (Joselit) and Elizabeth (Sussman) to work very intensely. I was involved in a very intense relationship with the board during the period between directors.

I have watched as Milena begins to reinvent the ICA. This has happened in a very exciting context. You have a million dollars to create an institution, then, how to do it? It's an exciting possibility. It's not a daunting task. It is daunting, however, in terms of changing people's expectations, while ratcheting in a different direction. It's not daunting and devastating in the sense that there is a future. It's a pretty terrific process and has been exciting to watch.

One of Milena's challenges is to be realistic about expectations and to help people to be realistic about what they expect from the ICA, about what it can deliver, and her incredible energy. There are a lot of people willing to work with her and she will maximize whatever she can. It's going to be tough to do the programming that she wants. If anyone can do it, then it's Milena.

Her timeframe has to expand in order to do certain things, and she'll make the right decisions, because she will be realistic about the resources of the staff. For the moment, it is very much touch and go. You can't change the structure of the institution and expect to produce the same product. Milena understands that.

Again, that doesn't mean that the product can't be exciting and develop a loyal following. But she has to be clear about the product, relative to resources.

CG Do you have a sense of that product under these circumstances?

MT It will be an institution where artists have a clear voice. Collective collaboration projects will be encouraged. Exhibitions will be linked to public programming. They won't be an add-on to satisfy the fifteen people who want to come to a lecture. Programming has to be thought about in a more organic manner, as a part of the presentation of the exhibition. I think the ICA will take council from artists and individuals in the community. That doesn't mean it will exclusively show works from the arts community. Projects, however, will be pitched in terms of their relevance to the community. That approach is quite healthy.

CG That approach to programming was not notable in the prior (Ross) administration.

MT I will say something you are not likely to agree with. Why that's not possible at the ICA is because of the institution that David (Ross) and Elizabeth (Sussman) built together. The ICA that Milena reinvents may be vastly different. But it's built on the foundation that David and Elizabeth left. It is an ICA of serious investigation and wide-ranging curiosity. It is an institution of the highest professional standards. Most importantly is a willingness to go in directions it does not fully understand.

Those are all positive elements. It is often that curators make a mistake. I said that in my conversation with Cate McQuaid (*Boston Globe*). I'll say it to you slightly differently. When you enter a creative project (putting together an exhibition is a creative project) you have a set of possibilities open for the longest possible time. There is a judgment about when you have to close them down. Believe me, I have made a mistake by keeping them too open. But, if you start with the question: What is it you want the content to be? What are the sets of relationships? Then you're asking a less exciting question than: Why do I want to do this? Why do I want to have a dynamic relationship with the issues that are being raised?

Why do I want to put Allan Crite's work from fifty or sixty years ago in the ICA? (Alan Crite, 1910–2007 was a graduate of The Museum School, and Boston's foremost African American artist of his generation.) Answer questions about "why," without being locked into the specific questions of "what," then you can open up a full set of possibilities in which the "what" comes pretty quickly. The problem with much curating is that you come up with the product seamlessly composed in terms of the answer to what. David and Elizabeth had the urge to ask: Why?

CG How might we rephrase that? Starting with the "what" rather than "why"? Is it the priority between what and why that we are discussing?

MT Right. I think you enter the field of inquiry, which consists of a whole set of questions. Why is this important? Why do we have to think about it now? Why do we want to present it to our public?

If you can ask yourself these questions, you can create a field of activity in which a whole bunch of things slot in.

We did this with *Dress Codes*. In the beginning of the project there were a small number of artists we were committed to. Nan Goldin was one of them. From the beginning (Japanese photographer Yasumasa) Morimura was another one. Ron Davilla had two works. One was a painting of an asshole sticking you in the face. The other was a Papal poster of a guy in a little dress. Actually, we started with another artist who didn't end up in the exhibition. We started with the question why and moved into what.

This might be one of your criticisms of the exhibition. If you leave in "the why" too long you don't end up with the works you want. You haven't focused on what the content is. But, as a methodology, you have left yourself open from the beginning. The exhibition was done in four months. That's not meant as an apology. It's a fact.

We had an historical component. We had plans to acknowledge cinema. We planned to include historical forebears, but scrapped all that. We didn't have enough time or money. That doesn't mean that we might have done it with the necessary scholarship. I'm not saying we had a perfect thing and that we couldn't do it. What I'm saying is that a part of our argument was missing. Our thesis was that this is not just a contemporary phenomenon. It came out of a condition that evolves from a set of historical facts. We tried to acknowledge that in the videotape. That was not a part of the exhibition and its construction. (Branka Bogdanov created remarkable video documents of ICA exhibitions.)

CG If you had more time and money, what might have been different?

MT We would have done that. But we didn't, because of specific circumstances. That is the problem that starts so rigorously with the question why, and by the time you get to what, you may not have enough time. You want somehow to ask the question, what, as quickly as you can. That level of curiosity, which I like to think I have as a curator, and what I believe David and Elizabeth brought to the ICA, allowed us to work together as well as we did.

CG Now that you are leaving town, what shape is the ICA in?

MT I feel that there are parts of Boston still opening up for me. There are parts of the city that I don't know. I truly believe there are some exceptionally intelligent artists of outstanding merit in this community that are doing things.

CG Milena tells me she plans to be here for the next decade. Do you think there is enough to keep her here that long? Is Boston a sufficiently dynamic community to hold its best talent?

MT The ICA has a role that allows us to talk to each other and to reach the public more directly, not as individuals, but as part of a dialogue, and that will keep Milena here.

CG As a native Bostonian I have accepted being provincial. With proximity to highways and airports, however, it's less relevant where you are from, than where you have been, and whom you are talking to. Critics and curators become provincial when they don't travel. There are too many examples of that in our community. One can be both provincial, planting roots and working with the community, as well as involved with global issues.

MT The ICA has that role to play there. You're talking about access to information and experience that may, or may not, be rooted in Boston. You have access to other experiences where you don't feel strange or isolated. The ICA plays a role by allowing access to greater information.

David and Elizabeth opened Boston to that new information. They made it accessible to individuals who need and benefit from that.

CG It often felt that a direct connection was lacking. If you include more people in the dialectics, make them part of the process, there will be wider interest and acceptance of programming. It isn't effective for the ICA to be an elitist laboratory and think tank. That's a part of why attendance remains marginal.

MT The challenge is to get Boston's artists involved with what's presented by the ICA.

Below, the 2019 interview.

Charles Giuliano It's been a long time.

Matthew Teitelbaum It was thirty years ago when we met. I joined the Institute of Contemporary Art (ICA) in 1989 and was there until 1993, for three and a half years.

CG Did you come from the Courtauld Institute of Art?

MT No, I came from a regional museum in Canada, the Mendel Art Gallery in Saskatoon.

CG Are you Canadian?

MT Yes, from Toronto.

CG From the ICA, you returned to Canada and the AGO (Art Gallery of Ontario in Toronto).

MT I came to Boston because my wife, to whom I was recently married, got a job in Boston. I left my job in Canada and came to live with her. Then I got a job at the ICA. I moved to Boston for love and then it worked out that I actually got a job.

CG I hope you have returned for love.

MT Yes, and then we went back to Toronto when I was asked if I would consider working at the AGO. It was my childhood museum and I started as chief curator. I was hired by Glen Lowry, who then left to become director of MoMA. Max Andersen (Maxwell L. Andersen) came to be director of the museum. He left to become director of the Whitney (Museum of American Art). Then I became director. I was chief curator for just under five years.

CG In 2018 Astrid and I visited the AGO and I recall its depth in sculpture by Henry Moore. Keeping up with you, I understand that you made many changes.

MT (laughing) Yes, I did. First of all, I made physical changes. There was an expansion project with Frank Gehry. We did a building project with him. The collection changed somewhat through acquiring major collections that changed the narrative in the galleries.

I was thinking of this recently. When I left, I was there for sixteen years, I had hired all of the people. One way that you change a place is to hire people.

CG Talk to me about First Nations artists. What was your role in that at AGO?

MT I have had a personal interest and a professional interest in the art of First Nations people. I felt for a long time that their history was the history of Canadian art. Under my watch, we acquired the first, historical, First Nations art ever. The museum hadn't collected that material. We integrated First Nations art into displays of Canadian art on a consistent basis. I was very proud and pleased when we hired Gerald McMaster as the head of the Canadian Department. It was the first time a First Nations leader had been appointed to lead a department other than First Nations. The notion of putting his voice in the middle of development of history was very important to me.

(Gerald Raymond McMaster, born 9 March 1953, North Battleford, is a Plains Cree and Blackfoot curator, artist, and author. He is enrolled in the Siksika Nation. Currently he lives in Toronto and was curator of Canadian art at the Art Gallery of Ontario until 2012, when he was succeeded by Andrew Hunter.)

He and I worked together for just about four years.

CG I was fortunate to visit Montreal a number of times, often invited by curators like René Blouin and Claude Gosselin to cover major exhibitions. The first time was essentially a tourism junket for travel writers promoting summer festivals. I asked if I might stay a bit longer at my own expense and extend the return flight.

The galleries I visited, based on the local gallery guide, were mostly commercial ones on Sherbrooke Street. By coincidence, that day there was an article about the René Blouin Gallery. After lunch I visited and was amazed. When I asked about other galleries, he wrote down a number of alternative, government sponsored, Parallel galleries along Rue St. Laurent. I left Montreal with a very different overview than what was presented as part of the tourism package.

That summer, I returned with my mother. We got to know René and the galleries better, as well as the museums. When Barbara Rose was editor of *The Art*

Paper I wrote features on Canadian artists including Betty Goodwin. There was a major project in multiple museums and galleries in Montreal and Quebec City that Rene curated and I was invited to write about it.

It's probably relatively unique that I have some interest and knowledge of contemporary Canadian art. We last visited two years ago, although, from the Berkshires, it's not a long drive. In general, mainstream American critics and curators have not paid close attention to our neighbors.

(In 2012 Denise Markonish curated *Oh Canada* for MASS MoCA. Mostly a hodgepodge, it was not well reviewed. The *New York Times* wrote, "Oh, Canada, a 62-artist affair that sprawls over most of Mass MoCA's first floor, wants to be that kind of national-scale mega-show. But in trying, it becomes something much quirkier. Seesawing between bigness and intimacy, the personal and the communal, it may tell you more about Canada's identity crisis than it does about Canadian art.")

In the 1960s, when I lived in New York, I worked for the East Hampton Gallery. They represented several Canadian artists who had participated in *The Responsive Eye*, which Bill Seitz curated for MoMA in 1956. We represented Guido Molinari, Claude Tousignant, and Jacques Hurtubise. They would drive down now and then to deliver new work. Marcel Barbeau was then living in New York, so we saw a lot of him. I always respected their work, particularly Molinari's stripes and Tousignant's circles.

Like much Canadian contemporary art, they have been undervalued. Late in his career Molinari was represented by Blouin.

Considering Boston, many of those problems may be applied here as well. The reputations of the best artists don't extend beyond Route 128.

The MFA has a sad history of involvement with 20th century art. From 1971 to 1984 Kenworth Moffett was curator of twentieth century art. That launched the department and program, but he was narrowly focused on formalism.

In terms of modern and contemporary art the MFA is a mess, and how are you going to clean it up?

MT I don't know that it's a mess, but like all large institutions, there needs to be some change. Very high on my priorities is to think about 20th and 21st century art. If we are going to continue to be a great encyclopedic museum, we have to do better. It doesn't mean that we haven't enjoyed support or that great artists haven't shown their work here. It means that we haven't done it consistently enough.

I agree with what you've noted, which is that the museum needs to be more grounded in or connected to work in Boston. We're thinking about how to do that. I believe that we should be a platform for artists who work here, both historic and contemporary. We have to think about how to do that in a way that will have real impact.

The reality is that it isn't just the lack of MFA support that leads artists to leave Boston. It also has to do with rentals and the cost of living. Boston is a really tough city to live in.

CG New York is more expensive.

MT It may not be more expensive. It may be the same with greater opportunity. It's a very complicated thing. The reason why I say that all large institutions need to change is because we are also realizing that you take New York institutions out of that, because New York is a freak of nature. As someone said to me, "New York is to the rest of the world as Picasso is to art." It's a freak and you can't actually use it as an example.

Glen (Lowry, MoMA) and Adam (Weinberg, Whitney Museum) can just open their doors and they will get thousands of people. They get ten thousand people on a Saturday. It's tourism, and just the way those institutions are imbedded is fundamentally different from the MFA. Putting aside New York, all institutions have the same challenges. How do you express, which is part of our strategic planning, invitation and welcome? How do we say, "You belong here come on in?" How do we make it a place that people want to go to? How do you make it friendly? How do you make it interesting? How do you make it less elitist? How do you make it more responsive? How do you make it more urgent? These are all things that we are talking about pretty actively.

I would hope that people who are following programming here see that there are shifts about how we are putting exhibitions together that mark a difference from the past. The question of how that reflects on collection building is slower. It's not that there haven't been adventurous and ambitious collectors of 20th century art in the 1930s and 1940s.

CG Can you name some?

MT There were a lot of people who did really great collecting in the '30s and '40s. There are a lot of great collectors today, but they are mostly aligned with the ICA. The question is: How does the MFA become a part of that dialogue? How do we have the platform that people want to be a part of? We're talking about that.

CG You're unique in the sense that you've had a foot in both institutions. You were a curator at the ICA and know it inside out. Now, amazingly, you are director of the MFA.

I want to comment that, with this interview, I have now interviewed every MFA director since Perry Rathbone.

MT Really, including Perry.

CG Rathbone plays into the history of the ICA in an interesting way. At one point, during its many moves and transitions, the ICA was installed on the second floor of the Museum School (in 1956).

Under its director Thomas Messer (February 9, 1920–May 15, 2013), the plan was that the ICA would merge with the MFA as its contemporary department with Messer as its curator. At an ICA's 50th anniversary event, during a press conference, I asked and Messer confirmed that. There is a transcript of a Messer interview that, in part, discusses his Boston years. It's online at the *Archives of American Art*.

When the ICA was on Soldier's Field Road in Brighton, he did important exhibitions. It was difficult to get there by public transportation. When I was in high school, I saw an Egon Schiele show there that I believe was the first in America. That went along with Boston's well-known interest in Germanic art.

MT Did the ICA actually exist as such at the Museum School? Also, correct me if I'm wrong, but didn't the ICA once exist in a fruit market? There was a period of time when the ICA had no physical presence and did exhibitions in a fruit market.

(In 1959 the ICA installed an exhibition at a Stop & Shop on Memorial Drive, *Young Talent in New England*. In 1968, at the end of the tenure of Sue Thurman, the ICA left space on Newbury Street at New England Life Hall. The content of the ICA, including an extensive library, was stored at its former site on Soldier's Field Road. Under Drew Hyde, then working on *Summerthing* with new mayor Kevin White, he installed ICA shows in various pop-up spaces including *Act Now* in a South End warehouse. He had access to a gallery in then-new City Hall. Drew and

I co-curated an exhibition, *Images*, on the new realism, in that space. Eventually, the gallery was taken over as office space for City Councilors. The ICA went back to Soldier's Field Road, and eventually moved to the mayoral mansion, The Parkman House, on Beacon Hill. Through Mayor White, Drew negotiated a lease on the abandoned police station on Boylston Street. From there, under current director Jill Medvedow, it built on the waterfront.

Another "fruit stall installation" was the ICA benefit staged as a part of the opening of the newly renovated Quincy Market. The ICA was known for raucous benefits and inventive locations. One memorable event *Fellini's Basement* was held at Filene's basement. That night, Bostonians were not so proper.)

CG During Messer's brief relationship with the MFA, he advised on some acquisitions. They included a portrait of Willem Sandberg by Karel Appel and *Rowboat* (1958) by the former Bostonian and later Bay Area figure artist David Park.

(The MFA information on the Park painting states, "1959, sold by Stæmpfli Gallery, New York, to Mr. and Mrs. Stanley X. Housen, Boston; 1959, to the Institute of Contemporary Art (provisional collection), Boston; 1963, sold by the Institute of Contemporary Art to the MFA. Accession Date: December 11, 1963." Funds for the purchase were provided by Lewis Cabot. Messer left to become director of the Solomon R. Guggenheim Museum in New York.)

MT What's interesting about that is that Perry Rathbone was a part of the group at Harvard that was very interested in modern art. (They were students of Paul Sachs, November 24, 1878–February 18, 1965, an American investor, businessman, and museum director. He served as associate director of the Fogg Art Museum and as a partner in the financial firm Goldman Sachs.)

Rathbone had that sense that he could probably do it. (Curate and collect modern art for the MFA.)

He probably wanted that space because he thought he could make it happen.

CG His curatorial partner was Hanns Swarzenski who, while a medievalist, was connected to the German-born art dealer Curt Valentin. Beckmann painted a double portrait of them that Swarzenski gave to the MFA.

I recall during the late 1950s and early 1960s that the MFA's modern/contemporary gallery was next to the Fenway entrance. For a number of years it featured, on loan, a multi-piece, bronze Picasso sculpture, *The Bathers*. There was a large abstract painting *Rue Gauquet* by Nicolas de Staël (Russian/French 1914–1955), as well as paintings by Fannie Hillsmith (1911–2007), Loren MacIver (1909–1998), Kenzo Okada (1902–1982), and Donald Stoltenberg (born 1927).

That's what passed for modern/contemporary art. When I commented to Rathbone about those works, he replied that they bought the de Staël for a few thousand dollars and that it was then worth many times that. (Current auction prices range from one to twelve million dollars.)

In recent years, there were media reports of antipathy between MFA director, Malcolm Rogers, and ICA director, Jill Medvedow. They were both fundraising for expansion and new construction. Particularly in the fine arts, there are only so many deep pockets to call upon. Now that we are past the brick and mortar period, I assume there are better relationships between the MFA and ICA. Is it possible one day to work together on exhibitions, acquisitions, or projects?

MT When you're never the big one. That's to say that you're not New York or Los Angeles, and you're Boston, you're still pretty big, but not the big one. And you want to compete; you have to think of all institutions as one thing, a whole. You have to think of the Gardner Museum and the Harvard Art Museums. You have to think of us as a circle, and we're all inside the circle. I think, for sure, the ICA and MFA have to think of doing some projects together. I don't think that includes collections.

CG Of course they collaborated on the *Binational*.

MT That was happening just as I was coming on board at the ICA

Jill (Medvedow) and I respect each other, are comfortable with each other. I would say that we mutually admire the quality of what is being achieved at both of our institutions. We haven't yet got to the point of joint programming. We have spoken about a couple of things, but haven't gotten any momentum behind them yet. I think in the end, we will want to work together.

We are just putting together our contemporary department. Reto has only been here for six months.

(Formerly with The Cleveland Museum, Reto Thüring will oversee programming, including special exhibitions and gallery installations throughout the building. This will draw on work from the contemporary art department, which was established in 1971, and comprises over 1,500 works of various mediums. Edward Saywell, who formerly chaired the department, has been promoted to the position of Chief of Exhibitions Strategy.)

Akili Tommasino, associate curator of modern and contemporary has been with us since October. (Previously Tommasino was at MoMA as a curatorial assistant. He is now at the Metropolitan Museum of Art.) We are just about to hire our crafts curator.

CG In doing research for a book, I have been looking at the social and political aspects of art in Boston, particularly as it pertains to the MFA. There have been shows that celebrate its Colonial and Anglo Saxon heritage.

It is significant that the MFA stopped celebrating Boston artists after 1930, in the Fairbrother show, and up to 1940, in Hirshler's project. Those cutoff dates are hardly arbitrary. The 1930s is precisely when the mainstream of the Boston art world transitioned from "elegant" and genteel to Jewish. The leading artists were the Boston Expressionists. Jack Levine and Hyman Bloom were South End residents and sons of Eastern European Jewish immigrants. Karl Zerbe was born in Germany. The Lebanese poet and artist, Kahlil Gibran, lived in the dominantly ethnic South End. The Brahmin MFA shunned these artists who are still inadequately represented in the MFA's collection and programming.

Major works by Bloom and Zerbe were acquired through the William H. and Saundra B. Lane collection. I understand that Hirshler is planning a Bloom show.

(Hirshler's *Hyman Bloom: Matters of Life and Death* was a well-reviewed exhibition in 2019.)

In 1976, I wrote a cover story for *Boston After Dark/Phoenix* about a paradigm shift of leadership at the MFA and issues of anti-Semitism. It is well established that Boston has a history of racism. The resistance against school bussing to achieve integration was an example. The museum had its first Jewish trustee, Sidney Rabb, in the 1960s.

My understanding was that the old money ran dry. To attract new money, changes were in order. Sitting in your seat, how does the museum address historical problems? In addition to non-inclusion of Boston's Jewish artists, are related issues related to African American artists. Looking at galleries in the Art of the Americas wing, Native American culture is poorly represented. Historical artifacts are jammed in with a hint of contemporary artists, like a small work by

Jaune Quick-to-See-Smith. There is a need for the museum to reflect the diversity of its citizens. Touring the country, we see that many museums have taken strides to address issues of representation and balance in their collections.

(The MFA has since acquired a major work by Jaune Quick-to-See-Smith.)

Activists like Dana Chandler, Jr. knocked on the door and reminded the museum of its proximity to Roxbury. Near the end of his tenure Perry T. Rathbone responded. That's when Barry Gaither was appointed adjunct curator of the MFA while also director of the National Center for African-American Artists. In 1970, he organized a major exhibition *Afro American Artists New York and Boston*. He went on to curate seven important shows for the MFA.

MT I think you put your finger on it. It goes back to the notion that I believe that institutions have to be more open and accessible. That is the future, and it goes to exactly what you said. Which is that our audiences are themselves diverse. Our audiences bring different life experiences. Once that you acknowledge that, you want to expand, and want to be an institution for your city, then that notion leads you to different community leaders. You then have to invite them into the work of the institution. Which is why boards start to diversify.

I don't know, per se, that money dried up. Or enthusiasm.

(As sources related to me, the old money didn't "dry up." It went elsewhere. There were legacy slots on the MFA passed from generation to generation. With that came a shift in philanthropy. Money that might have come to the museum went to other interests. Over the past decade there has been an entrepreneurial boom. The real estate has changed, evident in the increase of traffic and access to the inner city. The once run down South End, for example, has seen a glut of construction with high-end condos. The MFA, ICA, and other arts organizations have developed strategies to tap into these new resources. The Pandemic, however, has burst that balloon.)

CG If I may insert an observation, because I was a witness at the time, it was a fallow period. By 1993, at the end of Alan Shestack's tenure, the museum had lost momentum. There was a reduction of galleries on view in rotation. The Fenway entrance was closed as an economic decision. There was a need for renovation and change, including climate control of the painting galleries. Major traveling shows were bypassing Boston, including the Tutankhamun show. Given the importance of the MFA's Egyptian Collection, that was a major blow. All of that expressed a need for new revenue. That called for a paradigm shift.

MT For whatever reason, and we could talk about that, there was a lack of risk taking.

CG In 1970 there was an ad hoc policy report that defined mandates for the future. One resulted in hiring Ken Moffett. Initially, he was part time while a professor at Wellesley College. There were few resources to support his programming and acquisitions. Overall, in the final phase of Perry Rathbone as director, there was a low point for the museum. The museum was demoralized. What followed for the next three years only made matters worse.

The unilateral appointment of Merrill Rueppel (1973–1975) by Seybolt derailed. A palace revolt was reported in the *Boston Globe*, and the director was pressured to resign that week. Jan Fontein, curator of Asiatic art, was made acting director and later permanent director. His tenure proved to be problematic.

MT I'm fascinated by what you are saying. It's true to some degree. At some point, when institutions need to open their arms wider, it narrows ideologically. So when they set up a contemporary department, it was an ideologically driven contemporary department. It was relatively narrow in scope. It's exactly the opposite statement you want to make about contemporary art.

CG Ken did a lot of good things.

MT He sure did and he left a legacy in terms of his collection. It would be very hard for anybody to argue that his collection and commitment reflected the broad engagement of artists with the ideas of contemporary art, making of contemporary art, and critical discourse about contemporary art, not just in New York, but in Boston itself. In some degrees it was an exclusionary practice.

CG He advocated formalism, which was the focus of the trustee Lewis Cabot who backed him. It is what he collected and was known at times to deal in. Allegedly, with Cabot, there were levels of conflict of interest. But I would not accuse Ken of that. To me, he was always a gentleman and a scholar with a true passion for the artists he promoted and believed in. I had many discussions of that with him. After the MFA, he became director of the Fort Lauderdale Museum of Art.

MT I think there is a simple truth that leads to greater diversity. It goes as follows:

We have leadership in the institution that understands it; Complex times need diverse points of view. It's a very simple truth. It exists at the staff level, as much as it exists at the board level. We're starting to open up dialogues and inviting more points of view. It comes from the idea that we need some good problem-solving skills to get through some of these issues. How are we going to get there? By having more points of view around the table.

Your historical observations may very well be true. You say that you have done the research. I would say that's not the feeling at the MFA today. The question is, how do you actually achieve it? Allow us five years to look at the board and the staff and say, yes, there has been a change. We're still working that through. Conversations we're having, people are telling me, they're fundamentally different then they were before.

CG The MFA seems reluctant to celebrate itself. Because of its puritanical traditions, Boston doesn't seem comfortable with blowing its own horn. We were in San Francisco in 2017 for the fiftieth anniversary of The Summer of Love. There were many celebrations including a stunning museum exhibition. It included all of the hippie culture from rock bands, posters and costumes, film and photography. It was a very successful project. There is a new documentary film by Bill Lichtenstein *WBCN: The American Revolution*. Viking press has published the well-reviewed book by Ryan Walsh *Astral Weeks: A Secret History of 1968*. The Lichtenstein film takes the approach that in 1968 the counter culture shifted to Boston with a mandate for social and political activism. I published a book, *Counter Culture in Boston: 1968 to 1980s*.

That period was a time of enormous change for Boston. The ICA more or less died in 1968. It was forced out of Newbury Street and its material was put into storage in its former home on Soldier's Field Road. Drew Hyde was working with Kevin White and Summerthing. With the backing of Kathy and Lewis Kane, she worked for the Mayor, Drew became acting director and slowly revived the moribund ICA. There was a proliferation of media and emergence of major rock bands.

Through a number of projects, there is new attention to the unique role of Boston's golden age. Shouldn't the MFA be a natural platform for its celebration and education? It is interesting that there is a current MFA video installation focused on aspects of the Black Panther Party in Boston at that time. That's a glimpse of a larger picture of major social and political change, including the National Student Strike and Moratorium that started on Boston Common. The MFA doesn't appear to be interested in that counter culture history

(From the museum's PR, "The MFA exhibition was *Bouchra Khalili: Poets and Witnesses*. Charting the essential connection between poetry and activism, an exhibition of works by Berlin-based artist Bouchra Khalili (Moroccan, b. 1975) bridges discourses of resistance from the 1960s to the present. Making its US debut at the MFA, Khalili's *Twenty-Two Hours* (2018) is a testament to her deep research into the Black Panther Party in New England and their unexpected ally, the French poet Jean Genet.

"In 1970, Genet toured the US in support of the Panthers, delivering his first speech in Cambridge, Massachusetts, where Khalili recently completed a fellowship at the Radcliffe Institute for Advanced Study at Harvard University. In Twenty-Two Hours, two young Bostonians, Quiana Pontes and Vanessa Silva, perform on camera in Cambridge, combining fragments of images, sounds, memories, and film footage to retell the story of Genet's visit and reflect on the civic poet as a witness to history.")

MT One of our priorities, and I think about it a lot, is to celebrate Boston. It's not the way the institution has thought. I think you're right to mention something about Puritanism, that notion of propriety and not drawing attention to yourself. I get that. On the other hand there are a lot of hidden histories that would make us feel better about ourselves. I would even say something more strongly. Knowing that history will change some of the conversations here today.

CG Who will change that?

MT You, and other people who are going to write it. Then, whether institutions get involved in some way, celebrating the complexity of what happened here.

CG Will you read those books?

(There is a bibliography of some thirty books, past and recent, about media, jazz, rock, and folk music in Boston and Cambridge from the 1950s through the present. For further research there are growing archives. Northeastern University has the Stephen Mindich *Boston Phoenix* collection and Kay Bourne's *Bay State Banner* documents. The David Bieber archive has a million items and U Mass Amherst Archive is a major and growing resource.)

MT I think it's really important to know where you are.

CG I urge you to see the WBCN documentary. You were here at that time, but may not have participated in the counter culture that much, being married and such.

MT I was completely square. (both laughing) But recognizing that I am interested in how understanding our past generates understanding of our present, in terms of energy and possibilities. Knowing more about that would be really, really powerful.

CG The ICA was adamant about its position as a kunsthalle (non-collecting museum). Just imagine, if from those shows, they acquired one or two pieces over the years.

MT I look at it differently and here I am a little tough on the MFA. I'm not so sure that the ICA should have been collecting then. But the MFA should have been buying out of every show. Can you imagine today what a collection it would have? That's if we see ourselves as one institution. Now we can't do that. They do what they do, and we do what we do. At the time, I often thought about that. (When he was with the ICA.)

CG What do you do about the 20th century? Is that gone and just too expensive?

MT Yes, if you buy. But it's not too expensive if you can find a way to create a home for great collections.

CG What made the MFA great was that Bostonians were collecting impressionism and post-impressionism during a time when Parisians weren't.

MT They also had the support of collectors who were interested in having that happen. It was the MFA collecting and the community collecting. Now we have the community collecting, but we're not in the mainstream with those collectors in the way that the ICA is.

ICA curator Matthew Teitelbaum. Giuliano photo.

Teitelbaum today as director of the MFA. Giuliano photo.

Boston Expressionists Jack Levine, left, and Hyman Bloom, until recently were snubbed by the MFA. Giuliano photo.

Matthew Teitelbaum, from the ICA to MFA

Cliff Ackley curator of prints, drawings, and photography enhanced the modern and contemporary collections. Giuliano photo.

A gallery is named for Lois and Michael Torf collectors of modern and contemporary prints. Giuliano photo.

Architect and collector Graham Gund funded the special exhibitions gallery and has donated major modern and contemporary works. Giuliano photo.

A prize for women artists is named for Boston artist Maud Morgan. Giuliano photo.

Made in the USA
Las Vegas, NV
15 October 2021

Made in the USA
Las Vegas, NV
15 October 2021